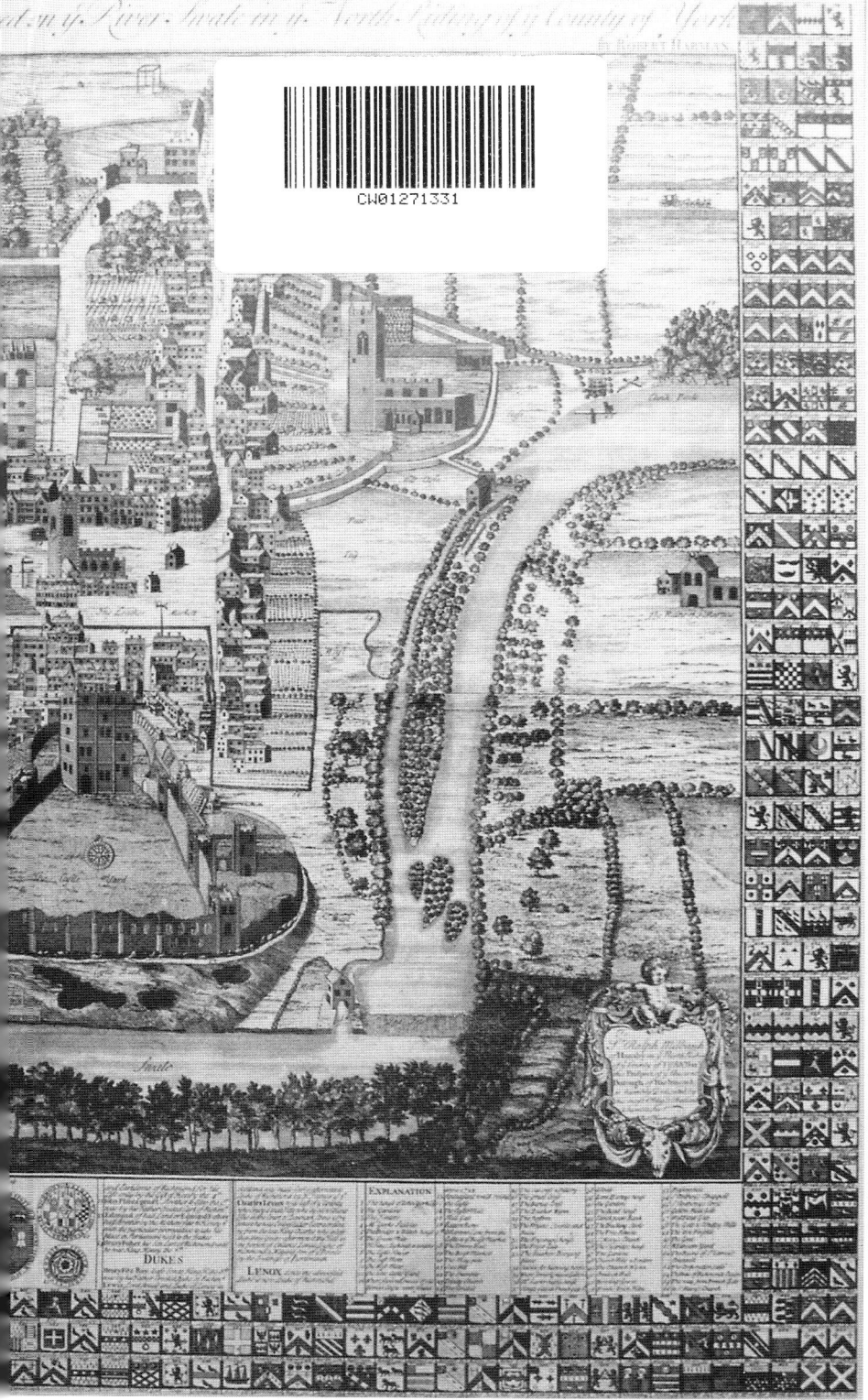

THE HISTORY OF
RICHMOND
NORTH YORKSHIRE

From Earliest Times to the Year 2000

by

JANE HATCHER

Jane Hatcher
30 xii 00

BLACKTHORN PRESS

Blackthorn Press, Blackthorn House
Middleton Rd, Pickering YO18 8AL
United Kingdom

www.blackthornpress.com

ISBN 0 9535072 6 2

© Jane Hatcher 2000

All rights reserved. No part of this publication may be reproduced, stored in a retrieval system or transmitted, in any form or by any means, electronic, mechanical, photocopying, recording, or otherwise, without the prior permission of the Blackthorn Press.

ILLUSTRATION CREDITS

The publisher and author are grateful
To the following for help with
Providing illustrations:

John Fletcher, Iris Murdock, Richmond Town Council, Richmondshire Museum, Studio 5, Mark Whyman, Bridgeman Art Library, British Library, Jane Hatcher, Alan Avery, English Heritage, Darlington & Stockton Times, Society of Antiquaries.

AUTHOR'S PREFACE

I am grateful to the Blackthorn Press for commissioning a volume, which was much needed. The publisher requested that the history be made as accessible as possible, and I have tried to achieve this. The brief included a preliminary contextual introduction to each chapter. The chapters follow a chronological pattern as far as possible. All dates are New Style. The publisher's contract specifically excluded detailed references but provided for a detailed bibliography which I hope goes some way towards a compromise with the requirements of academic studies.

My first acknowledgement has to be of my many debts to the late L.P. Wenham, for involving me in historical research many years ago, and for bequeathing me a huge quantity of material on the history of Richmond in various stages of preparation and completion. For helpful comments on the draft text I am grateful to Alan Avery of the Blackthorn Press, Linda and Michael Drury, David Kirby, Shirley Thubron, and Mark Whyman who not only read through all of the text while moving house but applied both stick and carrot to ensure the project was completed within the short time-scale requested by the publisher.

Jane Hatcher
Richmond
October 2000

PUBLISHER'S FOREWORD

This book on the history of Richmond is the first in a series which will tell the story of our towns and cities in an academically sound and readable form. It is aimed at the intelligent reader who may have no formal historical training but who is curious to know more about the place in which he or she lives.

A feature of the series is the full bibliography and index, which will enable readers to pursue their interest in greater depth by private study or on a more formal course.

We are frequently told that the world is becoming a global village and that the British must subsume their nationality and look to Europe or the United States for their future identity. This may be so as a nation but as individuals most of our lives are spent at the local level. On meeting someone new we want to know what he does and where he comes from.

Even with greater social mobility when few people spend all their lives in one place, let alone where they were born, we all seem to want to know what went on in the past in the place we live now. What sort of people were they and how did they spend their lives?

This series attempts to answer some of these questions whether they are from someone whose family has lived for generations in the same place or from a newcomer to the town, wanting to know the history, which has shaped its fabric and people.

AA

Dedicated

to the memory of

Leslie Peter Wenham

(1911 – 1990)

Historian of Hadrian's Wall, York and Richmond.

With affection, gratitude and humility

For the breadth and depth of his knowledge and research.

CONTENTS

Richmond before its history began	1
Norman Richmond 1066 – 1154	15
Medieval Richmond 1154 – 1485	31
Tudor Richmond 1485 – 1603	57
Stuart Richmond 1603 – 1714	93
Georgian Richmond 1714 – 1837	125
Victorian Richmond 1837 – 1901	173
Twentieth Century Richmond 1901 – 2000	201
Bibliography	239
Index	255

1

Richmond before its history began

The National History
  This chapter sets the scene before Richmond was founded about the year 1071. People have lived in the area since the earliest times, with evidence of occupation from the Bronze Age, from perhaps 1000 B.C., onwards. There is evidence of several local settlements dating from the Iron Age (about 650 B.C. to the Roman conquest of Britain in the 1st Century A.D.). Iron Age Britain consisted of many independent kingdoms, the largest of which was Brigantia, extending from the river Tweed to the river Trent.
  Late Iron Age Brigantia was ruled by Queen Cartimandua, a very clever woman who was a contemporary of the more famous Boudicca, queen of the Iceni in East Anglia. The Romans invaded the south of England in A.D. 43 but did not conquer 'Yorkshire' until A.D. 71, after which time there was busy traffic travelling on Dere Street (the Great North Road, or present A1) between the great fortress of Eboracum at York and Hadrian's Wall.
  With the withdrawal of the Roman army by A.D. 410, the country entered the so-called 'Dark Ages' as Germanic invaders established new independent Anglo-Saxon kingdoms. The legendary Celtic figure of Arthur was perhaps one of those who offered heroic resistance to such invasions. The Richmond area was in the Anglian kingdom of Deira, which stretched north from the river Humber to the river Tees on the east side of the

Pennines. In A.D. 597 Pope Gregory sent a Christian mission to England, and Kent was established as a Christian kingdom under Augustine as first archbishop of Canterbury. During the early years of the 7th century, Deira was annexed by the more northerly kingdom of Bernicia - between the rivers Tees and Tweed - to create the greater realm of Northumbria under King Edwin of Deira. Missionaries were sent from Kent to Northumbria, notably Paulinus who established an important base at York, and after he baptized King Edwin at York in A.D. 627, Christianity began to spread through Northumbria. This process was accelerated under Aidan, bishop of Lindisfarne, and his successors, and in the second half of the 7th century the Northumbrian church emerged as a powerful institution under Wilfrid, Bishop of York.

Northumbria absorbed other northern kingdoms to become one of the most important areas of England politically and militarily, and also an intellectual beacon of light in the 'Dark Ages'. Learning, culture and artistic endeavour were immensely cherished, particularly in biblical studies, as exemplified by great stone crosses, and the famous Lindisfarne Gospels written and illuminated about A.D. 720. The Venerable Bede (c.673-735) has left us a record of events both ecclesiastical and secular from Anglian times. Alcuin of York, a great Northumbrian scholar, teacher and theologian, was persuaded by Charlemagne, king of the Franks, to settle in Aachen in 781. Sadly, Northumbrian culture was eradicated by the Viking raids, which began in 793 and continued throughout the 9th century. The old kingdom of Northumbria was overthrown in 866 when York was captured by a large Viking force, and Whitby was also sacked. York emerged as the centre of a Scandinavian kingdom having close links with the Viking kingdom of Dublin in Ireland. Even after the annexation of York by the West Saxon successors of Alfred the Great in 954, North Yorkshire remained part of the Danelaw until the Norman Conquest. This confusing period of history has bequeathed us fine sculpted stones from the Northumbrian artistic flowering, and local place-names and dialects of Anglo-Scandinavian origin.

Richmond in Yorkshire, the 'mother' of all the fifty and more Richmonds all over the world, is a picturesque and historic town overflowing with character. It has jealously guarded its ancient traditions and customs. Here is (usually) still rung each evening the Curfew Bell allegedly introduced by William the Conqueror to require the inhabitants to 'cover' their fires, and similarly each morning the 'Prentice Bell rings to wake young shopkeepers, while the Pancake Bell each Shrove Tuesday reminds cooks to use up their eggs before Lent! The ancient Saturday outdoor market is signified by the placing of halberds outside the mayor's front door, and each autumn the first local farmer to complete his harvest presents a 'goodly sample' of grain to a begowned Mayor in the First Fruits ceremony. Every seven years the town's boundaries are 'ridden' or ceremonially walked by a large crowd of residents. Richmond has for centuries attracted the attention of artists and writers, and more recently of photographers, and owners of video cameras. In many ways nowadays, Richmond can seem rather a quaint little backwater, just another small and charming market town of the beautiful Yorkshire Dales. Yet here can be found the nearest thing to those eternal values so difficult to define, but which are sensed when found. Here is neighbourliness, and a sense of community.

Among the many quaint old customs, which remain, is the habit, clearly horrifying to some visitors from the south of England, of speaking not only to acquaintances but also to total strangers. Typical greetings while passing in the street demonstrate extreme forms of the Yorkshireman's use of abbreviation and litotes, or understatement, in speech pattern. "How do?" is often used instead of "Hello" or "How are you?". "Oh, champion" is a substitute for "Very well, thank you", whereas "Only moderate" indicates a poor state of health. The exclamation "Grand Day!" indicates splendid weather, while

"Terrible, in't it?" is a commiseration in very wet conditions. The outstanding beauty and impressive history of Richmond is rarely remarked upon by the town's long-established residents, who seem to take it all for granted, unless some change is threatened. The sight and smell of smoke rising from the chimney pots of cottages huddling on the hillsides below the town centre characterize a place where old habits die hard.

Richmond's name foretells its spectacular setting, the Norman French 'riche mont' meaning 'a fine or noble hill' from the Frankish *ric*. The town huddles deferentially around its castle, which takes pride of place on its headland. Below that dominating limestone bluff the mighty river Swale runs over a bare bed of hard sandstone before hurling itself over a ledge, which creates a waterfall. The river, which gives its name to Swaledale, is sometimes benign but often awesome, especially when it rises rapidly and treacherously after heavy rain: its floods can even, on occasions, rise so swiftly that it comes down as a roll. Many people have drowned over the years after failing to treat the river with sufficient respect and, even as this book was in preparation, a flood in June 2000 washed away the river bed underneath the central pier of Mercury Bridge, near the former railway station, causing the bridge to be closed for several months.

The name of the river Swale is from the Old English *suala* - the same root as the word 'swallow' - and means swirling and rushing, which this river certainly does. Reputedly the fastest-flowing river in England, its winding course falls dramatically from its source, watched over by four giants of the Pennine Chain - Nine Standards Rigg, High Seat, Lovely Seat and Great Shunnor Fell. It concludes its journey in the lowland area of Myton-on-Swale, about 70 miles to the east of its source, by joining with Wensleydale's river Ure to become the Yorkshire Ouse.

In many senses Richmond is a meeting place. Geologically, sandstone here meets limestone, giving a random mix in the materials used for local vernacular buildings. The geographical interface of lowland plain, through which the Swale flows to the east of the town, and Swaledale's V-shaped valley to the west, can clearly be seen from the top of the Castle keep. *[see plate 1]* Even to this day, that junction is marked by age-old differences between the areas to the west and east of Richmond. For example, in agriculture, almost no arable cultivation is found to the west in pastoral Swaledale, and the dale has different place-names, and even dialect, from the area east of Richmond. The Swale itself drops over many waterfalls higher up in the dale but, having had its final fling over Richmond's falls - a 'force' in Dales dialect, pronounced 'foss' locally, giving the term Foss Head to the area beside the falls - contents itself with a more meandering journey eastwards. Never gentle, however, its power is now terrifyingly eroding its north bank just below the town at Easby. Easby, (from the Old Norse, meaning the farm or hall of a Scandinavian settler called Esi), and Skeeby (Skith's farm), like many local settlements have much older origins than Richmond itself, which is a relatively young place, begun only about 1071. So what was here before then?

It is hard to imagine our early ancestors ignoring such a superb defensive site, but no evidence of them has been found here - perhaps all trace of earlier settlement was destroyed when the Castle was built. Recent archaeology in Swaledale has demonstrated many overlying phases of prehistory, and Neolithic cup-and-ring stones are found on Barningham Moor a few miles to the north. In the lowland areas to the east of the town there is plenty of evidence of prehistoric occupation. This is particularly so in the Scorton area, where recent development has unearthed important archaeological material and quarrying has exposed evidence of a late-Neolithic cursus or ceremonial avenue. A Bronze Age sword perhaps used as a votive offering and dating from 1,100 B.C. was unearthed near Catterick Bridge in 1992. It seems unlikely that the local hill-top sites in and around Richmond would not have attracted prehistoric settlers. Old maps show features which may represent former prehistoric barrows much nearer to Richmond itself, such as the 'long hill' near where the present Reeth Road enters the town, which from its shape could have been a Neolithic long barrow, and a 'round hill' in the area of the old racecourse to the north-west of Richmond could have been a Bronze Age round barrow.

One of the country's most impressive late-Iron Age monuments can be seen about eight miles north of Richmond at Stanwick, and is partially open to the public under the guardianship of English Heritage. An enormous site, where 850 acres are enclosed by large ramparts almost five miles in circumference, it was an *oppidum* or defended town constructed by the Brigantes, a large group of northern tribes. The Brigantian queen at the time when the Romans were extending their Empire northwards in the middle of the 1st century A.D. was called Cartimandua. She established good trading relations with the Romans and, hoping to keep her kingdom free from invasion, negotiated a status of alliance termed a client kingdom by historians. Cartimandua's husband was called Venutius: their marriage must have been somewhat turbulent, for he led a faction, which rebelled against her pro-Roman policy. The Romans, unsurprisingly, supported Cartimandua against Venutius and when forced to rescue her they embarked on the military conquest of Brigantia which took a number of years to complete.

Sir Mortimer Wheeler, invited to undertake a major excavation anywhere in the country for the Festival of Britain in 1951, chose Stanwick. He suggested that the site might have been Venutius' headquarters and later the Brigantes' 'last stand' against the Romans. Subsequent excavations have found evidence of peaceful trade with the Romans over a thirty-year period. Whatever its precise role in the swashbuckling story of Cartimandua and Venutius, Stanwick was an extremely important Brigantian settlement, which reached the peak of its influence shortly before the Roman conquest of northern England. A hoard of very fine Roman cavalry horse harness, discovered on Fremington Hagg in the 19th century and now split between the British Museum in London and the Yorkshire Museum in York, dates from before the Roman conquest of Brigantia and may be associated with the struggle between the supporters of Cartimandua and Venutius.

The fortifications of Stanwick, north-east of Stanwick Old Hall

The Romans are said to have mined Swaledale lead in the area around Hurst, and although no Roman sites have been identified in the Richmond area itself, the lead would have to be brought down to Dere Street, the Roman 'Great North Road'. It has been suggested that Quaker Lane is part of the Roman road from Swaledale. Chance finds have provided evidence of activity in Richmond during Roman times, notably the discovery in 1720 of a hoard of over 600 Roman coins, plus a silver spoon, on the Castle Bank by two men quarrying stone there. The men, Peter Plummer, waller, and Jonathan Raine, stonemason, gave detailed evidence of their find to George Kay, the Mayor of Richmond in 1720. Some of these coins found their way into the collection of the Leeds antiquary Ralph Thoresby. Other Roman coins from Richmond include a silver *siliqua* of the Emperor Gratian found about 1956.

The most important Roman site locally was *Cataractonium*, an extensive area near Catterick mainly on the south bank of the Swale where it was crossed by a bridge carrying Dere Street. This site had an extremely complex history, its many phases including a fort guarding the bridgehead, a military supply depot for the development of Hadrian's Wall, a small but important town, a period as a fort again, and then a return to civilian use which continued after the withdrawal of the Roman army early in the 5th century. There have been several major excavations in the Catterick area, many of them connected with improvement works to the A1 as well as quarrying, and as well as extensive Roman finds an Anglian cemetery has also been found.

Richmond is one of a number of ancient settlements throughout the country with an Arthurian legend, according to which beneath the Castle the heroic King Arthur 'sleeps on until the day shall come for that Golden Age to be restored'. The story goes that one moonlight night, a Richmondian known as Potter Thompson was wandering somewhere below the Castle hill and saw a cleft in the rock which, when he entered it, became a passage leading to a huge chamber directly below the Castle keep. Here was the Round Table and, sprawled around it, King Arthur and his knights in full armour. As Potter Thompson handled the dust-covered weapons on the table, the knights began to stretch themselves, making their armour jangle ominously as they did so. In a panic, he fled back down the passage, but as he did so these sepulchral words rang in his ears:

> Potter Thompson! Potter Thompson!
> If thou had'st drawn the sword or blown the horn
> Thou would'st have been the richest man this day born!

There is also a small natural cave called Arthur's Oven in the cliff side below Billy Banks Wood. The Welsh bard Aneirin tells in his poems of the kingdom of Gododdin, based on Edinburgh, and of an important battle fought about the year 600 at Catraeth where a large number of brave warriors fell, including one heroic figure whose story may have been woven into tales of Arthur. A morsel of substance to the Richmond legend is offered by some scholars identifying Catraeth as Catterick, a strategic river crossing which might have been fought over, especially as it is known that at that time there was a power struggle between the kingdoms of Deira and Bernicia which converged in the Teesside area before their eventual joining up to become Northumbria.

The somewhat hazy period of our island's story which includes the battle of Catraeth links up with another important aspect of the history of the Richmond area. The eastern boundary of Richmond is a linear earthwork known as Scots Dike. The word 'dike' here means an embankment forming a boundary, not a water-filled ditch or dyke, and it was here before Richmond existed. Scots Dike runs north-south, crossing the river Swale from the south and continuing north at least as far as Stanwick. The date of Scots Dike has never been ascertained by archaeological excavation, although a 6th-century spearhead was found close to it in the 1970s, and archaeologically it is clearly of later date than the Stanwick fortifications. Scots Dike consists of a bank with a dry ditch to its east, indicating that it was constructed to defend or demarcate the area to its west. It therefore seems likely that it was constructed as an eastern boundary of the shadowy but formidable British kingdom of

Rheged, based on Carlisle and the Eden Valley, against the Anglian kingdoms of Deira and Bernicia.

That section of Scots Dike nearest Richmond is still well preserved, and easily visible to the naked eye in the fields immediately east of the town. In addition to being the official boundary of Richmond, Scots Dike serves as a dividing line in that drivers notice how often the weather seems to change at that point, particularly the transition to snow or fog! South of the river Swale, Scots Dike turns south-westwards at least as far as the area, which takes its name from a small tributary of the river Swale, the Sand Beck. Both elements of the name Sandbeck are of Old Norse origin, the word 'beck' being commonly used for a small stream.

On the south bank of the Swale opposite the western side of the town is a small hamlet called Sleegill, another Old Norse place-name, the first element being the root from which our word 'saliva' comes, and 'gill' is a narrow valley. From Sleegill an ancient lane climbs steeply up towards the village of Hudswell, the lane is called on modern maps Boggy Lane (and boggy it is) but it was once called Boggy Lonnen, the Old Norse word for lane, and it too is a name which was in existence before Richmond. At the top of Sleegill is a pub called The Holly Hill, a corruption of Holy Hill, for in the Richmond and Catterick area Paulinus is traditionally said to have baptized thousands to Christianity about A.D. 627.

Today it is hard to imagine that the small village of Gilling West, north of Richmond, was from the 7th century up until the Norman Conquest the administrative centre of the region. According to tradition it was one of the main bases of the kingdom of Deira with a 'castle' or, more likely, a defended royal residence, presumably consisting of wooden structures, at Castle Hill on Low Scales Farm. Bede tells of the establishment of a monastery at Gilling in A.D. 651 and elaborates on the circumstances behind it. Oswine, a cousin of King Edwin, was murdered by Oswiu, an aggressive king of Bernicia. As a penance for his crime, Oswiu founded the monastery at Gilling, so that the monks could pray daily for the soul of Oswine, and also for himself.

All the Yorkshire monasteries of Northumbria, and the Christian culture of which they were a part, were either destroyed by the Vikings or simply ceased to exist as monastic communities, including Oswiu's monastery at Gilling West. The Christian tradition, established here in the 7th century, was thus lost, and replaced in the 9th century by Scandinavian cultures, which were in turn superseded by another period of Christian influence in the early 11th century. The first part of this historical sequence is graphically illustrated by two carved stones dredged from Gilling Beck in 1976. The older piece is a complete stone, which bears on its front face a cross of Anglian form, set within a circle. This probably dates from the early 9th century, before the Viking invasions, and is a rare example of its type, with few parallels, possibly having been intended either as the dedication stone of a Christian building or as a Christian grave marker.

Anglian cross dredged from Gilling Beck in 1976

The second stone is part of a 10th-century hogback grave marker, an example of the Viking sculptural tradition using a stylised version of a simple house of narrow plan with a steep shingled roof. Both these stones are on display in the Richmondshire Museum in Richmond. The Gilling Sword, one of the best examples from the 9th century known, found at about the same time and famously featured on the BBC TV programme 'Blue Peter', can be seen in the Yorkshire Museum in York.

Detail of the upper panel of the plaster cast
of the Easby Cross in Easby Parish Church

Many local churches, including that at Gilling West, contain pieces of sculpted stones of Anglo-Scandinavian origin, but the highest quality local example of carving of the

Northumbrian 'Carolingian' period is the Easby Cross. Probably dating from the late 8th century, it is contemporary with the era of Charlemagne. Although found in several pieces, the cross shaft is fairly complete. Its carving, in shallow relief, is quite masterful in its illusion of three-dimensional depth.

At the top of the principal face is shown the Risen Christ - a seated figure with robe heavily draped over the knees, and hands lifted up to display the wounds in the palms - flanked by smaller depictions of St. Peter and St. Paul. Below are busts of the Twelve Apostles, arranged in seven vertical tiers rather like a school photograph but also set within three classical arches. Each head, adorned with a Roman hair-style, also has a nimbus or halo, and these are overlapped to give an additional sense of depth. Some Apostles hold a book. The rear face depicts a vine scroll, with naturalistic leaves and delicate tendrils, inhabited by birds and small animals, the feet of which, fore and aft of the vine, again give a sophisticated sense of depth.

The two narrow sides of the shaft bear the interlace decoration often found on Northumbrian cross shafts, but the rich quality of the sculpture on the two main faces raises interesting questions as to where the Easby Cross was carved. Its stonemason clearly had knowledge of the artistic schemes found on ivories produced in Europe around the time of the Emperor Charlemagne. Thus we find evidence of a pre-Viking settlement at Easby which was not only part of the Northumbrian Christian tradition but had the confidence, prosperity and trade links to commission a work of art of a quality comparable with the best in Europe. A plaster cast of the Easby Cross can be seen in St. Agatha's Church at Easby, the original is in the Victoria and Albert Museum.

During the 10th century parishes were grouped together for the purposes of local administration - the equivalent of today's local authority districts - into wapentakes, another Old Norse word, meaning a flourish of weapons - the manner of showing assent in Scandinavian assemblies. It is the equivalent of the southern 'hundred'. Groups of wapentakes formed shires. Gilling West became the name of a wapentake, and that name was never changed to Richmond despite Gilling losing its ascendance. The Gilling West wapentake was, however, one which was grouped into a shire, which became known as Richmondshire, taking its name from the much later place-name of Richmond. The name Richmondshire continued to be used for several centuries but occurs less frequently in the 19th century. Local government re-organization in 1974 created a new district to which the name Richmondshire was given. The modern boundaries are not, however, those of the historic Richmondshire, which was much larger than its modern name-sake.

Some time before the Norman Conquest a settlement called Hindrelac developed near Richmond. Authorities differ as to what the name Hindrelac means, but it has been suggested that it can be broken down into three Old Norse components: *hind* meaning female hart; *re* - of the; and *lac* - a wood, a clearing in a wood or a forest glade. Thus the name can be interpreted as the wood, clearing or glade of the hind. Another version is to interpret *lac* as the Old English *lacu* or stream, suggesting the stream of the hind. These two translations build up slightly different mental pictures of the site so described, and opinions as to whether Richmond fits the description vary with which is accepted.

The late Peter Wenham, an eminent historian of Richmond, was of the opinion that Hindrelac was situated in that area of Richmond called Aldbiggin (old building or settlement). In addition to the evidence from the place-name, he considered the three great open fields, which provided medieval Richmond with food - Westfield, Gallowfield and Eastfield - to pivot around that area. Such a field system is likely to date from pre-Norman times. Hindrelac is recorded in the Domesday Book of 1086 as a small village with a church and a priest, and Richmond would seem the most likely place in the area to match that description. Richmond is not recorded as such in Domesday because it did not exist in pre-Norman times, although the Castle, and a hamlet called Newton - the new settlement - are mentioned. But these belong in Chapter Two.

2

Norman Richmond 1066-1154

The National History
     The Norman Conquest of 1066 was the last successful invasion England has experienced, but it was also the last of a series going back several hundred years. England had only been an entity for about 140 years, the old kingdoms of Northumbria, Mercia and Wessex having been united under King Athelstan of Wessex in A.D. 927. Richmond was a Norman foundation, one of the first so to be established, and was part of a process of stamping the rule of the Conqueror not only on England generally but in particular on the North of England, where the people then, as now, were notably resistant to being told what to do by 'incomers'. Their resistance led in 1069-70 to the devastating 'Harrying of the North' by which King William I (1066-87) finally subdued the North. His famous Domesday Book of 1086 gives a relatively consistent overview of the country as a whole, but is of little help in painting a picture of Richmond at that time. King William II (1087-1100), known as William Rufus, was killed by an arrow while hunting in the New Forest in Hampshire. He was succeeded by his youngest brother King Henry I (1100-35). When he died his daughter Matilda challenged Stephen (1135-54) for the throne and, during the ensuing period of civil unrest, the power of the barons increased. The Normans brought

to England high standards of architectural design and construction epitomized by their castles and churches. Richmond Castle is one of the country's finest Norman monuments, and tells us much of those who ruled the area for almost a century.

When Halley's comet was visible in the skies above the small village of Hindrelac in the summer of 1066 the inhabitants there, as elsewhere, would fear it was an omen of disaster. Doubtless the priest of their little church exhorted them to pray to the God of their salvation that He would spare them. As they looked up in wonder from their ploughs, little could they have realized that momentous events would shortly take place which would lead to the establishment, only five years later, of a mighty fortress such a short distance away. In one sense their fears were well-founded, for that Castle would eventually attract about it a settlement, which was, in time, totally to eclipse their village.

The origins of Richmond can be traced obliquely to the death on 5 January 1066 of King Edward the Confessor, who had ruled from 1042. He had re-established the Anglo-Saxon dynasty after a period under Danish kings, Canute and Harthacanute, who had ruled England for much of the early 11th century after a series of Danish raids following the death in 939 of Athelstan, the first king to reign over England as a whole. Edward the Confessor had ruled his kingdom by creating three powerful earls to oversee the areas previously the separate ancient kingdoms of Northumbria in the North, Mercia in the Midlands, and Wessex in the South. One of the administrative centres of these earls of Northumbria was Gilling West. The first Earl of Northumbria appointed by Edward was Siward, a Dane, who died in 1055, and was followed by Tosti, son of Godwin, and brother to Harold, Earl of Wessex. Tosti became unpopular in Northumbria and was overthrown at York in 1065, to be replaced by Morcar, brother of

Edwin, Earl of Mercia. This effectively meant that Edwin became Earl of Northumbria also.

Several candidates were keen to succeed to the throne of the childless Edward the Confessor. They included the heir presumptive, Harold Godwinson, Earl of Wessex; Eadgar Atheling, Edward's half-brother Edmund Ironside's grandson; Sweyn, King of Denmark, nephew of Canute; Harald Hardrada, King of Norway, the greatest Viking warrior of his time; and William, Duke of Normandy. William had visited England in 1052 and been cordially received by Edward the Confessor. Indeed, William later claimed that not only had Edward promised him his crown, but also that Harold Godwinson had promised him his support. The day after Edward the Confessor died, he was buried in Westminster Abbey, which he had just finished building, and a few hours later Harold Godwinson was hastily crowned King. He reigned for only nine months, but had to face no fewer than three invasions in that short time. First, Tosti, who had been in exile since his expulsion from Northumbria, sailed across the English Channel from Flanders with a fleet of sixty ships. He was quickly repelled by Harold, but retreated to Scotland to begin preparing another attack with Harald Hardrada of Norway.

Next, in June, Harold began mustering his English fleet against an expected invasion by William of Normandy. The wind, however, prevented the Normans from sailing, and by September the English troops were anxious to return home to get in their harvest, so Harold retreated to the Thames. Harald Hardrada took this opportunity to bring his and Tosti's combined fleet of 330 ships down into the Humber. They sailed up the Ouse almost to York, and were met at Fulford by a huge army led by Earl Morcar and his brother Earl Edwin. On 20 September, the Norwegians inflicted heavy casualties on the English. Harold Godwinson, meanwhile, had marched north from London, and took the Norwegians by surprise on 25 September. The ensuing battle, at Stamford Bridge on the River Derwent, was hard fought, but eventually resulted in the deaths, first, of Harald Hardrada, and later of Tosti. Harold Godwinson of England had fought off two foreign invasions. Three days after the Battle of Stamford Bridge, the wind finally changed and enabled William of Normandy to land at Pevensey. This news only reached Harold on 1st or 2nd October. He immediately mustered what was left of his army, and began to march south. During the Battle of Hastings, fought on 14 October, he was killed. The English had been defeated by the third invasion, William, Duke of Normandy, had become King of England, and was crowned in Westminster Abbey on Christmas Day 1066.

One of the largest contingents of William's army consisted of Bretons, and they provided his rear-guard at Hastings. Among the leaders of this group were three of the many younger sons of Count Eudo of Penthiévre in Brittany, and a distant kinsman of William's. These three brothers would all, successively, play an important role in the early history of Richmond. Two were, to our minds surprisingly, both called Alan, the third was called Stephen. The two brothers Alan were differentiated according to their colouring as Alan Rufus and Alan Niger, such distinguishing features as physical characteristics being one of the categories which would eventually constitute surnames when these came to be used in the 14th century.

Alan Rufus was particularly close to William, supporting him not only in his successful initial campaign but also in the more troublesome subsequent establishment of his rule. Alan was subsequently granted, both as a reward for his sterling work during the invasion and at Hastings, and also as someone who William could trust with delegated authority, a vast extent of lands throughout England, and in particular in the North and in East Anglia. This would later be known as the Honour of Richmond, as will be explained later in this chapter. Much of it had belonged to Earl Edwin. Rather than merely taking over Edwin's local headquarters at Gilling West, Alan Rufus deliberately chose to make it clear that his was a new regime, and thus he began building Richmond Castle. The significance of Alan Rufus was summed up in a verse, originally written in Norman-French as part of a poem describing the glories of the

Norman Conquest by the Norman chronicler Gaimar sometime between 1135 and 1147. This is an English translation:

> Earl Alan of Brittany
> Struck well with his company,
> He struck like a baron.
> Right well the Breton did
> With the king he came to this land
> To help him in his war.
> He was his cousin, of his lineage,
> A nobleman of high descent.
> Much he served and loved the king,
> And he right well rewarded him.
> Richmond he gave him in the north,
> A good castle fair and strong.
> In many places in England
> The king gave him land,
> Long he held it, and then came to his end.
> At St. Edmund's he was buried.

The opening line of the poem has been translated to begin 'Earl Alan' but in fact he is always referred to in early Latin documents as *comitis*, or Count Alan.

The Castle which Alan Rufus began building about the year 1071, only five years after the Norman Conquest, must have seemed extraordinary at the time for many reasons, the main one being that it was constructed of stone, when most buildings other than perhaps some local churches were built of wood. It is one of the oldest stone-built castles in England, and was possibly the first to be built in stone from the outset, without a preliminary phase of timber and earthworks. Not only does it occupy a commanding site, and one with such strategic importance at the junction of upland Swaledale with the lowland of the lower Swale valley, but it was conceived on a very grand scale. The very monumentality of it expresses the Normans' political will to dominate this part of the country, and indeed its design was so successful, in both practical and political terms, that it would never be besieged.

The Castle's main court was laid out in 1071 as an equilateral triangle, the base line of which runs parallel to the river along the southern edge of the site. The other two, western and eastern, sides were built as stone curtain walls, meeting in an apex at the northern point, where the main entrance was located. The western curtain wall terminated in the south-western angle with a corner tower, and along the eastern side were three towers, the most northerly one having at its lowest level a small chapel, dedicated to St. Nicholas. This survives remarkably intact, complete with its stone barrel-vaulted roof. Daylight enters the chapel not only from the doorway but through three windows in its east wall, their small openings in the thick wall deeply splayed so as to diffuse the light they admit. Two are circular, the third a small round-headed light, the sill of which provided a stone altar, with small recesses nearby to form cupboards for the storage of the communion vessels and service books. The chapel walls were once plastered, the surface painted with red lines suggestive of the mortar joints hidden below, as was fashionable during the Norman period. Rather than having wooden furniture as today, high status buildings in those days had built-in stone furniture. Along the two side walls are low benches divided into stalls with round-arched canopied tops, originally with vertical stone shafts between the bases and cushion capitals.

These canopies, constructed of rectangular blocks of dressed stone each shaped into a round arch on the lower edge, resting on stone corbels, are typical of early-Norman architecture. Similar features, once supporting the roof beams, can be seen in Scolland's Hall in the south-east corner of the Castle, considered to be one of the oldest surviving great halls in the country. It was situated at first-floor level, and was entered by an external flight of stone stairs, the bottom steps of which can still be seen, leading up to an imposing round-arched doorway. The hall itself has in both its main walls elegant windows, each consisting of a pair of round-headed lights, separated by a slender shaft, within a larger round-arched opening in the thickness of the wall. There are no scars of leaded glazing, only rebates where wooden shutters fitted, and it seems the glass of the day was deemed too expensive even for this splendid room. There is also no evidence of a fireplace, but the presumption is that portable braziers were brought in as required. At the west end of the building is a spiral staircase, up which food was brought to the guests from the kitchen in a separate building immediately to the west.

At the east end was the high table, raised on a dais, where the most important personnel sat, the higher status being emphasized by a larger window. Behind them to the east was a smaller and more private room, called the solar, with a fireplace and access to the latrine facilities provided nearby in the southernmost tower of the eastern curtain wall, euphemistically called the Gold Hole Tower. On the ground floor below the great hall is an undercroft, used for storage and perhaps for household administration, and there was a doorway leading out to a gallery, since removed, projecting from the riverside elevation of the building. Here, according to tradition, the ladies watched their handsome knights practising their jousting and other military skills on the field across the river, which is now used for football.

The stonework of Count Alan's construction was of such high quality that it still forms the major part of Richmond Castle as it exists today. The most important elements of the late-11th century work, notably the doorway and windows of Scolland's Hall, and the original entrance archway below the later keep, are outstandingly fine and unusually early examples of the architectural style introduced by the Normans from France. Norman architecture was part of the Romanesque artistic tradition, originating in ancient classical architecture, and because the Castle dates from so soon after the Norman Conquest, it has to be assumed that these architectural details were carved by French stonemasons imported into Richmond. How hard they would find the local stone to carve and shape, compared with the fine stones of their home country! That there were too few of the Norman masons to complete more than the most prestigious features of the building is shown by comparing these with the rest of the early work. Extensive areas of stonework, particularly in the curtain walls, in the pitched style of construction known as herring-bone masonry, which is usually illustrated in text-books as being typical of Anglo-Saxon architecture, suggests that the plain walling was delegated to native stonemasons, who presumably had to be conscripted for the task.

Herringbone stonework in the west curtain wall of Richmond Castle

Scolland's Hall is named after Scolland, lord of Bedale, who was sewer, or steward, to Count Alan, a very important position. Not only did Scolland oversee the banquets and hospitality in the Castle, but he would often be left in charge during Alan's frequent absences in other parts of the Honour of Richmond. Nowadays visitors to the Castle see first a vast expanse of empty lawn, and hear perhaps the sounds of a few children running about and playing. This is very misleading. The Castle in Norman times must have been a hive of activity, of hustle and bustle, ringing to the sounds of horses coming and going, of messengers constantly bringing news - the equivalent of the mail, telephone, fax and e-mail business of a large corporate body today. Richmond Castle represented the immense status of the Honour of Richmond, but was also its administrative headquarters.

An 'honour' was a grouping of feudal holdings. In the Middle Ages all land belonged to the king but was held in a politically-structured society in return for military service, a system known as feudalism. The king, William the Conqueror, granted Count Alan his lands, which had belonged to Earl Edwin. The lands comprised 'fees' or holdings, each of which had to provide Alan with a knight - a unit of sophisticated military expertise the modern equivalent of which might be a tank or a jet fighter. The Honour of Richmond thus provided the means of staffing the castle - each knight had to do a forty-day tour of duty on a roster, known as castle guard. A knight would bring with him the equipment necessary for the duty - perhaps a war horse, armour and weapons, and a team of retainers to back them up - in return for the land he held. Below the knight were families who held their land in return for other services, often agricultural, paying in kind rather than cash. The Honour of Richmond formed one of the largest landholdings in the country, comprising 199 manors in Yorkshire, plus over a hundred others elsewhere, particularly in Suffolk. Richmond Castle was the administrative base of all these vast estates and the populations living on them, hence the hustle and bustle we should picture here.

There must have been additional noise from the building construction and alterations, which clearly continued for many years. As far as we can tell, the first phase of construction of Richmond Castle had been completed when Alan Rufus died in 1089. He was buried, the poem tells us, at St. Edmund's - the rich monastery at Bury St. Edmund's in Suffolk, which he had endowed generously. He was unmarried, and so was succeeded by his next brother, Alan Niger, who only outlived him by a few years before dying, also unmarried, in 1093. The next lord of Richmond was another and younger brother, Stephen who lived into ripe old age, surviving until 1135/6. He was buried in the

Cistercian Abbey of Bégard in Brittany, which he had founded in 1130. Stephen had a son, another Alan Niger, who until his death in 1146 was the fourth lord of Richmond, the third with the name Alan, and the second to be known as Alan Niger. This Alan Niger is the first to be named in documents specifically as Count of Richmond, for the place-name was not used in the early years of the castle or town's history.

    This second Alan Niger married Constance, daughter of the Duke of Brittany, and their son, Conan the Little, inherited the title Duke of Brittany in 1164. He was also the first lord of Richmond to be called Earl of Richmond. Conan seems to have been self-conscious about his size, but his dukedom enhanced the social status of the lord of Richmond, as well as adding extensive estates in Brittany to his English lands, and this increase in status is reflected architecturally at Richmond Castle. Significant changes were made in Conan's lordship - the quarter-century from his inheritance in 1146 until his death in 1171. Although this phase of the Castle's history takes us just beyond the end of the Norman period in 1154, these works are included in this chapter because they represent the fully-developed form of the English Romanesque architecture. Despite Conan's assigning, for reasons of political prudence, his dukedom of Brittany to King Henry II in 1166, this did not diminish the architectural quality of his alterations, for some of these works were actually completed by that king. The most obvious of Conan's achievements today is the erection of the magnificent keep, which so dominates the Castle itself, but also forms the most instantly recognizable symbol of Richmond today, and is visible from many distant viewpoints. *[see plate 2]*

    The keep, built onto the outside of the original entrance in the northern angle, has a tower form, which is typical of prestigious Romanesque military architecture in the third quarter of the 12th century. Over 100 feet (30 metres) high, the keep is built of even ashlar stonework, with shallow buttresses, which articulate its appearance as well as strengthening its immensely thick walls. It has on each of its two upper floors a large and imposing chamber occupying most of the floor plan, with small ancillary chambers in the immense thickness of the walls. The upper suite, being the more sumptuous, is likely to have been for the use of the Constable, a high-ranking official of the Castle. The office was hereditary and gave the name to Constable Burton in Wensleydale.

A mural staircase within the keep, showing typical Romanesque stonework of the 12th century

The walls of the keep also contain long, straight flights of stairs, which continue up to the roof and corner turrets. For defensive reasons, the entry to the keep was by an external staircase, which has been lost, leading up to the first floor. Only from this level was it possible to reach, by a narrow spiral staircase, the ground-floor chamber which contains a well, an essential precaution in case the Castle were ever besieged. To form this chamber the original Castle entrance was blocked up, and a new gateway formed alongside the keep. Other improvements carried out in Conan's time include the building of the curtain wall along the river edge of the site, the addition of a barbican with dry moat and drawbridge to strengthen the northern entrance, and also the enclosing with stone walls of another court to the east, which is known as the Cockpit, where English Heritage hopes to create a new garden as a Millennium project.

As soon as Richmond Castle was begun in 1071 people not officially connected with it were drawn towards it for the trading opportunities offered by its military personnel. Indeed, those based at the Castle were also presumably pleased to be able to obtain supplies. To regulate this situation, the civilian settlement was soon recognized by the granting of charters, which, in centuries long before there was a free market economy, conferred certain privileges on the inhabitants, particularly the right to hold a weekly market. It was customary at the time for such charters to be granted by the local lord, not by the king himself. It has sometimes been claimed that Richmond was granted a charter in the year 1093, but this is the result of confusion caused by there being so many lords named Alan, and the earliest known charter was actually drawn up between 1136 and 1145. It granted to the burgesses, or citizens, the borough of Richmond, and the land of Fontenais, at an annual fee farm, or rent paid to the Earl, of £29. The 'land of Fontenais' has never satisfactorily been precisely located, but was clearly close by. It is implicit in the charter that Richmond was already holding its weekly Saturday market - but where?

What is certain is that it was not in the present Market Place because in those early years of Richmond's history this was the Outer Bailey of the Castle, demarcated by a wooden palisade and a defensive ditch, and very much a part of the exclusive Norman zone of the Castle. From an early date there were two civilian suburbs outside the Castle. One suburb grew up in

Frenchgate, the street leading to the Castle, near which the parish church was built, and the other in Newbiggin. Newbiggin is the more likely to have been the first market place, as it has one of the levellest sites around the town, and the present streetscape exhibits the characteristics of early town planning, with two parallel rows of buildings flanking a wide street, wider than was necessary for traffic, but which could accommodate traders' stalls and booths. This suggested identity of Newbiggin as the area authorized by early charter to have privileges tallies with the Domesday Book entry for the small and obviously new settlement of Newton.

The survey carried out in 1086, transcribed into what became known as the Domesday Book, was intended as a thorough record of the Conqueror's new lands, and was compiled for fiscal reasons. The commissioners appointed for the survey had to establish the name of each place, the names of those who had held it before 1066 and afterwards, the extent of taxable plough land with the number of ploughs before and since 1066, the number of villagers, cottagers, slaves and free men (but not of their families), the number of mills and fishponds and the amount of meadow, pasture and woodland, and above all the extent to which the taxation potential had been increased or reduced in the twenty years since the Norman Conquest. No record was therefore made of non-taxable lands, such as those belonging to monastic foundations, or other exempt property such as Richmond Castle.

The settlements in the Richmond area are recorded as then belonging to Count Alan, and both Hindrelac and Newton came under Enisant - Enisant Musard, Alan's Constable of the Castle - having belonged to Thorr in Earl Edwin's time. The entry for Newton significantly does not have a 1066 valuation, as it had only come into existence after the Conquest. Hindrelac was recorded in two parts, each of which was assessed as having a value of 10s. before 1066. The two parts provide a contrasting picture in 1086, the larger part with population and a church had increased in value to 16s. whereas the other was waste, with no population mentioned, but a fishery, and a value of 16d.

Presumably these details can be interpreted that in 1086 major development on the site of the new town of Richmond was in progress.

Many northern settlements were recorded as being 'waste', or land with little productive value, in 1086. This is generally taken to reflect the severity of the 'Harrying of the North', William I's policy of subduing opposition to his Conquest. He had experienced rebellion in Northumbria almost from the word go, particularly in York which revolted as early as 1067. This prompted him to erect two motte-and-bailey castles - the castles of earthworks and timber, which characterized the early Norman period - to guard the river Ouse in York. Two more rebellions north of the Humber followed, and a fourth in York in September 1069 in collusion with the Danes - supported by among others Earl Edwin - resulted in William confiscating Edwin's lands.

Determined to teach Northumbria a lesson it would not forget, during the winter of 1069/70 William ravaged the countryside between York and the river Tees, burning hundreds of villages and slaying their inhabitants to such an extent that many areas had still not recovered from such a terrible episode by 1086. The death in 1071 of Earl Edwin, killed while on his way to Scotland, prompted the gift of his lands to Count Alan and set in motion the foundation of Richmond in 1071. According to tradition, it was because of the damage caused by fire during the devastation of 1069 that William ordered domestic fires to be damped down every evening, hence the curfew bell, which is still ring in Richmond when the town clock is working properly.

The Norman period was a time of contrasts. On the one hand there was the brutality with which rebellions were put down, on the other it was a time of great religious fervour and piety, with the foundation and generous endowment of many religious institutions, particularly monasteries, and the building of many thousands of parish churches. The same individuals were involved with these contrasting activities. The religious endeavours of the Normans fully re-established the country's Christian culture, eventually compensating for the losses under the Vikings. There is architectural evidence of church building in the Richmond area shortly before and soon after the Norman Conquest. Examples include the tower of the parish church at Gilling West, where Anglo-Saxon window details were seen during repair work in 1995, and the tower of Hornby Church, which seems to belong to a late phase which is Norman in date but still Anglo-Saxon in architectural style $c.1080$. At Easby, the fine Northumbrian cross had been superseded by a small parish church, parts of which still date from before 1100. Perhaps some at least of this area escaped the full effects of the Harrying of the North, and it has been suggested that some of the records of waste at the time of the Domesday survey may be attributed to Scottish raids.

It is clear that churches and chapels quickly appeared in both the Castle and civilian areas of Norman Richmond. In addition to the Chapel of St. Nicholas within the Castle itself, a larger Chapel, dedicated to Holy Trinity, was built in the Outer Bailey. There has in the past been debate by historians as to which came first, Holy Trinity Chapel or Richmond's parish church of St. Mary, which contains two rebuilt Norman arches. A charter dating from 1125-30, several years earlier than the Borough's charter of 1136-45, whereby Count Stephen endowed St. Mary's Abbey in York, which his uncle Alan Rufus had been instrumental in founding, mentions the church at Richmond. This is more likely to be the parish church of St. Mary, a parish church being a more generous endowment than that of a castle chapelry. The St. Mary's Abbey charter was witnessed by the Archdeacon of Richmond, the Archdeaconry tracing its origins back to 1089.

The first monastery to be established close to Richmond was St. Martin's Priory, on the opposite bank of the river Swale from the Castle. St. Martin's was begun in 1100 as a cell of St. Mary's Abbey in York, which Alan Rufus had founded, by Whyomar or Wimar, Count Alan's steward. There was already a small chapel dedicated to St. Martin, but Whyomar's gift of it to the great Benedictine house in York is an action very typical of his status and time. The popularity of the Benedictine order, which preferred urban locations, had not yet been challenged by, for example, the Cistercians who liked remote sites. St. Martin's Priory was a significantly early foundation, pre-dating the charters already mentioned.

Whyomar was probably also the founder of the Anchoress's Cell, which gave its name to Anchorage Hill. It was near Aldbiggin, and at the junction of the roads to Darlington and Brompton-on-Swale, on the north-eastern outskirts of the town. The Anchoress's Cell was either attached to or next to a small chapel dedicated to St. Edmund, which, although the date of its foundation is unknown, from surviving architectural evidence seems to date from the Norman period. Edmund, King of East Anglia, died in 868 during a Danish raid and was buried at Bury St. Edmunds. Before long he was being revered as a saint, and a cult developed about him, which was particularly popular in East Anglia. The first two lords of Richmond, Alan Rufus and Alan Niger, who also had extensive estates in East Anglia, were particularly devoted to St. Edmund, both being buried at Bury St. Edmunds.

By the time the last Norman king, Stephen, died in 1154, Richmond consisted of a large and impressive stone-built Castle with two chapels, and around it a small town divided into two areas, Frenchgate suburb with the parish church, and Newbiggin suburb with a market place. Just across the river was the small Benedictine cell of St. Martin's Priory, and somewhere on the same side in the Sleegill area, at an unknown location called Bordelby, was the small leper chapel of St. Thomas. The number of religious houses and secular chapels in Richmond would grow in the medieval period - as told in the next chapter.

3

Medieval Richmond 1154-1485

The National History

     The Plantagenet dynasty, named from the yellow broom flowers on their coat of arms, began with King Henry II (1154-89). Also ruling much of France through his great-grandfather William the Conqueror, and formidable wife Eleanor of Aquitaine, he introduced the King's Peace, or rule of law, and trial by jury, even though his Archbishop of Canterbury, Thomas Becket, his "turbulent priest", was murdered in his own Cathedral in 1170. His strong rule left England sufficiently stable to withstand the prolonged absences on the Crusades of his son King Richard I, the Lionheart, (1189-99). Another son, King John (1199-1216), was weaker, losing control of Normandy in 1204, and in 1215 conceding some of his own power to the English barons through the Magna Carta. Much of the long reign of John's son, King Henry III (1216-72), was dominated by the leader of the barons, Simon de Montfort.

     Henry III's son King Edward I (1272-1307) gave Parliament the right to pass laws and conquered Wales, building many fine castles on the Welsh border. His campaign against Scotland was less easily won, and the Scottish wars continued into the time of his son King Edward II (1307-27), who lost the Battle of Bannockburn to Robert Bruce in 1314, and was eventually deposed and murdered in 1327. The long reign of his son King Edward III (1327-77) saw the beginning of the Hundred Years War with France in 1337, and the devastating plague known as the Black Death of 1348-9, but also the writings of Geoffrey Chaucer and the use at court of the English language. Following the death of his son, the Black Prince, in 1376, his successor was his grandson, King Richard II (1377-99), whose attempts to raise revenue for the on-going wars with France led to the Peasants' Revolt against the Poll Tax in 1381, which accelerated the breakdown of the feudal system. Richard was murdered at Pontefract Castle in 1400, Henry Bolingbroke, son of King Edward III's son John of Gaunt, Duke of Lancaster, having usurped the throne to become King Henry IV (1399-1413). Thus began the ascendancy of the House of Lancaster. His son King Henry V (1413-22) won a decisive victory over the French at Agincourt in 1415. His son, the scholarly King Henry VI (1422-61), was only a baby on his accession, which created a power vacuum, and in adult life was prone to fits of madness. Having finally lost the Hundred Years War with France in 1453, England was from 1455 rent asunder by the Wars of the Roses, a power struggle between the Houses of York and Lancaster. Henry VI, murdered in 1471, was ousted from the throne in 1461 by the Yorkist King Edward IV (1461-83), whose turbulent reign nevertheless saw the printing press introduced into England by William Caxton in 1477. Edward was succeeded by his brother King Richard III (1483-5) whose defeat at the Battle of Bosworth by Henry Tudor in 1485, started the Tudor dynasty.

Inevitably over such a long period, medieval England witnessed many changes. At its start, most of the population lived in manorial villages, by the end more were living in towns like Richmond, where there were markets, fairs and trade guilds. Most of the population lived in timber-framed houses, but grander buildings reflected the development of Gothic architecture through its Early English, Decorated and Perpendicular phases. The majority of surviving medieval buildings apart from castles are parish churches and ruined monasteries, and this reflects the high priority given to religion in the Middle Ages. Later centuries were to see greater religious upheaval, but one of the first theologians to challenge the might of the Church was John Wycliffe, Foxe's 'Morning Star of the Reformation', who was born about 1330 in the Richmond area, possibly either in the village of Wycliffe on the river Tees, or in the village of Hipswell near Catterick Garrison.

The medieval history of Richmond, and its Castle, was closely interwoven with the complex descent of the Honour of Richmond, and further complicated by that of the titles of Earl of Richmond and Duke of Brittany. Sometimes, but by no means always, these descended together: sometimes, but by no means always, they passed by direct inheritance, often reverting to the Crown by forfeit or other default, and being re-granted, sometimes repeatedly, by the king. Sometimes they were held by Englishmen, sometimes by Frenchmen: sometimes they were confiscated and re-granted in accordance with the politics between the two countries. Due to the ensuing incredible complexity, only some of the events and personalities will be highlighted here.

Conan died in 1171 and was buried at the Abbey of Bégard in Brittany, where his grandfather Stephen and his father Alan lay. Conan had married Margaret, sister of King Malcolm IV of Scotland, and left as his heir their young daughter, Constance. She had been betrothed as an infant to Geoffrey Plantagenet, third son of King Henry II, who acted as her guardian until the marriage took place in 1181. During this time Richmond Castle briefly featured in national history as the prison of King William the Lion of Scotland, captured at Alnwick in 1174, and said to have been held in the tower chamber above the Chapel of St. Nicholas.

Constance inherited the title of Duchess of Brittany, and also held the Honour of Richmond. Constance and Geoffrey's marriage was brief, as he died in 1186, but they had a daughter, Eleanor, and posthumous son, Arthur. Arthur, named after the heroic legendary King Arthur, a name which was also of great significance in Brittany, had some claim on the English throne, and was murdered as a threat to King John in 1203, after Constance's death in Brittany in 1201. She had married twice more after Geoffrey's death, and her third marriage had produced two daughters. The elder, Alice, married Peter de Braine, who became Duke of Brittany and received part of the Honour of Richmond in 1218. After a lengthy period of exceptionally frequent confiscations and re-grants the Crown granted the Honour in 1240 to Peter of Savoy, who held it through to 1266, when it reverted to the Duke of Brittany, whose son John de Dreux had in 1260 married King Henry III's daughter Beatrice and became the first of many Earls of Richmond to be called John. A late-14th century John, Earl of Richmond, was King Edward III's second son, John of Gaunt.

Richard II granted Richmond to his queen, Anne of Bohemia, in 1384, then in 1399 the Honour was granted to Ralph Nevill, 1st Earl of Westmorland, by his brother-in-law King Henry IV as a reward for his support for the House of Lancaster. The long connection with Brittany was now broken, and the Castle was old-fashioned and of little interest to those to whom it was granted, but the Honour was still a valuable asset bringing in considerable income. Those endowed with this were from now on all connected with the English royal family. After Ralph Nevill's death in 1425, the Honour and earldom were granted to Henry IV's son John, Duke of Bedford, who held them until his death in 1435, when both reverted to the Crown. The Honour was given in 1453 to Edmund Tudor, and he was also Earl of Richmond until his death in 1456: his son Henry Tudor, who became King Henry VII, belongs in the next chapter. In the 1460s the Yorkist King Edward IV gave the Honour and Richmond Castle to his brother George, Duke of Clarence and, when he was executed in 1478, they went to another brother, Richard, Duke of Gloucester, later Richard III, who was based at Middleham Castle.

The keep was probably just about finished when Conan died in 1171. The Pipe Rolls (so called because the parchments were wrapped round rods), annual records of the expenses laid out on the Crown's behalf by county sheriffs, show that King Henry II, as Constance's guardian, paid for the completion of the keep in 1172, and then for the completion of the remainder of the large-scale building programme begun by Conan in 1146. After this, nothing of significance was added to the Castle for just over a century, until a new addition expressed an increase in status of the perpetrator, and indeed another royal connection, just as Conan's work had done.

The first John, Earl of Richmond, about the year 1278 added a second chapel to the Castle. Situated on the first floor of a new building erected near the south-west corner, its size led to it being called the Great Chapel. It was staffed by no fewer than six chaplains, Premonstratensian canons, like those of Easby, but from Egglestone Abbey situated on the Yorkshire bank of the river Tees near Barnard Castle. The canons were to live in the Castle, near to the new chapel, unless an outbreak of war necessitated their recall to Egglestone. They were to celebrate divine office in perpetuity, and to sing Mass for the soul of his late wife Beatrice, daughter of King Henry III, whom John had married in 1260, and in due course for John's. The Great Chapel no longer exists, all that is left is its large west window in the west curtain wall. Below it is a sallyport doorway, or hidden exit through which the garrison could sneak out to confront any attackers besieging the Castle.

The Calendar of Close Rolls, records of the Court of Chancery so called because the parchment rolls were closed with a seal, provide several references to Richmond Castle during the reign of King Edward I. On 18 August 1295 the Sheriff of York was ordered to receive Welsh hostages and to send ten of them to Richmond, 4d. per day maintenance allowance being provided for each one. On 20 August 1297 the Constable of Richmond Castle, Roald of Constable Burton, was ordered to deliver to the wife of Miles Stapleton some suitable houses in the Castle "wherein she may dwell with her household until the King shall otherwise order as Miles is shortly going to Gascony in the King's service by his order". Perhaps the lady found fault with her lodgings, for in November of that year the Constable was ordered "to cause that Castle to be repaired where necessary and to cause it to be kept safely so that no peril shall arise to the King or to the Castle for lack of custody".

A few years later, early in the 14th century, the second John, Earl of Richmond, made improvements to the living accommodation at the solar end of Scolland's Hall, adding a new private chamber and yet another chapel. By standing near the base of the staircase outside Scolland's Hall, visitors can still see the chapel's piscina, or small wash-basin for washing the Mass vessels, also an opening which enabled people in the chamber to see the priest celebrating Mass at the altar. Other modifications carried out at about the same time included increasing the height of some of the curtain wall towers, and the insertion into the keep of stone ribbed vaulting springing from the central Norman pier over the well. By standing in the ground floor one can see on the ribs the mason's marks, or 'signatures' of the medieval stonemasons who constructed the vault. After this time there were few repairs or alterations made to the Castle.

Among the ancient manuscripts in the Cotton collection of the British Library is a 14th-century coloured drawing of the castle, an amazing diagram showing the positions of the castle-guard service performed by knights holding lands under the Earl of Richmond *[see plate 3]*. Their coats of arms are shown by their placements, and a list of their names defines the eight locations. Brian Fitzalan (of Bedale) was responsible for the 'Great Hall of Scoulande' - the sketch of Scolland's Hall shows it with a lead roof, and the external staircase is recognizable. The place of Thomas de Burgh (of Brough Hall near Catterick) was west of the Great Chapel, which is depicted as we might expect the chapel to have looked. In St. Anne's parish church at Catterick, where he lived, is the tomb of Walter de Urswick, appointed Constable of Richmond Castle by John of Gaunt in 1371, and who died about 1415. The tomb is decorated with his coat of arms and that of his wife, a daughter of Henry Scrope of Masham. Walter's recumbent effigy shows him wearing a helm over chain mail, the rest of his body protected by plate armour, with his feet resting on a mastiff dog.

At some stage the Outer Bailey, the large area immediately to the north of the main Castle entrance, ceased to be a military zone and became a civilian area, then or later becoming the Market Place. We do not know when this change occurred, only that it had taken place in 1312 when permission was granted for a defensive wall to be erected around it to protect the inhabitants against Scottish raids. Although early medieval pottery has been found during archaeological investigations of various sites in the Market Place, it has not been possible to ascertain if the fragments dated from before or after 1312, and whether they had been in military or civilian use. King Edward I's unsuccessful attempts to conquer Scotland led to an intensification of England's Scottish wars in the early years of King Edward II's reign, with England generally coming off worse, particularly around the time of the defeat at the Battle of Bannockburn in 1314. The Scots made many raids down into North Yorkshire, a particularly severe incursion in 1310 affecting Richmond considerably, as can be seen from the following account given by the late-medieval chronicler Raphael Holinshed.

> Lord James Douglasse and the Lord Steward of Scotland went abroad to harrie and spoile the countrie (of) England on each side, the one of them passing forth towards Hartlepools and Cleveland, and the other towards Richmond. The inhabitants of Richmondshire having no captain amongst them, gave a great summe of monie in like manner as at other times they had done to have their countrie spared from fire and spoil.

Following this raid, on the petition of the second John, Earl of Richmond, the Crown in 1312 gave the burgesses, or town council, of Richmond permission to construct a defensive stone wall around their town to protect them against attacks. This was an immense undertaking, far beyond the means of the inhabitants, and so the permission was backed up by a grant of 'murage', or the right to generate income for building the wall by levying tolls on certain specified goods sold in the market. The initial murage grant was for five years, and subsequent grants were made for either three or five years in 1332, 1338 and 1399 for further works and repairs after more damage by the Scots.

The lists of items on which tolls were to be levied gives some idea of the range of merchandise available in Richmond market in the 14th century, and also the quantities being sold to produce such income. As well as the local produce of corn and vegetables, horses, cows and sheep, and their hides, fish, cheese and butter, honey, firewood and nails, cloth and dye-stuffs which one might expect, there were many goods imported from far afield, including dried fish from Aberdeen, "mulnells, conger and stikar eels" from the North Sea, Irish cloth and wax from Spain, Poland and Lübeck. The 1332 list enumerates 76 different commodities to be taxed. The levy was a farthing per cartload of bark, 1000 faggots, 1000 roof nails or 2000 onions, a ha'penny per 1000 herrings, 10 hams, 100 wool fells (skins), 100 skins of foxes, cats or squirrels, a cartload of charcoal, a 'wey' (measure of weight probably 40 bushels) of butter or cheese, or one millstone. One (old) penny was levied per 1000 turves and a tun of wine brought in one and a half pence.

There were only two places in the wall for vehicular ingress or egress, the two main gateways, called bars in northern dialect, one in Finkle Street, the other at the bottom of Frenchgate in the low-lying area known locally as the Channel. These two locations identify the main approach routes to the town at the time. Frenchgate Bar was used by all traffic approaching from the east and north, coming in from the Great North Road at Catterick through Brompton-on-Swale or Scotch Corner by Skeeby, and also from the western part of County Durham and Greta Bridge by Gilling West. Horse-drawn vehicles must have found the road down Frenchgate very trying, with its sharp bend at the top, the long steep route down, and then the pull up at the bottom from the boggy Channel. Finkle Street Bar took traffic from Swaledale coming down Hurgill Road, and also that from the south, which crossed the river Swale by the Green Bridge and climbed up Bargate towards Newbiggin and into Finkle Street.

Bargate is a good example of a local place-name of Scandinavian origin, describing the street leading to the bar, the suffix 'gate' meaning street. 'Finkle' means crooked, and there is an angle where the bar stood near the Black Lion Hotel.

The main bars were long ago demolished as traffic obstructions, but two postern gates, for pedestrian use, remain. One, known as The Bar, stands at the top of the attractive Cornforth Hill, which is clearly far too steep for wheeled vehicles. Close by, following the contour line northward, can be seen the line of the dry ditch which lay outside the rampart on which the wall was built. The Bar has a pointed arch, which is stylistically typical of Gothic architecture in the 14th century. The other postern, in Friars Wynd, has a round arch and is of slightly later date, having been inserted into the town wall after its main defensive purpose had ceased, to enable the townspeople to fetch drinking water from the house of Grey Friars situated immediately outside the wall.

Friars Wynd Postern, with tram-lines laid down in 1895 by ironmonger Robert Spence to connect warehouses with his shop in the Market Place

The site of Richmond had been chosen as a good location for a castle, but was not particularly well suited to being a town, not having a plentiful supply of water, and with few flat sites suitable for holding markets. At the bottom of Ryder's Wynd the sound can still be heard of the water gushing down from the Grey Friars' site, having emanated from springs on Bolton Crofts.

The openings of both posterns are rebated so that they could be barricaded in times of attack, but it is unlikely that any of the Richmond bars was equipped with a portcullis, which required a superstructure into which it could be raised. The town wall encircled the present Market Place, seemingly following the line of the older timber palisade and ditch around the horseshoe-shaped Outer Bailey, but the precise location of its full circuit is unknown. The line of the wall to north and west between the openings can be deduced, but there is scant documentary evidence. Some old boundary walls have been suggested as possible surviving sections of the town wall, but it is very difficult to date rubble walls, and none are as thick as the fragments in which the posterns are set. The section about which least is known is that along the lower, east end of the Market Place towards the Cockpit of the Castle, where archaeological observation has failed to locate the wall. The term Bailey, sometimes spelled Bayley, was in common use into the 18th century, and indeed the building now occupied by Woolworths was known as Bailey House into the early years of the 20th century.

The town wall had to be manned by guards on watch, and these were probably initially found by the inhabitants, but it seems that by late-medieval times paid watchmen were employed, to give the townsfolk peace of mind while they slept, against burglaries, or fire breaking out. As in other medieval towns, Richmond's Watch evolved into the Waits, a small band of civic musicians, complete with official livery, who provided entertainment at public functions as well as proclaiming the night hours and the assurance that all was well. The present Town Mayor of Richmond's entourage still includes two halberdiers who carry ancient but still-sharp weapons - to defend the town's leading citizen if need be! The Beacon, situated alongside the old road leading up Swaledale, on the highest point within the borough boundary at 1061 feet above sea level, may also have been introduced at the time of the Scottish incursions. It can be seen clearly from the top of the Castle keep, and is also in sight of similar beacons on Penhill in Wensleydale and Roseberry Topping in Cleveland.

Several medieval charters were issued to Richmond, most simply confirming the established privileges previously given to the town in Norman times, but some are more noteworthy for granting something new. In 1268, during the reign of King Henry III, the first John, Earl of Richmond, augmented the lands available for agriculture by additionally giving the burgesses Whitcliffe Pasture, a large area of grazing land to the west of the town. The annual fee farm rent was increased from £29 to £40 in consequence. The weekly Saturday market had long been established, but medieval towns gained additional prosperity from holding fairs, special trading events held over several days. As with markets, these were not a right, but a privilege, which had to be granted by charter.

In 1278 King Edward I granted to John, Duke of Brittany, Earl of Richmond, an annual four-day fair to be held at Richmond "on the vigil, on the day, on the morrow of the Exaltation of the Holy Cross, and for one day following". In medieval times it was conventional for dates to be identified not by the calendar but by a religious feast day. Holy Cross Day was observed on 14 September, and the crucifix was often referred to as the rood, so it became known as the Rood Fair. A September fair continued to be held into the 20th century. The town acquired two other annual fairs as the centuries passed. Later medieval charters included that issued in 1329 by King Edward III, which ratified that of 1278.

Common Seal of Richmond dating from 1278

It is in the late-13th and early-14th centuries that we begin to glimpse some of the individual residents of Richmond and their occupations. A list survives of those eligible in 1301 to pay Lay Subsidy, a tax levied to raise money for the Scottish wars of one-tenth on the 'movable' possessions, not lands, of householders. It excludes, for obvious reasons, the very poor, and also all clergy, of whom there would be many in Richmond, but gives a list of 67 names contributing a total of £15 7s. 10d. They paid amounts varying from 4d. to 65s. 2d. with most paying about 3s. The figures probably suggest a population of about 600, most villages having had about a dozen taxpayers.

Little did those Richmond inhabitants realize that within a few years they would be faced with the need to construct defences for their town. As the 14th century progressed they had other hardships to face. Bad weather, particularly in the mid-1340s, caused a series of poor harvests, which meant people had little to eat, and there was less to sell in Richmond market. Perhaps general health was undermined, for in 1348 the country suffered the Black Death, an epidemic of severe illness, probably bubonic plague. Estimates of the proportion of population to die during the Black Death vary from 20% to 50%, and we have no way of knowing the extent to which Richmond was affected. In general the huge loss of life is known to have had immense socio-economic effects, leading to an acceleration in the breakdown, which had already begun, of the feudal system. More payment was made in money rather than service, and more people moved from the country into towns. This would certainly seem to have happened in Richmond, for the population evidence later in the 14th century shows an increase to about 800 in 1377, when 370 people over the age of 14 paid 4d. per head Poll Tax.

Although the picture of medieval Richmond is generally of a gradual increase in size and prosperity, there were times when the picture was less rosy. During the reign of King Henry VI, in 1440, the inhabitants petitioned the king to request a reduction in the annual fee farm rent of £40, citing loss of trade, and inhabitants, and a general decline, as the grounds for their being unable to raise that sum.

> Richmond consists of many burgesses, merchants and victuallers insomuch that foreign merchants and workmen, and other people from the parts adjacent and the counties of Lancaster, Cumberland and Westmorland trafficked in their market every Saturday, and carriers of grain and bread from the said counties and from the parts of Lonsdale, Craven, Dent and Sedbergh and other distant parts, wherein fruits grow not plentifully, wherefrom by the constant flocking of men thither, the burgesses for many years passed were able to levy the greater part of the fee farm.
> .....because markets are now held at Masham on Wednesday, at Bedale on Tuesday, at Middleham on Tuesday, at Staindrop, County Durham, on Thursday and at Barnard Castle on Wednesday, all within eight miles of Richmond,

whither the whole county around resorts and further that a great part of the grass of the pasture of Whitcliff has been so destroyed by underwood, thorns, fern and other growths and also because inhabitants have been consumed by pestilence and plague..... many have left with their wives and children as beggars so that the remaining burgesses have been unable to raise more than a third part of the fee farm.

Henry VI set up a commission of four to investigate the problem. Sixteen 'jurors' drawn from the surrounding area were to find out if the claims made by the petitioners were true, and report back. They found that the claims were correct, and that the burgesses had only been able to raise just under £20. In response, Henry VI granted Richmond a new charter in 1441, which duly reduced the fee farm, but this was done in a complicated way. Certain grants out of the fee farm were to be paid during the lifetime of the recipients, but the amount paid to the Crown was reduced to £12. An annual fee farm rent of this amount is still paid to the Crown, but nowadays it is returned to the town and distributed charitably as 'audit money'. The 1441 charter, written in Latin, which survives among the town's treasures, has a very elaborate initial letter H, for Henricus. This incorporates a rebus, or word picture, of the name Richmond, with the name *ryche* written across an orb, or mont, representing the suffix. Below *ryche* is shown water, for the river Swale, and above it a deer and a castle. A simplified version of this rebus became the logo for the Richmondshire Museum when it was opened in 1978.

The corporate life of medieval Richmond was organized by its burgesses, four of whom served each year as Bailiffs to administer the town. Below them were guilds, fraternities of religious and craft groups, which took responsibility for smaller scale matters and operated a simple welfare system, looking after their poor or sick brethren, and the widows and orphans of members. Among the religious fraternities was that of St. Mary, another was dedicated to St. John, and had a guildhall on the site of the present Town Hall which seems to have provided a home base for much of Richmond's corporate life, perhaps because the patron saint of the earls of Richmond was St. John the Evangelist. We do not know how many craft guilds there were in medieval Richmond, but later there were 13, some of which represented several crafts, suggesting that there had been more until some amalgamated. The craft guilds or companies governed the town's trade, perpetuating their skills through apprenticeship, and exercising strict quality control on products sold. Only guild members were freemen of the town, only they could trade freely from their premises, whereas others, such as outsiders coming in to sell their wares in the Saturday market, had to pay tolls to do so. Tradesmen became freemen of their guild either by birth - the eldest son of a freeman was automatically himself a freeman if he took up his freedom and paid his dues to the town - or by successfully completing a recognized apprenticeship, usually of seven years, with a Richmond freeman.

The medieval Market Place was surrounded by mainly timber-framed buildings in which tradesmen both lived and worked. In the Market Place was a free-standing building called the Toll Booth, from which market tolls were collected, and where were kept the town's standard weights and measures, against which those of traders could be compared. The Market Cross stood roughly where the present Obelisk stands, it consisted of a stone cross, mounted on a square base which was buttressed at each corner, each buttress being surmounted by a stone dog. All this was raised up on a mound of square stone steps. Nearby was a smaller cross, the Barley Cross, where corn was sold, and into which were fixed rings to which could be tied those felons sentenced to a public whipping. Lesser miscreants might be sentenced to the pillory, or stocks, both of which also stood nearby. The area where butchers worked, a notoriously messy operation, was known as the Shambles, and this consisted of an open timber-framed structure sited towards the northern side of the Market Place. The remains of this were uncovered during road-surfacing works in 1993.

Some occupations required a water supply, and craftsmen such as tanners congregated around the Green, down beside the river Swale. Just below the Green Bridge was a dye house, first mentioned in a document dated 1280, so there must have been a sizable textile trade in Richmond as early as that. The river powered a number of watermills, the most important being the Castle Mill at the Foss Head, probably almost as old in origin as the Castle itself. It was common for owners of corn mills to give the income they produced, or a proportion of it, to some good cause, such as a monastery, and one of the 12th-century Earls of Richmond had granted Castle Mill to the Abbey of Bégard in Brittany. Because of the esteem in which Bégard was held by the early earls, the abbey owned a considerable amount of property in England, and its northern estates were administered from the small cell it had established at Moulton, near Scotch Corner. When there were hostilities with France, the property of 'alien priories' such as Bégard was confiscated. During these periods their properties could not be administered, and as mills need constant maintenance, this meant that Castle Mill could not always be kept in repair. During one such spell when Castle Mill was inconveniently idle, it seems that the borough built its own corn watermill, Whitcliffe Mill, some little distance upstream of the town.

About half-way between the Castle and Whitcliffe mills, near the Green, yet another corn-grinding watermill was established by a mid-14th century inhabitant called William de Hudswell. Of entrepreneurial disposition, wealthier and more aggressive than many of his contemporaries, he was taking the law into his own hands, because corn mills were protected from competition by medieval manorial custom, called soke. He was legally challenged by Geoffrey, a Bégard monk, but the Green Mill continued for many centuries. William de Hudswell's authority-challenging character is further indicated by his building a pele tower, or fortified house, on the hill above the Green - during the quarrelsome 14th and 15th centuries, many pele towers would be built in the villages around Richmond. Both the Green and Whitcliffe mills were worked not only as corn mills but also as fulling mills, using water power to pound lengths of the woollen cloth woven in local cottages into a stronger fabric. The cloth was then dried outdoors on large wooden frames called tenters, and the hillside above the Green became known as Tenter Bank.

The expansion of Richmond's corn-grinding capacity reflects the growth of its population. Some of the corn ground would have been bought in the market; much was probably still grown on Richmond's open fields, those once belonging to the village of Hindrelac. The three fields, Westfield, Gallowfield (named from the town gallows being there) and Eastfield totalled 344 acres. They were cultivated in rotation, each year one field being sown with a cereal crop (probably barley, oats and rye), another with less hungry crops such as peas and beans, and the third left fallow. The fallowed field, rested and manured, would become the corn field the following year. Each field was divided into strips, which were ploughed by teams of oxen whose passage up and down the field created the ridge-and-furrow profile, which can still be detected on Westfield under a dusting of snow. Oxen were slow tractors but efficient to 'fuel' on grass, horses being faster but more extravagant to feed, needing oats for heavy work. Eligible inhabitants were allocated a different batch of strips each year, in order to share out better and worse land fairly. Animals were grazed on the 950-acre Whitcliffe Pasture. In Easby Parish Church there are late-13th century wall paintings illustrating some aspects of medieval agriculture - digging, sowing, pruning and hawking, birds being a challenge to cultivators then as now!

An additional source of medieval Richmond's trade was the archdeaconry of Richmond, the largest in England, covering an area from the Vale of York to the shores of the Solway, for it stretched from Northallerton in the East to near Lancaster in the West, and from the river Ure in the South to the river Tees in the North. Because of the great extent, and also the wild nature of much of the area, the Archdeacon of Richmond had unique authority, being the equivalent of a bishop excepting powers of confirmation and ordination. The archdeaconry, then part of the archdiocese of York, was based in Richmond, and here was held the consistory court. All parishes within that vast area, except those, which were ecclesiastical peculiars (areas outside the jurisdiction of the local bishop), had to deal with Richmond for all church business including church buildings and clergy, and tithe disputes. Many other matters now dealt with by civil authorities then came under ecclesiastical jurisdiction, so not only were clergy licensed by the church, but also schoolteachers, surgeons and midwives. What brought a great number of people to Richmond was the administration of probate in the archdeaconry courts.

Easby Church medieval wall painting

It is hard nowadays to appreciate the importance of the church in the everyday life of ordinary people in medieval times. It was not a Sundays only importance, but part and parcel of the fabric of society, not an optional choice but a universal embracing common factor throughout all ranks of people. The poor gave what they could, but the rich generously endowed a range of religious institutions, the nature of which varied according to changing fashion throughout the medieval period. In the 1150s one of the most favoured religious orders was the Premonstratensian, founded by St. Norbert at Premontré near

Laon in northern France in 1120. Members of the order were, and are, canons working as parish priests, not monks living an enclosed monastic life, and were known as the White Canons from the undyed woollen cloth of their habits. In the mid-1150s, at a date not known more precisely, Easby Abbey was founded by Roald, hereditary Constable of Richmond Castle. Typically of his status, he had already been a generous patron to St. Martin's Priory. Endowed for an abbot and 13 canons, the house was dedicated to St. Agatha, the Sicilian Christian martyred in the mid-3rd century to whom the pre-existing parish church at Easby was dedicated. The abbey precinct enclosed the parish church, and the parishioners had to pass through the abbey gatehouse for their baptisms, weddings and funerals as well as to attend Mass, but although this seems strange now, it would not at the time because the Premonstratensians were so much part of the everyday world, and indeed later served as the parish priests at Easby.

The abbey gradually developed into a large and prosperous organization, becoming the wealthiest of the three Premonstratensian houses in Yorkshire, the other two being at Coverham and Egglestone, both relatively close to Easby, in similarly rural locations. In addition to Easby's cruciform abbey church, domestic buildings were constructed around a cloister, and there was also an infirmary. Some of the original buildings were later rebuilt on a grander scale, and the buildings which survive most complete are the impressive gatehouse and refectory. The spacious guesthouse demonstrates the warm hospitality extended by the canons to those in need of it, either the poor or travellers. The abbey had property in Frenchgate, and the white-habited canons would be a common sight in the town, as well as contributing to the town's medieval economy by buying goods at the fairs and markets, and, particularly in later medieval times, employing many lay servants who would spend their wages locally.

The abbey church is not well preserved, but some of its wooden furniture and fittings survive and will be mentioned in the next chapter. In the north wall of the choir are two tomb recesses where members of the Scrope family were buried, eligible for this privilege because, having in 1336 purchased from Roald's descendants his property, they inherited the status of monastic founders. Their tombs, painted with their heraldic arms, were described by John, the then abbot, when he gave evidence in the so-called Scrope-Grosvenor controversy of about 1390. Both families had claimed the same coat of arms - *azure a bend or*, and each was trying to establish that they had used them first. The Scropes won, and went on to add considerably to Easby Abbey's fortunes by enlarging it and establishing a chantry chapel in 1393.

Evidence was also given that Scrope coat of arms was to be seen in the church and other buildings in the Richmond house of Grey Friars. This had been founded in 1258, a date which reflects the fashion for the mendicant, or begging orders such as the Franciscans, founded by St. Francis of Assisi, who wore coarse grey habits. Their houses were usually located in or near towns of size and importance, because their commitment to total poverty necessitated a regular source of donations, and their popularity rested on their learned and dynamic preaching, which assumed a nearby congregation. Thus the founder of the Richmond house, Ralph FitzRandal, lord of Middleham, provided a site just north of the town centre, beyond the line of what would become the town wall half a century later.

The friary consisted of simple buildings, even the small church being built only of rubble stone. A south aisle was added to the nave in the 14th century, to accommodate more of the laity who came to hear the friars' sermons. As well as the Scrope family, donors to the Richmond Grey Friars included the Nevill family and William de Hudswell. Recent archaeological work has confirmed that the cloister and domestic ranges were built on the north side of the church, not as in most monasteries to the south. The bell tower, added much later, will be included in the next chapter. The rest of the Grey Friars' site was cultivated, utilizing its plentiful springs of water.

The Richmond Grey Friars were involved in another dispute in 1490, when the Warden, William Billyngham, and the abbot of St. Agatha's, William Ellerton, could not agree about the disposal of the goods of the recently-deceased Richmond anchoress, Margaret Richmond. The town's four Bailiffs became involved in the dispute, which was referred to the arbitration of a small panel chaired by a canon of York Minster. Their judgement was that the Grey Friars were to have Margaret Richmond's goods, those of the next anchoress were, when she died, to be given to St. Agatha's, and the corporation of Richmond was to appoint future anchoresses! The Grey Friars of Richmond also received another controversial gift, a ferocious sow presented by Ralph Rokeby, which proved difficult to transport to Richmond and became the subject of a 15th-century comic poem *The Felone Sowe of Rokeby*.

    The Grey Friars preached not only in the nave of their church, which was open to lay people, but also outdoors in public spaces. The appeal of their sermons meant that they received many of the donations and church fees, which would otherwise have gone to parish churches. This made them very unpopular with parish clergy including, presumably, those of St. Mary's Parish Church in Richmond, especially as the friary was more conveniently situated for residents of the walled town. The Parish Church developed its present overall 'footprint' during the medieval centuries, that of an aisled nave and chancel, with tall west tower, but it was built gradually. The windows in the north and south walls, with their various designs of Gothic tracery, illustrate the piecemeal nature of the building. The large east window, with its fine Perpendicular tracery, is of higher quality and probably dates from the mid-15th century. At least some of the windows contained stained glass, a few fragments showing heraldic shields having been allowed to survive are now gathered together in the tracery of two of the windows of the south nave aisle. An interesting detail can be seen by looking up inside the north porch, where the ribs of the 14th-century stone vault meet in a 'green man' boss. For the medieval tombstone near the north porch, see the section on the Hospital of St. Nicholas later in this chapter. In the south porch can be seen the tombstone of a 15th-century priest, carved with a floreated cross, an elaborate letter *M* (for Mary) and the sacred monogram *ihc* (Jesus). It was found under the floor of the north aisle in April 1860 during the Victorian restoration of the church.

The tall and handsome west tower was added to the church about 1400, being a gift from Ralph Nevill, 1st Earl of Westmorland, who was granted the Honour of Richmond in 1399, and whose coat of arms, a saltire cross, can be seen at the top of the tower on the outside of the west face. Inside the tower is a ribbed vault, the ribs stopping at a central circular opening allowing bells to be raised and lowered through it. Ralph Nevill died in 1425, and was buried in the parish church of Staindrop, of which he was also a benefactor, and his effigy, flanked by those of his two wives, can be seen there. In old pictures of Richmond, the church tower looks much taller than now because before the Victorian restoration the roofs were lower, having flat slopes suitable for covering with lead, probably of 15th-century date. As can be seen from the two 'Norman' arches, the medieval arcades were also much lower than now, for the nave had a clerestorey despite its lower roof. The chancel was very long, extending further west into the nave than it does now.

Relatively little remains of the medieval fabric of the church due to the severity of its Victorian restoration, but some information on what survived up to 1820 is provided by Christopher Clarkson, the early-19th century historian of Richmond. A feature still in the church today, which late-medieval worshippers would have known is the fine black 'marble' font, of a limestone probably quarried in Teesdale, dating from the early-15th century. Perpendicular in style and octagonal in plan, it has shields on each face, some of which bear in abbreviated Latin the inscription *The Font of Jesus and John the Baptist*. Some corner of the parish church may have been used as a medieval grammar school, for there are references in the 1390s to two masters of it in the abstract of the Registers of the Archdeacon of Richmond compiled by Matthew Hutton, Archbishop of York 1747-57. Further evidence that there was a medieval school of some note in Richmond occurs in a letter written about 1486 by John de Auckland, Prior of Durham, concerning the schoolmaster of Richmond, whom he was hoping would take up a post in the Almonry School at Durham. The Elizabethan refoundation of Richmond Grammar School features in the next chapter.

Holy Trinity Chapel was of considerable size for a non-parochial chapel, though never as grand as the parish church. It too developed from its Norman origins in a somewhat random architectural manner. Most of the surviving fabric appears to be of 14th and 15th century date, and it retains late-medieval roof beams designed for a flat lead roof. The tower became the town's property, because the bells hung there were used for civic purposes, such as the curfew bell and, later, for the town clock. In addition to the Chapel of St. Edmund the King mentioned in the last chapter, two more were built to serve travellers leaving or entering the town. Little is known of the Chapel of St. Anthony, which stood at the corner of Quaker Lane and what is now Wellington Place, and served those coming down Hurgill Road from Swaledale. Nearby is the area called Nuns' Close, the name being all that remains of a short-lived medieval nunnery.

The name of Chapel Wynd, a narrow lane running from the bottom of Bargate through to Cravengate, is a good example of the meaning of the Norse word 'wynd', a narrow lane, which goes through rather than being a cul-de-sac. Some people pronounce it to rhyme with 'find', but it seems it should be a softer sound, as in 'tinder', for it is spelled 'weind' and 'weynd' in old documents. The name of this wynd is a reminder of the Chapel of St. James the Great, a popular medieval saint whose shrine at Santiago de Compostela in northern Spain was by the 12th century the most important centre of Christian pilgrimage after Jerusalem and Rome. The east window of the chapel, with Perpendicular tracery, was discovered when an old cottage was demolished in May 1828. The chapel stood on the north side of the wynd at the Bargate end, and served travellers using the Green Bridge. It is not known when the medieval bridge was first built, but it seems to have superseded a ford, and was certainly in existence by the 15th century. The medieval bridge was about half the width of the present bridge, and had four arches. Its three piers, with pointed ends and unequally spaced apart, can still be seen in the river bed immediately upstream of the present bridge when the river is running low.

St. James' Chapel included a chantry, or endowment for a priest to say Mass for the soul of the benefactor, or his nominees. As has already been seen, Richmond Castle had a chantry chapel from 1278, but most chantries were founded in the 14th and 15th centuries when the Catholic Church put theological emphasis on the efficacy of the Mass as a means of reducing the time a soul spent in Purgatory. About thirteen chantries were founded in Richmond in all, several being in St. Mary's Church, and some in Holy Trinity Chapel. Chantry priests received modest sums for celebrating Mass each day, and were not usually very well educated: some spent the rest of their time in good works such as helping other clergy and teaching children, others enjoyed their light work-load! The Richmond chantry priests lived together behind the Market Place between Finkle Street and Friars Wynd in the College, the word originally meaning a religious institution where people shared communal catering and housekeeping facilities.

There were yet more religious institutions in medieval Richmond. The street-name Maison Dieu recalls a lost 'house of God' or medieval hospital, a religious community of poor, infirm and chronic sick, particularly the aged. Nearby was the medieval hospital of St. Nicholas, the foundation date of which is not known precisely, but the earliest documentary reference which has been traced is of 1171/2, when a donation was made to it on behalf of King Henry II. This shows the prestige of the institution, and indeed the Mastership of St. Nicholas was a sought-after sinecure. Some Masters, however, misappropriated the Hospital's endowments, and by the late-14th century it was in very poor repair. King Richard II set up a commission to investigate, headed by Ralph Nevill, 1st Earl of Westmorland, and for a time the advowson of the Hospital, or right to appoint its Masters, was vested in the Earls of Richmond. As a result, further endowments were forthcoming, and the buildings were renovated in the mid-15th century. The Hospital had a chapel, and a chantry priest was shared with the Chapel of St. Edmund the King. St. Nicholas survived as a hospital into Tudor times and then became a private residence. The chapel bell, with the letters *Deo Cana* cast in mirror image by an illiterate bell founder, was during the 20th century returned to the house from a location in Swaledale to which it had found its way in the intervening centuries. The inscription should probably have been *Canan Deo* - I will sing to God.

A fine tombstone from St. Nicholas which, from the elaborate cross-head carved on it was of mid-13th century date, and from the chalice on it seemingly marked the grave of a medieval priest, can be seen outside the north porch of St. Mary's parish church. Discovered in 1841, it was presented to the Museum then in Tower Street, and later given to the Mechanics Institute (see Chapter 6). When that closed it was moved to its present position. An archaeological excavation at St. Nicholas in 1987 uncovered a number of skeletons carefully buried, but it was not possible to deduce their status at the hospital as there were no grave goods with the burials. In a nearby garden in 1989 was discovered part of a large free-standing medieval cross, perhaps an upright grave marker. Now in Richmondshire Museum, it seems to have been carved about 1200-1250, as it bears traces of dog-tooth motif and also has fleur-de-lis emblems, both of which are typical of the Early English period of Gothic architecture.

In the mid-15th century the country was involved in yet another conflict, the Wars of the Roses. Although no battles were fought in the Richmond area, it seems unlikely that before the medieval period ended in 1485 there was any improvement on the economic situation recorded in 1440. The area's cloth industry in particular suffered as cloth production grew in the West Riding of Yorkshire. The histories of the Honour and earldom of Richmond are complex and both changed hands many times at this period, but none of those who held them showed any interest in Richmond, and merely took the income generated.

King Richard III as Duke of Gloucester was closely associated with, and very generous to, Middleham, where the famous late-15th century gold pendant, the Middleham Jewel, was found in 1985. It was from Middleham that Richard in effect ruled the north on behalf of his older brother King Edward IV. Richard was held in high regard in the north, administering justice firmly but fairly, arbitrating in disputes and bringing about a more settled situation than the north had perhaps ever experienced before. Richard III's short rule began at Easter 1483 with the unexpected death of Edward IV, and ended on the battlefield at Bosworth in Leicestershire on 22 August 1485. A few days later, the civic records of the City of York famously provided his obituary: "King Richard, late mercifully reigning over us ..... was piteously slain and murdered to the great heaviness of the city". Richmond, whose Honour he held, probably felt the same, but was soon to find its name becoming surprisingly better known.

4

Tudor Richmond 1485-1603

The National History

The Tudor era began at the Battle of Bosworth Field with the victory of King Henry VII (1485-1509) of the House of Lancaster. He ended the Wars of the Roses by marrying King Edward IV's daughter, Elizabeth of York, whose portrait is familiar from playing cards. Coloured glass white and red roses in the Rose Window of York Minster commemorate their marriage, in 1486. Henry Tudor's weak claim to the English throne was based on his descent from John of Gaunt, and he was accused of being a usurper, having to resist two 'pretenders', Lambert Simnel and Perkin Warbeck. A shrewd and patient man, he brought to the strife-torn country a period of stability and economic growth. One of Henry VII's few titles was that of Earl of Richmond, inherited from his father, Edmund Tudor, at his posthumous birth in 1457. When he rebuilt the royal palace at Sheen, in Surrey, after it was destroyed by fire about 1500, he renamed it after his earldom, and so it became Richmond Palace. The little town alongside it then became known as Richmond, and thus was named the first of over 50 settlements throughout the world to be called Richmond after the Yorkshire Richmond.

It was during Henry VII's reign, in 1492, that Christopher Columbus discovered America. Henry VII was succeeded by his second son, Henry VIII (1509-47), in youth a 'Renaissance Man', attractive, intelligent and cultured, but a repugnant figure in older age, corpulent and greedy for both power and money, famous for his six wives. He determined to divorce his first, Katharine of Aragon, when she did not give him a male heir, and broke away from the Church of Rome to do so. The establishment of the Church of England, initially a change of authority rather than theology, began a long period of religious upheaval which included the Dissolution of the Monasteries. This had devastating social and economic repercussions, but also led to a major redistribution of land ownership.

King Edward VI (1547-53), the son of Henry VIII's third wife Jane Seymour, was too young and sickly to rule effectively, and there was a swing towards a more Puritan form of Protestantism during the Protectorate of the Duke of Somerset. Edward was followed by his older half-sister, Queen Mary (1553-58), a lady greatly embittered by the appalling treatment meted out to her mother Katharine of Aragon and her own designation as a bastard, who turned the country back to staunch Roman Catholicism. Childless and anxious to placate her husband King Philip II of Spain, she became more extreme as her reign continued, culminating with the burning of Protestant martyrs, mainly in London and Oxford, but with a notable northern exception in Richmond.

Her younger half-sister Queen Elizabeth I (1558-1603), daughter of Henry VIII and his second wife, Anne Boleyn, was a more pragmatic sovereign. She too had suffered the stigma of being declared illegitimate, and was at pains to show she was her father's daughter, not just genetically but in stature - Richmond's contemporary portrait is one of many stressing the physical resemblance. Queen Elizabeth had to face a number of challenges during her long reign, several of them rebellions inspired by her cousin Mary, Queen of Scots. Having encouraged swashbuckling heroes such as Sir Francis Drake, Elizabeth also had to repel the famous Spanish Armada, an invasion planned by her half-sister Mary's husband Philip of Spain, at which time Richmond's beacon played its part. The third and last of Henry VIII's children to fail to produce an heir, the death of the Virgin

Queen in 1603 saw the Scottish king James VI ascend the English throne as King James I, and so began the Stuart dynasty.

The uncharismatic King Henry VII was an astute monarch. He knew that after thirty long years of expensive conflict during the Wars of the Roses, Englishmen were relieved to have peace at last, but would not willingly pay taxes for foreign wars. So he needed other sources of income, both personal and national, and income from the Honour of Richmond brought him much needed revenue, especially as he increased the rents of his lands and property, by now paid in money rather than the old system of military and agricultural service, and also exacted feudal dues from those nobles who owed him allegiance. To increase national wealth he encouraged cloth exports, which generated customs duties as well as benefiting sheep farmers, weavers and merchants, and created further income from fines levied by the various courts he instigated to dispense speedy, fair and firm justice, notably the Court of the Star Chamber.

Medieval monarchs had established the tradition of leaving the unhealthy water and air of the City of London whenever possible, often sailing the relatively easy and quick journey up the river Thames to the pleasant country surroundings of their palace at Sheen in Surrey. Sheen Palace, surrounded by a defensive moat, was a fairly small complex, built in the early-15th century and so only perhaps sixty or seventy years old when Henry VII became king. It became a particular favourite of his, and he was in residence there some time in 1499 when fire broke out and, spreading rapidly, destroyed so much of the complex that it could clearly not be readily repaired. Although not normally an extravagant man, Henry decided immediately to rebuild it, along more modern architectural lines in the newly fashionable material of brick. It was completed in 1501 and Henry renamed it

Richmond Palace after his earldom, the source of the revenue, which had helped to pay for the rebuilding.

Richmond Palace continued to be not only his favourite, but also that of his queen, and both spent a lot of time there. When his queen, Elizabeth, died in 1503, following the birth of her eighth child at the age of 37, Henry built for her, and himself, a chantry chapel at the east end of Westminster Abbey. Beneath the King Henry VII Chapel's amazing stone pendant fan vault, their recumbent effigies rest on the elaborate tomb commissioned by their son King Henry VIII. By the Florentine sculptor Pietro Torrigiano, a contemporary of Michelangelo, it is an outstanding and early English example of Italian Renaissance design. Henry VII died, at his Richmond Palace, on 22 April 1509. It continued to be a favourite palace of Henry VIII, but eventually decayed, and only small fragments survive today. Richmond in Surrey is, however, famous throughout the world, and is usually incorrectly assumed to be the oldest Richmond.

While Richmond Palace was being rebuilt, Richmond Castle was already in decay. A survey of 1538 mentions roofless buildings and falling walls, and it was described as ruined by the antiquarian John Leland, visiting Richmond about 1534. The description, from two entries, generally matches the picture of late-medieval Richmond painted in Chapter 3, is in his spelling:

> Richemont is pavid. Richemont towne is waullid, and the castel on the river side of Swale is as the knot of the cumpace of the waulle. In the waul be iij. [3] gates. Frenchegate yn the north parte of the towne, and is the most occupied gate of the towne; Finkel-streete gate, Bargate, al iij be downe; vestigia yet remayne. In the market place is a large chapel of the Trinite, the cumpace of the ruinus waulles is not half a mile abowt. So that the towne waulle cumpasith litle but the market place, the howses about hit and gardens behind them. There is a suburbe withowt Frenchgate. Finkelstreat suburb strayt west from the market place and Bargate suburbe. But Frenchgate suburbe is almost as bygge as bothe the other suburbes. In Frenchgate

suburbe is the paroch chirch of al the hole towne. A litle beyonde the ende of Frenchegate-streate is, or was, a late a chapel of a woman anachorete. Bargate suburbe cummith down to the bridge ende of Swale, the wich bridge is sumtime chaynid. A this side the bridge is no building. In this suburbe is a chapel of S. James. At the bakke of the Frenchgate is the Grey Freres, a litle withowte the waullis. Their howse, medow, orchard, and a litle wood is waullid yn. Men go from the market place to hit by a posterne gate. There is a conducte of water at the Grey Freres, els there is none in Richemont. Not far from the Freres waul is a chapel of S. Antony. Al the towne and suburbes be on the farther side of Swale.

  The castel is nere hand as much yn cumpace as the circuite of the town walle. But now it is in mere ruine.... I cam thoroug a great long strete in Richemont or [ere - before] I cam to the top of the hille, where [is] the best of the toune caullid the Bailly and the Castelle. Sum think that the place wher the Baily was ons [once] *extima area castelli* and sins [since] buildid with houses; waullid it was, but the waul is now decayid. The names and parte of 4 or 5 gates yet remaine..... There is a chapel on Richemont toune with straung figures in the waulles of it. There people there dreme [dream] that it was ons a temple of idoles..... From Richemont to Midleham first a mile by ille [ill] rokky ground, but first over Richemont bridge of 4 arches, and the vj [6] miles all by mory [miry] grounde and litle wood nere in sight.

  The dereliction of the town wall Leland described is consistent with its diminishing importance, especially after the Battle of Flodden Field in 1513 at which the English defeated the Scottish king James IV, to whom Henry VII, a great believer in dynastic marriages, had paired his elder daughter Margaret. Leland seems to confirm that the postern gate in Friars Wynd was an insertion into the wall, describing it separately and referring to its use for the collection of water from the Grey Friars' conduit.

Frenchgate was the largest suburb, with Newbiggin not specifically mentioned, being in the Finkle Street suburb 'straight west from the Market Place'. The chapel with strange figures is probably Holy Trinity Chapel, which maybe retained some Romanesque carvings, perhaps grotesques, until its Victorian restoration. Leland's concern over the poor road from Richmond Bridge to Middleham will be seen to be justified in Chapter 6.

Richmond changed dramatically almost immediately after Leland's visit, due to the Reformation when King Henry VIII broke away from the Church of Rome and established in its stead what would later be called the Church of England. The consequences of the Reformation were many, at national, regional and local levels, some being felt immediately, others in the future. The scale of the effect the Reformation had on Richmond justifies a brief summary of its background, beginning with Henry VIII's birth as his parents' second son. Henry Tudor had hoped that his first-born child would be a son whom he could name after the legendary King Arthur and his Knights of the Round Table, to convey the message that, despite his poor claim to the English throne, his Welsh blood would restore the ancient Celtic blood of England's glorious, chivalrous past. In anticipation of this he had repaired and painted in Tudor livery colours the huge Round Table, which still hangs in the Great Hall of Winchester Castle, and he arranged for Elizabeth of York to give birth at Winchester. The baby, born in 1486, was indeed a son, was named Arthur, and was created Prince of Wales. As a baby, Prince Arthur was betrothed to Katharine of Aragon, a Spanish princess, a dynastic match cementing an alliance between England and Spain. Then, in 1502, Arthur died of consumption, and thus Prince Henry, the second son, became the heir-apparent. Henry VII, wishing to continue the dynastic alliance, subsequently betrothed Henry to Katharine.

Shortly after becoming king, Henry VIII married Katharine in 1510, having first sought a dispensation from the Pope to do so, it being forbidden by church law for a man to marry his dead brother's widow. Katharine bore him many babies, but only one, a girl, Princess Mary, born in 1516, lived.

Ironically, as his reign was to be so dominated by the need for a male heir, Henry VIII in 1519 fathered an illegitimate son, known as Henry Fitzroy. This little boy, whom the king would have liked to make his heir, was created Duke of Richmond in 1525, the title showing that Henry VIII, as much as his father, appreciated the income from the Honour of Richmond. Henry VIII was of a much more extravagant disposition than his father, as had been seen in 1520 when he met the young French king Francis I in dazzling splendour at the Field of the Cloth of Gold. The Dukedom of Richmond lapsed when Henry Fitzroy died in 1536, at a time when the king's problems were at their worst.

As Katharine of Aragon grew older and it became obvious that she was not going to produce a son, Henry petitioned the Pope to annul his marriage so that he could marry a younger wife of child-bearing age. The Pope, restricted by Papal Infallibility regarding the earlier dispensation, and an unfortunate prisoner of the Holy Roman Emperor, who happened to be Katharine's nephew, declined to do so. Cardinal Thomas Wolsey, unable to persuade the Pope to change his mind, fell from Henry's favour in 1529. Over the next few years the Reformation Parliament passed a number of Acts which, although ostensibly reforming corruption in the Church, vested authority over the Church in England in the king and directed much church revenue into the king's coffers. Henry VIII's marriage to Anne Boleyn was finally accomplished late in 1532, and was followed in 1533 by the birth, not of the longed-for son, but of Princess Elizabeth.

Also in 1533 Thomas Cranmer was consecrated Archbishop of Canterbury, and became one of the two key figures in the Reformation, the other being Thomas Cromwell, Henry VIII's powerful minister who, though only a secular politician, rose to the title of Vicar-General in 1535 and proceeded during the next five years to facilitate the confiscation of the monasteries' assets by the king. One of Cromwell's first acts was to initiate a two-fold survey by Doctors Layton and Leigh of the religious houses, to investigate the moral condition of them all and, with an augmented commission, to produce an inventory of all their possessions. The latter was compiled meticulously, the religious houses clearly having had warning of the impending visitation to prepare their accounts as if for a modern audit. The former was carried out differently, the surviving evidence showing that, if the commissioners did not find sufficient evidence of moral corruption, they fabricated it. They worked with great rapidity, in teams, which each surveyed the religious houses of a county, and claimed generous expenses.

The Archdeaconry of Richmond was treated as a separate county, and was visited early in 1536. The first phase seems to have been accomplished late in January, by Layton and Leigh accompanied by a civil servant called William Blytheman. At Easby Abbey, out of the 13 canons there they allegedly 'found' five sodomites and one fornicator! For the survey of monastic possessions the team consisted of three commissioners, an auditor, a receiver and a clerk. The receiver was William Blytheman, who already knew his way around from his previous visit. They arrived at a gross value of Easby Abbey's property, and then deducted the financial obligations for which the abbey was responsible, such as the finding of various chantry priests and the vicar for Easby parish church, and also obligations to the five corrodians, or aged persons who had entered into contracts to live in the abbey and be looked after, rather as in a present-day retirement home. The resultant figure for Easby's net annual income was £111 17s. 11d.

On 4 February 1536 the Act of Parliament was passed for the suppression of the 'lesser' monasteries, those with a net annual income of £200 or less. Easby Abbey clearly fell within that category, and plans for its closure were immediately put in hand. Blytheman returned on 17 June to arrange the handover of the abbey's seal, charters, and precious jewels and other valuables, and also to put in hand making the abbey uninhabitable. During that summer the lead was taken off the roofs to be melted down into pigs of lead for transporting to Boroughbridge by land, and then by water to York. To melt the lead, roof timbers were used, and when that supply ran out, 350 trees from the abbey's woods were cut down.

Arrangements were made to hand over the abbey's assets into a new government department, the Court of Augmentations, which continued to honour monasteries' financial obligations, and also to pay pensions to those members of the religious orders who agreed to leave. In theory they were offered the alternative of transferring to larger houses of the same religious order, those worth more than £200 p.a. and not being suppressed at this time, but none of the Easby canons took up that option. The abbot, Robert Bampton, took an annual pension of 40 marks, and 9 of the canons were granted dispensations to take up clergy posts in parishes. Meanwhile negotiations took place between the commissioners and Henry, Lord Scrope of Bolton Castle, the descendant of the Scrope family who had been generous patrons of the abbey, to lease to him the abbey's estates. While these arrangements were being made and the buildings dismantled, outside events overtook all concerned.

The 'Pilgrimage of Grace', a series of rebellious incidents, started in Lincolnshire on 1 October 1536. The rebellion, mainly about religious grievances but also with economic content, was instigated by a London lawyer who had northern origins, Robert Aske. The rebellion spread first to the East Riding, then to York, and by 11 October to Wensleydale. Two days later the whole of Richmondshire, particularly Richmond, was up in arms. The Richmond ringleaders included two of the town's four bailiffs, and among the local gentry who took part were William Conyers of Marske and Richard Sidgwick of Walburn, and County Durham lawyer Robert Bowes. Shortly afterwards the rebels, usually referred to in contemporary documents as the 'commons', reinstated Abbot Robert Bampton and all or some of his canons into the partially-dismantled abbey buildings, and there they stayed until early in 1537. Local feeling for Easby Abbey was so strong that the rebels said "But rather than our house of Saint Agatha should go down, we shall all die."

Attempts were made to reconcile Robert Aske with the Crown late in 1536, but then the situation was exacerbated by a further outbreak of the rebellion set off by Sir Francis Bigod, the absentee part-owner of the manor of Healaugh in Swaledale.

Henry VIII then instructed the Duke of Norfolk, the commander of the royal army, to crush the rebellion and make examples of the ringleaders, specifically citing St. Agatha's among the religious houses he blamed most. Surprisingly, in view of the part he had played, Robert Bampton was not punished, but Aske and Bigod, and other scapegoats, including the abbot of Jervaulx, were executed for treason late in January 1537.

Before his execution, Aske defended the monasteries, paying great tribute to their work both spiritual and material in tones giving no hint of any corruption or malpractice, at least in northern England, and somewhat surprisingly also noting the beauty of their buildings long before ruined abbeys would be generally appreciated aesthetically:

> The abbeys in the north parts gave great alms to poor men and laudably served God. By occasion of the suppression, the divine service of almighty God is much diminished. Many of the abbeys were in the mountains and desert places, where the people be rude of condition and not well taught the law of God, and when the abbeys stood the said people had not only worldly refreshing in their bodies but also spiritual refuge. None was in these parts denied so that the people were greatly refreshed by the said abbeys, where they now have no such succour. Also the abbeys were one of the beauties of this realm to all men and strangers passing through.

Other local scapegoats included Anthony Peacock of Arkengarthdale, who was hanged on Richmond Moor for his part as the 'principal stirrer of the business beside Barney Castle' - an attack on Barnard Castle. The Pilgrimage of Grace had been robustly quelled, and the next stage of the Dissolution of the Monasteries, the suppression in 1539 of those houses with a net annual income above £200, passed without incident. It was in November 1539 that St. Mary's Abbey in York was dissolved, its number of black-cowled monks including some once at its Richmond cell, St. Martin's Priory, which closed in 1535. One wonders how they had viewed the doings of their former neighbours across the Swale, the white canons, in 1536 - did they support their opposition to the Dissolution, or tut-tut in horror at their indiscretion, or perhaps even flee to York?

One of the ramifications of the suppression of St. Martin's Priory was a legal dispute concerning Church Mill, a corn and fulling mill, which originally stood just below the parish church near the present Station or Mercury Bridge. A case was brought before the Court of Chancery in 1537 by Henry Cogell, who stated that about seven years previously he had bought some land on the riverside belonging to the King and subject to fee farm. He had erected on it two watermills (probably one for corn grinding and the other for fulling) which, with the expense of constructing a dam across the river Swale, had cost him £80. Shortly afterwards, John, the Prior of St. Martin's, "bearing inward malice and displeasure unto your orator and minding utterly to undo him for ever", had informed Cogell that half the width of the river belonged to the Abbot of St. Mary in York, who had commanded Prior John "to pull down the dam of the stream".

The assertion regarding the two halves of the river was correct, for the Richmond boundary extends to the middle of the river, the other half belonging to landowners on the other side, in this case St. Martin's Priory, which also had a corn watermill on their land. As Cogell could not work his mills without water, and "being a poor man and glad to obtain and get the good will and favour of the prior", he said that he had paid £4 13s. 4d. to Prior John, who had "faithfully promised and granted that ..... [Cogell] ..... should peaceably have and enjoy the stream for ever". Three years later the prior had broken his word, "pulled up the dam of the stream whereby the mills of your orator cannot grind", Cogell had lost "the profit that might have risen and grown of the mills if the prior had not pulled up the dam of the stream", and the prior had refused to repay the £4 13s. 4d.

John Matthew, the last prior of St. Martin's, was called to the court, and said in defence that he had only acted on the orders of the Abbot in York to protect the priory's water, had acted "upon no malice" but in a "peaceable manner pulled down the mill dam which was fixed and builded on the water belonging to the monastery" and denied he had received the money on the understanding "that the dam should stand". Frustratingly, there is no record of the outcome of the case, which must have been difficult to resolve as in 1537 St. Martin's Priory no longer existed, and before long St. Mary's Abbey would close also. Nevertheless, both Church Mill and St. Martin's Mill continued to function for several centuries more, as will be seen in Chapter 6.

The Grey Friars of Richmond lasted until the second tranche of the Dissolution, closing in January 1539 when the warden, Dr. Robert Sanderson, and fourteen friars surrendered, some of whom had come from friaries dissolved earlier. The friars' orders having embraced poverty more literally than others, friaries had fewer possessions than most religious houses, and so did not escape the 1536 surrender on the grounds of wealth, but their more intellectual approach to the religious life allowed them to accept some of Henry VIII's arguments on their own terms and thus they had been left alone for a while.

The effects of the Dissolution must have been felt both severely and instantly in Richmond. The familiar figures in their black, white and grey habits were now absent from the streets of the town, and with them had gone not only the money spent for them and their guests and corrodians, but also the purchasing power of their staff, who had lost their jobs. We know from documentary evidence, particularly of their wills, that a few pensioned members of the former religious houses, including nuns from the Swaledale nunneries of Marrick and Ellerton, settled in the Richmond area after the Dissolution, but their influence was much less than before.

Harder to define, and even more so to replace than this economic downturn, was the welfare role which the religious houses had provided for the sick, with expert knowledge of anatomy and herbal medicines, and the poor and the aged. Gone also was the education, not only the teaching of children but the wise counsel and benefits of literacy and learning of which adults could avail themselves. Monasteries had developed expertise to a greater extent than lay society of industrial and craft skills such as

Greyfriars Tower, drawn by W. R. Robinson for Christopher Clarkson's *History of Richmond*, 1821. To the right is the Friary, the home of Sir Timothy Hutton, later the boarding house of Richmond Grammar School and now the Friary Hospital corn milling, brewing, tanning, woodland management and farming. Above all they had offered up worship and praise to God, activities which may seem insignificant in our age, but there is no doubt that they mattered greatly to the inhabitants of Richmond at the time.

The local building trade in particular must have felt the effects of the Dissolution, for stonemasons, woodcarvers, plumbers and glaziers, even goldsmiths and silversmiths, had received generous patronage from the religious houses. Many had building work either still in progress or only recently completed when the end came. Greyfriars Tower, one of Richmond's favourite landmarks, and the best local example, aesthetically, of ecclesiastical Gothic architecture, had been added to the Grey Friars' church not long before their suppression. Frustratingly, there is no documentary evidence of the generous endowment, which must have funded construction of this new tower, and presumably also the founding of new bells, but on architectural evidence the tower would appear to date from about 1500. Built of good quality ashlar sandstone, which must have been brought in from a quarry at least a few miles distant, its height has elegant proportions, the bell openings have Perpendicular tracery, and its skyline is graced by crocketed pinnacles and pierced parapets.

Construction of Greyfriars Tower was a miracle of medieval technology. The four delicately-shafted piers on which the belfry stands are in effect stilts, yet they supported not only the heavy structure above but great vibrations when the bells were swung. Inserted within the narrow confines of an older building of inferior quality and considerably smaller scale, the erection of the necessary scaffolding and the handling of building materials must have been a nightmare. The surviving fragments of the friars' church - south aisle east wall and part of the choir north wall - and the watertabling from the steeply-pitched roofs which abutted the tower's west and east sides, illustrate the comparatively small scale of the rest of the church. Most of the friary buildings were used, after 1539, as a convenient quarry for stone for the erection of new buildings in Richmond, and doubtless the tower's ashlar stonework was much sought after, but its great height prevented dismantling from the top, and the danger of it collapsing on anyone attempting to take away the supporting piers at the bottom, made it impossible to demolish.

Easby Abbey had also undergone building work shortly before its dissolution, particularly in the south-east corner of the cloister, where the domestic quarters at first floor level and above show considerable evidence of re-planning. This area, above the chapter house, and conveniently close to the refectory, was altered to form flatlets for the corrodians taken in by the abbey. There are doorways and fireplaces with Tudor-style arches, and the vertical cylinder, obviously inserted, for a spiral staircase, which gave access to the flatlets.

About 1530, Robert Bampton, the last abbot, commissioned a new set of canopied choir stalls from William Brownfleet (sometimes called Bromflet), the Ripon woodcarver whose workshop was the leading supplier of late-medieval furniture to monasteries and large churches throughout northern England. Brand new at the Dissolution, the choir stalls were moved into St. Mary's Parish Church in Richmond, where they remain despite having been fitted in various configurations during the last four and a half centuries. The seat of each stall is hinged and tips up to form a misericord, or small bench for the canons to lean back on during long church services. Typically of such misericords, the undersides are richly carved with subjects by no means religious in content but popular in medieval times, including piglets dancing while the sow plays the bagpipes, a grotesque leering human face with protruding tongue, various mythical beasts such as a wyverns and cockatrices, fruit and flowers.

Slender colonnaded shafts rising from the arm-rests support a continuous canopy, carved along the front of which is a vine scroll wrapped round with a ribbon bearing, in Latin, minor faults of which canons might be guilty - negligent scholar, disobedient youth, indolent old man, obstinate monk, expensive food, rumour in the cloister, strife in the Chapter, dissolution in the choir. The screen behind the stalls is carved with Gothic tracery, and above one of the stalls is a shield bearing the rebus, or word picture, of Abbot Bampton's name with a crosier. Slightly older wooden furniture from Easby Abbey church also survives in Wensley Church where, behind the Bolton family pew, there is the parclose screen from the Scrope chantry, bearing much genealogical information on the Scrope family, and in the nave is a reliquary, or relic hutch, with attached alms-box.

After the suppression of the religious houses, and the seizure of their wealth, the pace of the Reformation slackened. For the time being, the parish church and the various chapels, chantries and hospitals remained much as before. Theologically, both Henry VIII, and the English Church during his lifetime, remained Catholic. While there was discouragement of the veneration of holy relics and the burning of candles before images of saints, and the more minor holy days were no longer kept as holidays, still the Virgin Mary and the saints were prayed to and chantry priests sang masses for the souls of their benefactors. Services continued to be said or sung in Latin, although the churchwardens of all churches were required to obtain a copy of the Bible in English from 1538 - a long time after John Wycliffe had argued for it in 1380! An innovation of great significance for later historians was the instruction by Thomas Cromwell in 1538 that all churches should keep a register of the baptisms, marriages and burials performed there. At first such records were unsatisfactorily kept on loose sheets of paper, but these were later ordered to be kept in bound volumes. For this reason it is rare for parish registers to go back to 1538 - Richmond's begin in 1556.

Henry VIII had achieved independence from the Pope by persuading Parliament to pass measures to achieve his ends, and this subsequent increase in parliamentary power would have immense repercussions for later monarchs, particularly King Charles I. In response to one of the grievances of the Pilgrimage of Grace, that northern England was a great distance from the seats of both government and justice, Henry VIII set up a regional parliament, the Council of the North, under a Lord President. It was based in the abbot's grand quarters of the former St. Mary's Abbey in York, now known as the King's Manor and the city-centre campus of the University of York. Other administrative changes included the transfer of the Archdeaconry of Richmond into the new Diocese of Chester in 1541, and a commissary was appointed to oversee the consistory courts. Tudor governments effected increasing amounts of administration through the parish and other ecclesiastical systems, including that generated by the higher proportion of the population making wills. These developments added to the workload of the archdeaconry courts, and generated more trade for Richmond as people travelled from considerable distances to do business, especially that concerning probate, in the town.

The wills of many hundreds of former Richmond inhabitants survive among the archdeaconry archives, now in the Leeds District Archives Office at Sheepscar. Accompanying many wills are the even more fascinating inventories of the testators' goods. As nowadays, Tudor wills followed a standard pattern. They began with an implicit declaration of truthfulness, in either Latin or English - In the Name of God, Amen, followed by the date - the testator was usually on his or her death-bed, and occasionally was either unconscious or already dead, in which case the will is termed nuncupative, and is a record of what the testator had earlier indicated were his or her wishes. The person is then named, often with a description such as a trade, and they invariably proceed to declare that although they are sick in body they are of sound mind.

The first bequest was of their soul to God, and the wording of this indicates their religious beliefs - those with Roman Catholic sympathies continued to refer to the Virgin Mary and the saints, while the increasing influence of Calvinism can be detected in assumptions about being among the elect of God. Then the testator requests the place of burial, which was still often within the parish church itself, references to various altars and other graves providing information on the internal arrangement of the church at the time. These preambles are followed by personal bequests, and lastly arrangements are made for business matters to be carried out, such as debts discharged, funeral expenses met, executors appointed, and the will is witnessed. Many testators were illiterate and signed with a mark. A week or two later, a handful of neighbours and friends gathered to 'appraise' the testator's property, listing and valuing for the inventory personal effects, especially apparel, household goods, trade equipment, farm animals, crops etc. Household furniture was generally sparse, and many homes consisted of a single room.

The Church of England became much more Protestant after Henry VIII died early in 1547, for the young King Edward VI, ruling with the help of his uncle the Duke of Somerset, could not resist pressures for change as his father had done. Moves away from the old Catholic ways included the enforced destruction of all shrines, images and pictures of saints, and the abolition of processing around the church during services. During the Communion, the laity were to share not only the bread, but also the wine with the priest, and stone altars were replaced by wooden communion tables in 1550. A conspicuous change was the introduction of services in English, the churchwardens of every church being ordered to obtain a copy of the Book of Common Prayer in 1549. Many of the prayers were in the exquisitely beautiful prose of Thomas Cranmer, who had worked on English versions of the old Latin services for many years. Archbishop of Canterbury since 1533, he had narrowly survived many difficulties, the greatest being that he had married, albeit while abroad, when clergy were still expected to be celibate. Another of the Catholic and Protestant differences, this was regulated in 1549 when clergy were allowed to marry, although only a small proportion initially chose to do so.

After dissolving the religious houses, Henry VIII had eyed enviously the chantries and their property, in 1546 ordering a survey of "all chantries, obits, lights, religious colleges and guilds, and free chapels", but the process of suppression was interrupted by his death. The first Parliament of King Edward VI's reign in 1547 passed an Act for their dissolution and another survey was made in 1548. In Richmond there had been 13 chantries, plus about 20 obits and lights - similar but lesser endowments, paying for candles to be burned - all funded by capital or property to support priests who said masses for the souls of their founders or for other nominated persons. In 1544 the Corporation of Richmond had seized for their own use these assets, and the chapel buildings of St. James and St. Edmund, acting in collusion with the chantry priests who acquiesced in this sequestration because both their incomes and their priestly functions were guaranteed by the Corporation.

Consequently, in 1546 and again in 1548, the Crown commissioners found only two Richmond chantries - that of St. Anne and St. Catherine in the Parish Church, and that of St. Nicholas in the Hospital of that name - plus certain obits in the Parish Church. The Corporation, astutely, had not seized these because by 1544 they were all already known to the Crown and therefore impossible to conceal: the chantry of St. Anne and St. Catherine having been endowed by Whitby Abbey, and these particular obits by Easby Abbey, they had been vested in the Court of Augmentations at the Dissolution of their respective religious houses, and the Wardenship of the Hospital of St. Nicholas was a Crown appointment. However, a few years later, a Richmond resident called William Wharton wrote to the Court of Augmentations informing it of the concealed chantries. An inquiry was held into Wharton's claims, but nothing came of the matter before Edward VI died in 1553, and it did not surface again until Queen Elizabeth's reign, as will be seen later in this chapter. The two chantries, the remaining obits, the Hospital of St. Nicholas and the Anchoress' Cell, were however suppressed under the 1547 Act.

In 1552 a second Book of Common Prayer was published, more Puritan in tone than the first, but destined for only a brief period of use as King Edward VI's short reign ended in 1553. He was succeeded by his older half-sister Queen Mary Tudor who had remained a staunch Roman Catholic, and had a deep resentment of the Protestant reforms, which had begun as a means of removing her mother Katharine of Aragon. Queen Mary returned the country to Roman Catholicism, restoring the papacy, Latin masses, the observation of saints' days, rood screens - and clergy celibacy, which resulted in married priests having to 'divorce' their wives! Many non-monastic religious institutions were refounded during Mary's reign, including Richmond's Hospital of St. Nicholas. This continued, though probably as a sinecure rather than as a home for the aged, until about 1585, when it was dissolved again and became the private house it has remained.

The Marian regime set great store by reinstated heresy laws, which were used to persecute Protestants. Many of the Protestant martyrs were leading churchmen, including Thomas Cranmer, but others were humble men and women who had strongly espoused the religious changes of the last twenty or so years. Protestants put to death by Queen Mary mostly came from centres such as London and Oxford, but one of the few northern martyrs was burnt at the stake in Richmond, in one of the most appalling and harrowing episodes in the town's long history.

The Richmond parish register of burials begins in January 1557. Among the early records, for the year 1558, is the stark entry *Richard Snell burnt 9 September.* Two brothers from Bedale, John and Richard Snell, had been brought before the ecclesiastical courts in Richmond for refusing to revert to Roman Catholicism. The church authorities made long and strenuous efforts to persuade them to recant and thus avoid the ultimate penalty, but they were extremely stubborn. After a prolonged period in gaol, they were brought out for the last time. John did recant, but then drowned himself in the river Swale; Richard was burnt to death at the stake, according to tradition outside the old county gaol at the west end of Newbiggin. One of the editions of John Foxe's *Book of Martyrs* gives this account of the trial:

> At Bedale a market town in Yorkshire were two men in the later days of Queen Mary, the one named John Snel and the other Richard Snel. Who being suspected for religion, were sent into Richmond where Dr. Dakins had commission from the Bishop of Chester to have the examination of them.
>
> This Dr. Dakins many times conferred with them, sometimes threatening fire and faggot, if they would not

recant and sometimes flattering them with fair fables if they would returne into the holy Catholik Church. But they stood constantly to the sure rocke of Jesus Christ, in whom they put their whole trust and confidence, whilest at last, being so sore imprisoned, that their toes rotted off, and the one of them could not go without crutches, they brought them to the church by compulsion, where the one of them heard their abominable Masse, having a certaine summe of money given by the benevolence of the people, and so departed thence; but the first newes that was heard of him within three or four days, was that he had drowned himselfe in a river running by Richmond, called Swaile. Immediately after Dr. Dakins giving sentence that the other should be burnt, came home to his house, and never joyed after but died. The commissary of Richmond, named Hillings, preached at his burning, exhorting him to return to the church; but his labour was vain, the constant martyr standing strongly to the faith he professed.

Then being brought to the stake whereunto he was tied by a girdle of iron, there was given unto him gunpowder and a little strawe was laid under his feete and set round about with small wood and tarre barrels; the fire was put under the strawe, which by and by flaming about his head, he cried thrice together Christe Helpe me. Insomuch that one Robert Atkinson being present, said: Hold fast there, and we will all pray for thee. Thus this blessed martyr ended his life.

This incident affected Richmond people deeply. What made it cruelly ironic was that when Queen Mary died only a few weeks later, on 19 November 1558, England reverted to Protestantism. One of those sorely affected was Foxe's 'Dr. Dakins', who himself died on 9 November. John Dakyn was a priest who, living and working through this period of turbulent religious changes, had achieved high office through his ability to 'move with the times' as each change was introduced, being first a Catholic priest, then an Anglican priest and lastly a Catholic priest again. It has been said that he began his career as a Benedictine monk at St. Mary's Abbey in York, but recent research has disproved this, although he certainly had links with St. Mary's as the abbey was his patron as rector of Kirkby Ravensworth from 1535. During the Pilgrimage of Grace in 1536 he was the most senior local cleric on the horns of a dilemma, sharing the rebels' opposition to the Dissolution but expected to persuade his congregation to accept the new religious ways. Dakyn tried to keep in with both camps, defending himself to both commons and Crown, and as was usual for him, doing so successfully.

Dakyn was a close friend of another priest, William Knight, who held high office, being Archdeacon of Richmond from 1531 until 1541, when the archdeaconry was transferred to the new diocese of Chester, and Knight was promoted to Bishop of Bath and Wells. When he died in 1547, he made Dakyn his executor and requested him to found a school and hospital in his memory. It seems that Dakyn was somewhat tardy in doing so, but as he grew old and approached his own end his conscience pricked, and in 1555 he obtained a licence from Queen Mary, and her husband Philip of Spain with whom she ruled England. This enabled him to establish the school and hospital of St. John the Baptist at Kirkby Ravensworth, and he erected a large new building in the churchyard, which was opened on 11 May 1556 by John Dakyn himself. He laid down 37 statutes specifying exactly how the charity was to be run, how the staff appointed or dismissed, the scholars and alms-folk selected, and even the school curriculum.

The charity still exists, although the grammar school closed in 1957 and the almshouse moved to a new building in the village in 1754, now called Dakyn House. The original building has been split into a house, a village hall and a holiday cottage run by the Landmark Trust. The Dakyn charity still elects its two wardens by the archaic method laid down by the founder, picking two names from six, written on scraps of paper set within balls of wax, kept in a pitcher of water. Its endowments include land and property in Sleegill, just across the river from Richmond, some of which once belonged to St. Martin's Priory.

When Queen Elizabeth I succeeded her half-sister Mary, England became Protestant again with a Prayer Book in English and the Queen as Supreme Governor of the Church, but Elizabeth deliberately sought to tread a middle path inclusive of those of both Puritan and Catholic inclinations. Among the urgent problems facing her was the shortfall of welfare and similar provision caused by the Dissolution of the Monasteries. Her reign saw various measures attempting to succour the disadvantaged, notably the Statute of Artificers of 1567 regulating employment and wages, and the Poor Law Acts of 1597 and 1601. A parallel phenomenon of late-Tudor times was the foundation of grammar schools in many towns and cities, several of which still bear a monarch's name. Richmond too received a royal charter for a school, but in different circumstances.

The investigation of William Wharton's complaint to the Court of Augmentations concerning the 'concealment' of most of the Richmond chantries, begun in King Edward VI's time, had remained dormant during Mary Tudor's reign. Then in January 1560 all Richmond's concealed chantry lands were included in a grant made by Queen Elizabeth to Sir George Howard, her master of the armoury. Soon afterwards Howard contracted to sell on these lands to Thomas Warcoppe of Westmorland, but Richmond Corporation refused him entry to 'theirs', and he complained to the Court of Requests in February 1560. A Commission of Inquiry set up to investigate heard numerous lengthy depositions in Richmond.

The town's case, unsurprisingly, was weak, and the Crown brought an action against the Bailiffs and Burgesses of Richmond to be heard in the Exchequer Court in London. Due to difficulties in empanelling there a jury of knights from the Richmond area, it was transferred to York Assizes. The vast quantity of recorded evidence included details of all the chantries, their founders, chantry priests, silver chalices and richly embroidered vestments, and other property. The judgement when finally delivered early in 1563, quite amazingly, found Richmond not guilty. The verdict was clearly not impartial and has to be interpreted as an example of northern opposition to the Queen's religious policies.

The Corporation realized its victory was hollow and, anticipating further trouble, considered it prudent to petition the Queen to endow and erect a Free Grammar School out of the properties under dispute. The request was granted, and a charter of incorporation duly issued on 14 March 1567 to 'The Free Grammar School of the Burgesses of the Borough or Town of Richmond in the County of York'. This was a re-foundation, there having been a grammar school in the town since at least the 1390s, and indeed a chantry priest, John More of the chantry of Our Lady in the Parish Church, is known to have been the master of the grammar school in the 1540s, a position he may have continued to hold until his death in 1571.

The Corporation only had to endow the school with lands to an annual value of £40, far less than the value of property seized, and they could accept further endowments from individual benefactors. In the north-east corner of the churchyard they erected a school building which, typically of Tudor grammar schools, consisted of a single room, at one end of which on a raised dais was the Master's desk and seat, with its high back with Gothic panelling between classical pilasters. The Corporation had to employ one master, and the four Bailiffs of the Borough were *ex officio* to be the School Governors. The school was to have a common seal, which survives. It portrays St. James the Greater, whose shrine at Compostella was a favoured destination of medieval pilgrims, as a bearded figure in pilgrim's garb with bare feet, a rosary in one hand and a palmer's staff in the other, and on his head a broad-brimmed hat on which is a scallop-shell - his emblem. St. James was chosen because one of the main endowments given to the School in 1567 was that of St. James Chapel in Bargate. The Elizabethan Grammar School's successor, the present Richmond School, a large and highly regarded comprehensive school, still has the figure of St. James as its badge, and within the present school there survives the venerable Master's desk. The Grammar School will feature in later chapters.

As Queen Elizabeth's reign progressed, it became harder for her to maintain her religious tolerance. There were several attempts to put on the throne her younger cousin Mary, Queen of Scots, the daughter of her father's sister Margaret who had married James IV of Scotland. Mary was the focus of many aspirations hostile to Elizabeth. As well as being queen of Scotland, still a separate country and England's old enemy, she was a Catholic and so had the support not only of English Catholics but also powerful continental ones including Philip of Spain who, as Mary Tudor's husband, had been king of England also.

The first serious rebellion against Elizabeth occurred in 1569, spearheaded by two northern earls, Thomas Percy of Northumberland and Charles Nevill of Westmorland. In November of that year the rebels entered Durham Cathedral, re-erected its old stone altars and restored the Mass, and then marched to Darlington. Their followers increasing to 1,000 horse and 4,000 foot, by early December they were in Richmond, where they burned English Bibles and Prayer Books. Marching south to Northallerton, they then headed for Ripon where they held a Mass in the Minster, and then returned north, to Richmond again, and then to Barnard Castle, which they besieged until its garrison capitulated.

When the rebellion was eventually suppressed, sufficient of the rebels as would serve as a public example were executed for High Treason, some of them at Richmond. A more expedient punishment was imposed on many of the more prosperous ones, who were attainted, and had their estates confiscated. Of the ten men from the Archdeaconry of Richmond who were attainted, three came from Richmond - Ralph Conyers, whose estate was valued at £6 13s. 4d. John Gower (£10 18s. 8d.) and Robert Heighington (6s.), all of whom seem to have escaped death by fleeing abroad. Others, including 47 from Richmond, were pardoned on the receipt of fines, some clubbing together to pay theirs in groups of ten.

As a result of this Rising of the Northern Earls, or Northern Rebellion, and subsequent similar revolts, life was made more difficult for those with Catholic sympathies. For each non-attendance at church on Sunday a fine of 12d. was imposed, with larger fines for more radical acts of non-compliance. Nevertheless many families remained loyal to the 'Old Religion', especially in North Yorkshire. Among the most notable Roman Catholic families, vituperatively referred to as recusants or papists, were the Lawsons of Brough Hall, who remained true to their faith through thick and thin, century after century, maintaining a private chapel, and supporting priests to serve it.

Kings Henry VII, Henry VIII, Edward VI and Queen Mary (and Philip) had issued charters to Richmond, which perpetuated the town's medieval form of self-government under which four Bailiffs acted on behalf of the burgesses. Queen Elizabeth's charter, granted in 1577, made radical alterations, broadly in line with national social and economic changes of its time. The corporate body was now to consist of an Alderman and twelve Capital Burgesses, who were all named, the Alderman being chosen each Feast of St. Hilary (13 January), from two candidates. The Saturday market was confirmed, with the Alderman as clerk of the market, and a second annual fair was granted, to be held on the Eve of Palm Sunday. Among the town's judicial privileges was to be a Recorder sitting in a Court of Record in the Tollbooth, the Alderman was to be a Justice of the Peace and coroner, and the borough was to have a prison. There were to be two Serjeants-at-mace carrying maces of silver or gilt, assisted by Constables. The Corporation was to have the right of perambulating the bounds of the borough and of making bye-laws. Almost as an afterthought the charter mentions the Borough being given full power and authority, whenever a Parliament was assembled, to choose 'two discreet and honest men, Burgesses of the town, to be Burgesses of Parliament at the burden and cost of the said borough'.

Richmond seems at first to have considered it an unnecessary expense to send two Members to Parliament, and neglected to do so for some years. The clause had, however, been inserted deliberately, for Queen Elizabeth was anxious to balance the traditional 'knights of the shires' in Parliament with 'new men' who she hoped would be more sympathetic. Richmond, it would appear, received some gentle reminders, and sent two members from 1584. The town's parliamentary representation became an important aspect of its history, as will be seen in Chapter 6. Richmond still appoints two Serjeants-at-mace who carry fine maces, and the town's oldest mace, now carried by the mayor, is a small silver one which is probably of Elizabethan date. The bounds are now ceremonially perambulated or 'beaten' every seven years in what is called the Boundary Riding, but in the days before maps were available it was essential to make sure the local population understood where boundaries lay.

The first Alderman of Richmond, as named in the town's Elizabethan charter, was James Cotterel. Born in Dublin and educated there at Trinity College, he became a lawyer and moved to Richmond for the career opportunities afforded by the Archdeaconry courts. Having established his reputation, he then moved to York where he spent his latter years as a judicial 'examiner' at the Council of the North. He died in York in 1595 and was buried in York Minster where his grave was marked by a large brass tablet, chaste with his portrait. This still exists and is one of the few old brasses surviving in the Minster.

In his long and complex will, Cotterel bequeathed a silver salt-cellar to each of the three places which had played large parts in his life. Dublin's salt has long since disappeared, York's was melted down with other civic plate during the mid-17th century Civil War, but Richmond's survives and is the oldest piece in the town's important collection of civic plate. With the town's status enhanced by its new charter, one can imagine his desire to see official banquets in the town befittingly graced with an elegant piece of table silver. Cotterel also bequeathed to the Corporation the sum of £100 from which £8 was to be paid to the Rector of Richmond for an annual sermon - "and I hartilie praie and require the said Alderman and Burgesses for the glories of God and the good of the toune of Richmond to do their best endevors for a godlie grave sufficient learned preacher to succede there from time to time". This annuity is still paid to the Rector.

The Cotterel salt of 1595

James Cotterel was typical of the new 'middle class' of men who held public office during Elizabeth's reign. Often lawyers, many made money from lands newly-acquired from the Crown in the aftermath of the Dissolution of the Monasteries and chantries. Some families produced several individuals of similar importance, others intermarried with them. One such was the Gower family. Ralph Gower was wealthy enough to become the re-founded Grammar School's first benefactor as early as 1567, giving the School land, called Gower's Paddock, on the north side of Quaker Lane. He had gained some of his wealth from supplying lead for major building projects such as at Durham Castle, and also by marrying as his second wife Anne, daughter of Thomas Wray who had acquired St. Nicholas from the Crown.

The Pepper family produced several notable members, starting with William and his son John who invested in several local corn watermills. John became one of the town's first Members of Parliament in 1584. A cousin, Cuthbert, qualified as a lawyer and became Chancellor of Durham and a member of the Council of the North, before serving as Recorder of Richmond 1586-1603. He lived in, and may have built, Hill House, and also bought the former estate of the Grey Friars in 1605. Sir Cuthbert was succeeded as Recorder by John Pepper's son Christopher, who held the post 1603-35. Both Cuthbert and Christopher also served as Members of Parliament for part of the time they were Recorders.

Another name of even greater importance in the Tudor history of Richmond was that of Bowes, a leading northern family based at Streatlam in County Durham. A Robert Bowes was involved in the Pilgrimage of Grace, and his nephew Sir George was largely responsible for putting down the Northern Rebellion. Among their North Yorkshire estates was Aske, acquired early in the 16th century when Sir George's father Richard Bowes married Elizabeth, heiress of the Aske estate. In 1548 Richard Bowes was appointed Captain of Norham, the Scottish frontier's largest castle seven miles from Berwick, and Elizabeth and their many children joined him there. Elizabeth Bowes found the life of well-born women in the Scottish borders different from what she had known at Aske. English law forbade women to read the Bible, despite Protestant arguments in favour of an English Bible that people must be able to have direct access to it. Scottish women were not only permitted to read the Bible but were encouraged to do so, and to discuss matters of theology, which had developed their education and liberated them more than their English sisters. Elizabeth Bowes developed an interest in Protestant theology, and became deeply involved with the Scottish Calvinists, particularly their leader, John Knox himself.

This was very much against the wishes of her husband, Richard Bowes, whose diplomatic position required a non-controversial wife, especially as the women in this group were prepared to disobey their husbands over religion, and indeed the degree of involvement between Elizabeth and John Knox was such as to cause considerable embarrassment. John Knox was in Berwick 1549-51, and when he met Elizabeth Bowes he was a middle-aged man and she was older, having been married for nearly 30 years and the mother of 15 children, many of whom were by then grown up. To complicate matters further, in 1553 John Knox married her fifth daughter, Margery, about twenty years his junior, again against Richard Bowes' wishes. Margery and John Knox had two sons, Nathaniel and Eleazer, born in the late 1550s. Margery acted as Knox's secretary, and her mother helped to raise the children. Ironically, in 1558 John Knox published his famous book condemning women rulers *The First Blast of a Trumpet against the Monstrous Regiment of Women.* In the same year died Richard Bowes, still estranged from Elizabeth, who continued to live with the Knoxes, even when they moved briefly to Geneva. Margery Knox died in 1560, and Elizabeth continued to live with John, bringing up her young grandsons Nathaniel and Eleazer who, according to tradition, were later educated at Richmond Grammar School. John Knox remarried in 1564, and Elizabeth Bowes died about 1568, but when Knox himself died in 1572 he left as trustee for the education of his sons and its endowment, her youngest son, Robert Bowes who inherited Aske.

  This Robert Bowes married twice, first a distant Bowes cousin who died young, leaving one son, Ralph, who inherited Aske but died in 1622 shortly before his father's second wife Eleanor Musgrave of Eden Hall in Cumberland, whom he married in 1560. This second marriage was a long one but produced no children. In 1575 Robert Bowes was appointed by Queen Elizabeth, probably on the strength of his father's career, as Treasurer of Berwick, a high position on the Scottish border. Later he became the Queen's ambassador to the Court of Scotland, a post which required him to fund an expensive and protracted espionage operation spying on Mary, Queen of Scots and her son, since her enforced abdication in 1567 King James VI of Scotland, who would one day be Queen Elizabeth's successor.

Robert Bowes' letters have been published. As he became older and frailer, and poorer - the Queen never paid his expenses - he wrote to her ministers, secretary Sir Francis Walsingham, and treasurer Lord Burghley, begging to be reimbursed, and then to be allowed to return to his home at Aske, to manage his estate there, describing in one letter his desire "that my neck may once be delivered out of this halter". It was never convenient, either to settle up with him, or to grant him leave, and although he did manage to obtain his recall as Ambassador in 1583, he remained Treasurer of Berwick and continued to be engaged on diplomatic missions. In 1596 he wrote that he must "either purchase my liberty, or at least lycence to come to my house for a tyme to put in order by broken estate before the end of my dayes", but despite this plea he died at Berwick in 1597.

Unlike her mother-in-law, Eleanor Bowes seems to have stayed at Aske looking after the estate during Robert Bowes' long absences on the Scottish border. The couple made considerable improvements to the house at Aske, adding a new great hall onto the 15th-century pele tower he had inherited, perhaps in anticipation of a possible northern progress of the royal court. One of the problems during their time at Aske was a long-running dispute over the estate boundary. The argument was about whether the tithes from some land were due to the rector of Richmond or the vicar of Easby, in other words whether the land in question lay within the boundary of the borough of Richmond, or the Aske estate, which is in Easby parish. Various inquiries were held in the 1560s and 1570s, and numerous witness statements and sworn affidavits were taken, but despite the bundles of surviving documents the outcome is unclear. However it is probably the origin of the Aske estate agent's customary challenge made until recently to the Mayor of Richmond during the Boundary Riding.

It is through Robert Bowes' position as a courtier, and his widow Eleanor's subsequent benefactions to Richmond (to be described in the next chapter) that Richmond possesses the fine contemporary portrait of Queen Elizabeth I, which now hangs over the seat of the Town Mayor of Richmond in the Council

Chamber in the Town Hall. Painted on a wooden panel made up from three boards, within what is probably the original frame, it has been dated by experts to around the time of the Spanish Armada in 1588. Richly begowned, and holding a feather fan, her many jewels include the pearls which symbolized her virginity. *[see plate 4]* Tudor monarchs used their portraits as political propaganda, and her colouring, athletic build and long thin fingers, are all exaggerated in order to emphasise her physical resemblance to her father King Henry VIII. The 60-year old queen's image is flattered, a delicate lace ruff gracing her neck, her serious expression disguising the loss of her teeth, her bald head hidden by a red wig. This great treasure was mislaid by Richmond Corporation for over 30 years until it was brought back to the town in 1986. It was cleaned of the blackening effect of centuries of candle smoke and its beauty can now be fully appreciated.

      The later years of Queen Elizabeth's reign were still affected by Roman Catholic rebellion. Having had a Protestant martyr during Queen Mary's reign, Richmond now produced a Catholic martyr. John Acrige was a member of an established Richmond family and, described as having "a good knowledge in music and competent understanding in the Latin tonge", had probably been educated at Richmond Grammar School. He became priest of St. Thomas' chantry in Holy Trinity Chapel, and later curate in the Parish Church but, troubled by his acceptance of Protestantism, during the Northern Rebellion of 1569 he threw in his lot with the Catholic rebels. When the rebellion was crushed he fled abroad, but became homesick for Richmond and, after some years, ventured back to his birthplace. Arrested in his sister's house in Richmond, he was arraigned before the Alderman who, ironically, was a kinsman and namesake. He was then sent to York for further examination by Matthew Hutton, the Dean of York whose son Timothy would at the end of the 16th century purchase the estate of Marske in Swaledale. Acrige refused to renounce his Catholic views and was imprisoned, first in York Castle "to be put in irons" and, finally, in the notorious Blockhouse at Hull where he died on 2

March 1585. In 1588, when the Spanish Armada threatened England's shores, Richmond Corporation was on alert, with the town's beacon prepared ready for lighting as part of the national chain of defence in the event of invasion.

A selection (with modernized spelling) of Richmond's Elizabethan bye-laws gives some insight into everyday life in the town then.

> Mr. Alderman shall control the Wool House and have the profits from all things weighed there
> At the ringing of the Common Bell at any time all the inhabitants are to report to Mr. Alderman. If the bell rings on account of a fire the inhabitants are to proceed at once to the scene of the fire and with all speed assist in extinguishing it
> At all elections and consultations the youngest of the 12 burgesses shall first speak and so ascend in order to the eldest burgess. The "reason, voice and assent of Mr. Alderman to be last". Every person arrested and committed to gaol shall receive victuals from the gaoler and shall pay him at the rate of 7s. a week. Any person making an affray within the Town on a Market Day shall be fined 40s., on a Fair Day £5 and on a week day 3s. 4d. If any blood be shed there shall be an additional fine of 6s. 8d. The keys of the Common Box belonging to the Free Grammar School shall be kept in this manner: the Bailiffs of the School for the time being to have one, Mr. Alderman one, the "most ancient burgess" one and the Schoolmaster one. Every butcher shall from time to time clean out his stall and shall not sweep his filth down the Shambles but carry away the same. The butchers shall not leave tup horns lying in the street nor lay in the Shambles any calves taken out of a cow's belly. All mastiffs to be kept under control by being muzzled. No one shall make a dunghill except in the areas staked out for such by Mr. Alderman's officers. Every townsman not keeping the front of his premises clean shall be fined

6d. Fishing in the River Swale is forbidden without a licence from Mr. Alderman and then only with "angle rods". No one is to kill salmon by "any manner of engine". No person shall sell meat, drink or other victual in the time of Divine Service on Sundays or Holy Days. No one without reasonable excuse shall absent himself from church in time of Divine Service. No one shall harbour a vagabond or evil person in his home nor "lodge any dishonest woman to be delivered of child". No one shall winnow corn in the street unless he carry away the chaff. No one shall leave his carriage, cart or wain standing in the streets on Sundays, Fair Days or Market Days. No one is to wash any fish or other thing at the conduit or at any of the Town's wells whereby the filth may "corrupt the water". All weights and measures are to be checked against the standard ones in the Toll Booth. All lime sacks are to be measured against the "Toll Booth bushel", every sack is to contain 4 bushels and to have a mark affixed to it by Mr. Alderman. No cordwainers are to offer any wares for sale until the Corn Bell is rung. Upon proclamation by Mr. Alderman in the event of some emergency every burgess must appear himself carrying a halbert or supply a proxy. No corn shall be ground in a Town mill on a Sunday between 8 a.m. and "until evening prayer be said". No one shall hire any other person to knit for money without also supplying him (or her) with meat, drink, lodging and "competent apparel". Every common baker is to have two marks designed by Mr. Alderman and shall mark his loaves with them. Bakers shall sell in the market at the rate of 13 loaves to the dozen.

Many of the above ordinances relate to structures, which then stood in the Market Place. The Shambles and Toll Booth were mentioned in the previous chapter. The Wool House was somewhere on the south side west of the Town Hall. The common bell, said to have come from St. James' Chapel, was the smaller of the two bells in the tower of Holy Trinity Chapel. Salmon were found in the river Swale until the 18th century. The attempts to protect the purity of the town's drinking water refer to the Conduit, a covered cistern near the entry to Friars Wynd, erected in 1583 as Richmond's first public water supply. The Corporation undertook the cost of laying wooden pipes to bring the water from springs at Aislabeck, north-west of the West Field. One of these pipes, bored out from the branch of an elm tree, was discovered near West Field about 1885, and is on display in the Richmondshire Museum.

However, the new water supply did not prevent a severe plague late in Queen Elizabeth's reign. The first death from this plague is recorded in the parish register for 17 August 1597, and the last on 15 February 1599, with the total number of deaths given as 1,072, probably representing about half the population of Richmond at that time. A plaque in Penrith Church gives the figure of 2,200 for Richmond, but this may mean Richmondshire. A plain uninscribed stone in Richmond Churchyard is known as the Plague Stone, and tradition has it that it marks the place where many of the dead were buried in a mass grave. Other mass graves are said to have been dug in the Castle Yard and on Clarke Green near Clink Bank.

The historian Camden gave his version of Richmond and its history in 1590:

> ..... Richmondia, commonly Richmond, the chief city of this shire [is] enclos'd with walls of no great compass; yet by the suburbs which shoot out in length to the three gates, it is pretty populous.
>
> It was built by Alan, the first Earl, who (not daring to rely upon Gilling, his village or manor hard by to withstand the assaults of the Saxons and the Danes, whom the Normans had strip'd of their inheritances) grac'd it with this name, signifying a Rich Mount and fortify'd it with walls and a very strong castle situated upon a rock from whence it looks down upon the River Swale, which with a great murmur seems to rush rather than run among the stones.

Richmond historian Peter Wendham and Mayor Mrs Ella Devlin at the unveiling of the Civic Society's plaque to Protestant martyr Richard Snell in Newbiggin

5

Stuart Richmond 1603-1714

The National History

News of the death at Richmond Palace, London, on 24 March 1603 of Queen Elizabeth I was passed to her named successor, the 37-year old king James VI of Scotland. Now King James I of England (1603-25), he travelled south to London via York. An unattractive, slobbering character with obscene sense of humour, whose slurred speech compounded his Scottish accent, he was nevertheless an efficient ruler. His fervent belief in the Divine Right of Kings was interpreted as arrogance, making him increasingly unpopular with Parliament on whom he, particularly, depended for revenue due to his extravagant tastes and personal poverty. Despite being a Stuart he was a Protestant, against whom the Catholics planned the infamous Gunpowder Plot, with several Yorkshire participants. One of his greatest achievements was the King James Bible - the 'Authorized Version' - published in 1611, but religious discontent led to the Pilgrim Fathers and other early settlers leaving to establish colonies in America.

King Charles I (1625-49), a good and devout man although an ineffective king, was Protestant but the Catholicism of his queen Henrietta Maria alienated Parliament's growing number of Puritans, adding to his poverty. His adherence to the Divine Right of Kings led him to assemble no Parliament for eleven years, but a desperate shortage of defence revenue led to his levying nationally Ship Money tax, previously collected only from coastal regions. People argued that only Parliament should set taxes, and so the King reluctantly summoned one, but it refused to grant him money until he abolished Ship Money, so he angrily dismissed what is thus known as the Short Parliament of 1640.

The imposition on Scotland of the English Prayer Book provoked Scottish threats of war against England, and Charles had to call the Long Parliament, named because it sat from late 1640 until 1653. Puritans in Parliament accused him of Catholic sympathies and, in exchange for tax revenue for the army, forced him to make concessions such as forsaking the right to lead an army against the Irish, who had risen against the English. King and Parliament were now on a collision course. The queen was dispatched to France to raise funds, and Parliament began to organize its own army. Charles, having stronger support in the north, spent eight months of 1642 in York mustering his army, before raising his standard at Nottingham on 22 August. The English Civil War had begun, and Royalists and Parliamentarians fought for nearly seven years.

For almost three months in 1644 the Parliamentarians besieged Royalist York, with armies commanded by the Earl of Manchester and Sir Thomas Fairfax, plus the Scottish army, camped outside its walls. A Royalist army, brilliantly led by Prince Rupert of the Rhine, marched to relieve the city, but due to Royalist command incompetence, their advantage of surprise was wasted and they lost the Battle of Marston Moor on 2 July 1644. On 16 July the city surrendered, Charles saying, "If York be lost, I shall esteem my crown little less". Charles was taken prisoner and eventually executed on 30 January 1649, hence the inn-sign 'The King's Head' and England became a Puritan-influenced Commonwealth under the Protector Oliver Cromwell and, from 1658, his son Richard.

After eleven years of Puritan restrictions on enjoyment, the Restoration of King Charles II (1660-85) was greeted with feasting and celebration in 1660, followed by the disasters of the Plague of 1665 and the Great Fire of London in 1666. He was an immensely popular king despite his womanizing - one of his illegitimate sons being created Duke of Richmond - but without a legitimate heir he was succeeded by his brother King James II (1685-88). Unpopular for his Roman Catholicism, James fled to France where his descendants kept alive the Stuart cause. The Glorious Revolution resulted in the reigns of William III (1689-1702) and Mary II (1689-94), daughter of James II who had married the Dutch Prince William of Orange. The reign of Mary's younger sister Queen Anne (1704-14) saw wars with France, with some notable victories by the Duke of Marlborough, and the Union with Scotland in 1707.

King James I must have passed quite near to Richmond on his journey south from Scotland in 1603. Doubtless the residents of Richmond soon heard of Roman Catholic plans to depose the new king, and eventually of the unsuccessful Gunpowder Plot on 5 November 1605, with which some local people may have sympathized. Others would feel more support for the king in its aftermath. Meanwhile, life went on as before, and among those with both land and leisure, hunting was a popular sport. This activity led to an event in early-Stuart times, which has become one of Richmond's favourite stories.

One November day in 1606 Robert Willance, a prosperous Richmond draper, was a member of a hunting party above Whitcliffe Scar, a sheer drop just west of the town. His family owned property at Clints, a little further west, so he presumably knew the area well. Suddenly, a mist descended, blotting out all familiar landmarks, causing him to lose his sense of direction. The horse he was riding that day, a young inexperienced animal according to tradition, panicked and hurtled over the cliff edge. They fell over 100 feet. The horse was killed, but Willance escaped with a badly broken leg. Willance knew that he was unlikely to be rescued that foggy day, and needed to keep the leg warm to delay the onset of gangrene during the cold night ahead, so with his hunting knife he slit open the horse's belly and managed to get his leg inside it.

He was eventually found, and carried back to Richmond where his leg was amputated, and he made a good recovery. In recognition of his escape he erected on the top of the escarpment three identical monuments marking the last two bounds his horse took before plunging downwards, the stones being spaced 24 feet apart. Each was inscribed Glory be to our merciful God who so miraculously preserved me from the danger so great, and the place has ever since been known as "Willance's Leap". The event so fired the imagination of successive generations of Richmondians that on subsequent occasions the original stones have been replaced, in two cases by larger ones. Two stones remain, neither of them original. At the top is an obelisk within railings, set up by public subscription, and inaugurated on 19 September 1906 during the seven-yearly Boundary Riding. Below that is a flat upright stone placed there in 1815, with an inscription, which was renewed in 1843 and again in 1906. Willance also gave to the Corporation of Richmond a silver cup inscribed *This Boulle given by Robert Willance to the Incorporated Alderman and Burgesses of Richmond, to be used by the Alderman for the time being, and to be delivered by him, his executors, or assigns, to his successors for ever. 1606.* This cup is still in the town's fine collection of civic plate displayed in the Green Howards Regimental Museum in the Market Place.

Willance's recovery from his horrendous accident was so complete that in 1608 he was able to serve as Alderman of Richmond, and presumably to use his cup on civic occasions. His house in Frenchgate still survives as No. 24, its garden adjoining the churchyard. To make it easier for him with his disability to attend church, a doorway was made in the garden wall. When he died in February 1616 he was carried through that garden door for his funeral, and then was buried in the churchyard just beside the door. According to tradition, his amputated leg had been buried there ten years earlier! His grave was marked by a large ledger stone which is still there, the commemorative inscription was re-cut in 1906, but is now illegible again. Robert Willance was a wealthy man, and apparently quite a character. In his will he bequeathed money to the poor of Richmond, who were to be given 'dynners' on the day of his funeral, and among his personal bequests were a round hoop ring and a double ducat of gold to his widow, Elizabeth, his best horse and saddle and furniture, his best sword and dagger and his books to his nephew Brian Willance, his heir. He had no legitimate children of his own, but left small sums to each of his many god-children, called 'god barnes' in his local dialect, £50 each to his two nieces, and £300 and £100 respectively to his illegitimate son and daughter, by two named mothers!

"Boulle" or cup given to Richmond by Robert Willance, 1606

In the year following Willance's escapade the Bowes Hospital was founded by Eleanor Bowes, widow of Robert Bowes, Queen Elizabeth I's ambassador to Scotland. The former medieval Chapel of St. Edmund King and Martyr in Aldbiggin was converted to become the hospital, or almshouse, which was to house three poor widows, two from Richmond and one from Easby. Where the town's Elizabethan portrait once hung, the coats of arms of Eleanor and Robert Bowes can be seen on the outside of the building, and inside survives a fragment of a plaster frieze, depicting shields held by putti between pomegranate discs in bas relief, typical of the date 1607. The Bowes Hospital is still an almshouse although now occupied by just one widow. By the end of the 17th century the town would have a second almshouse, the hospital founded in 1699 by George Pinckney also for three poor widows. The original site was close to Frenchgate Bar, but new premises were built in Tower Street in 1825. Eleanor Bowes died after a long period of widowhood in 1623, bequeathing to Richmond Corporation the sum of forty pounds as the so-called Widow's Mite charity, to be used to lend money to up to eight poor tradesmen for up to three years.

The Bowes Hospital, still identified as 'The Ankriche', is the first of 19 buildings and places in the town specifically highlighted on John Speede's Map of Richmond of 1610, the earliest plan of the town. Although not drawn accurately to scale it nevertheless is an invaluable source of information for the layout of Richmond at this date. One of the intriguing features of it is that on the south side of the river Swale, Speede has drawn a cave entrance with the annotation "A Vault that goeth under the River and ascendeth up into the Castell", and near it the figure of a traveller with a staff in his hand and a pack on his back - or it might even be a drum! Perhaps this is a reference to Richmond's Little Drummer Boy legend, according to which there is a secret passage running from either the Market Place or the Castle to Easby Abbey.

The story goes that one day at some unspecified time in the past, a contingent from a regiment stationed in Richmond discovered an opening leading into an underground passage. The soldiers being too large to explore it, they lowered into it the smallest drummer boy with them, ordering him to follow the passage, beating his drum as he went so that they could trace its course above ground by the sound of his drumbeats. The route took them to a point in Clink Bank Wood about two thirds of the way to Easby, when the drumming ceased. The little drummer boy was never seen again, but his companions erected at the place a stone still to this day called the Drummer Boy Stone, and they do say that if you venture to that lonely spot at midnight, you can sometimes still hear his drumming!

Less well-known than John Speede's Map is Alexander Keirincx's painting of a prospect of Richmond from the east, dating from 1639. *[see plate 5]* He was one of two Dutchmen commissioned by Charles I to paint pictures of England and Scotland. There were to be two landscapes, while eight were of the "King's houses and towns", Richmond being one of the latter. The original is now in the Yale Center for British Art in the United States of America.

Religious strife was never far beneath the surface of Stuart society, and both Puritans and Roman Catholics continued to feel aggrieved. Sir George Calvert of Kiplin Hall near Scorton was one of those who chose to seek greater religious toleration for Catholics in the New World, and was responsible for the establishment of the Colony, later the State, of Maryland about 1630. The lengthy preface to the will of William Coates, a cordwainer or shoemaker of Richmond who died in 1621, shows that he had become a Calvinist, one of those who believed himself of the 'elect' and called by God to heaven.

> I William Coates of Richmond callinge to minde the uncertaintie of man's estait and continuance here upon the earth and seeing dayly before myne eyes howe death doth throwe his dartes round ni[gh]e on everye side, hittinge both yonge and old, whereby I am admonished not to withstand or resist deathes force, or to thinke my selfe out of his danger but rather prepare my selfe to be in such readiness as that I may without feare yeeld my selfe

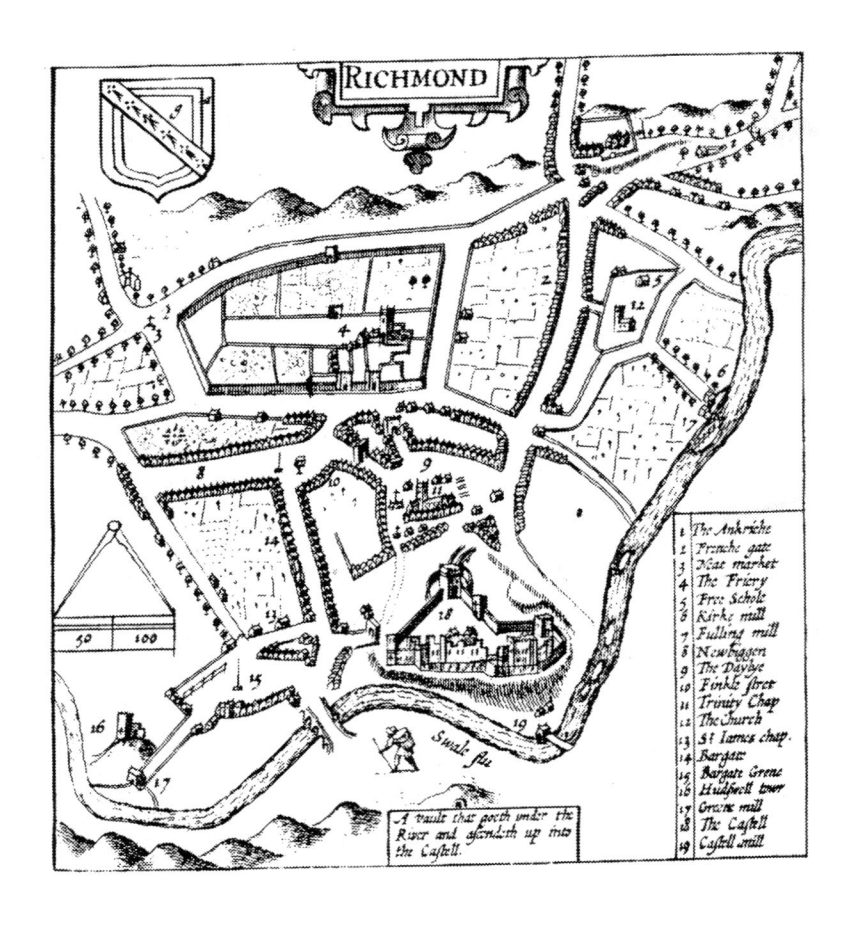

John Speede's Map of Richmond, 1610

not unprovided for his coming......
First I do commend my soule unto almightie god my maker and redeemer by the merite of whose passion and death I do assure my selfe to be made partaker of the glory of his everlastinge kingdome which I know is given to no man throughe his owne righteousness but through the rightesousness of our alone Saviour Christ Jesus whome I humbly beseech and earnestly pray to be an intercession for me unto God his father that through his mercye and everlastinge goodnes as a member of his Catholique Church I may be received amongest the number of his elect as I do faithfullie beleeve I shall and I do commit my body to be buried in the earth......

William Coates perhaps made shoes for, and would certainly have known, Sir Timothy Hutton. The eldest son of Matthew Hutton, Archbishop of York 1595-1606, Timothy was born in 1569, the year of the Northern Rebellion, put down by Sir George Bowes. When Bowes' third daughter was born shortly afterwards, the grateful queen had agreed to stand godmother to the child, who was named Elizabeth. This Elizabeth Bowes married Timothy Hutton in 1592, and the queen gave her goddaughter a beautiful silver-gilt standing cup. Archbishop Hutton gave Timothy the vast sum of £1,900, with which he bought property at Marrick, sold in 1598 when he purchased a better estate at Marske-in-Swaledale, owned by the family until 1957. Timothy Hutton built a new mansion at Marske, designed by the then leading northern architect Robert Smythson, now encapsulated within Georgian alterations made by later generations of Huttons.

Timothy Hutton was active in public life, both in Richmond and in Yorkshire generally. He was one of several members of the Hutton family to serve as High Sheriff of Yorkshire, being knighted by King James I in the year of his shrievalty, 1605. It was probably at this time that he first acquired a house in Richmond, a more accessible location than Marske. A Richmond base became even more necessary for him when in 1617 he first served as Alderman of the Borough. In 1627 he purchased from Sir Cuthbert Pepper the property formerly belonging to the Grey Friars, probably then building the handsome new house there, the Friary. Sir Timothy became Alderman for the second time in January 1629 and the speech he gave upon taking office still survives, remarkably similar to many such speeches made by present-day mayors - he was honoured to have been elected, unworthy though he was, would rely on his fellow officers whom he held in high regard, must not speak too long etc. etc. Then almost sixty years of age, he did not live to complete that second term of office, dying only a few months later, at the Friary. As Alderman, his funeral in the parish church must have been a grand civic occasion, and the Latin entry in the parish register is lengthier than most and very fulsome. Elizabeth Bowes had predeceased her husband, dying on the eve of Palm Sunday 1625.

A very fine monument, which still dominates the chancel south wall of the Parish Church, was erected to Sir Timothy and Elizabeth's memory by their son Matthew. *[see plate 4]* Kneeling facing east are full-size portrait figures of Sir Timothy and Elizabeth, in contemporary court dress, surrounded by the classical figures of Faith, Hope and Charity, below Fate with her trumpet standing on a Baroque pediment. Below the parents are the smaller bas-relief figures of their eight surviving children, and babes in swaddling clothes of the four, which had died in infancy. Below each child is an inscription. The text, in Greek and Latin as well as English, was composed by Sir Timothy's friend John Jackson, Rector of Marske-in-Swaledale 1620-1647, who had been Master of Richmond School 1618-20. Jackson was a distinguished theologian, and would in 1643 be a member of the Westminster Assembly of Divines, which attempted to re-shape the Church of England along Presbyterian lines. The Hutton Monument not only provides a great deal of genealogical information on a Stuart local family but, also by architect Robert Smythson, is of a design quality making it a monument of national importance.

Sir Timothy's will and inventory show that he had extensive property which he bequeathed generously, not only to relatives and friends in Richmond and Marske but in places further afield with which the Huttons had links, including Poppleton near York and Warton in Lancashire. He had lived at the Friary in some style, the furnishings of twelve rooms, plus well-equipped kitchen quarters, are described in the inventory, and his silverware weighed over 650 ounces. Typically of the time, eleven rooms contained beds, the best bed chamber having a very grand bed-stead. The great hall was still furnished in the medieval tradition with long tables and benches, but the nearby parlour was more up-to-date and contained a 'Germaine' clock.

Despite the gentry status of Sir Timothy Hutton's mansion, the area around the Friary included the more mundane House of Correction. An Act of Parliament of 1576 had ordered every county to set up *one two or more Abyding Howses or Places convenient in some Market Town or Corporate Town to be called the Howse or Howses of Correction for setting on worcke [work] and punishinge such as shall be taken as Rogues.* The North Riding Magistrates chose Richmond for theirs and sited it at "the howse called the Frieries". There was considerable delay in implementing the scheme and it was only opened in 1620, continuing at the Friary until 1665. The first Master was George Shaw, a Leeds clothier, knitting and weaving being the two principal occupations taught to the inmates.

The names and offences of many of the men and women imprisoned in the House of Correction are known. One of the commonest punishments was whipping, usually in public at the Market Cross on Market Day, but there were other types of punishment. In 1654 Mary, wife of George Outhwaite of Firby near Bedale, was

> to be set in the ducking stool and publiquely ducked for being an incorrigible and notorious scould [scold] and abusing her neighbours.

The Ducking Stool was sited alongside Clink Pool in the grounds of what is now Clink Bank Cottage, and again it is shown on Robert Harman's Plan of Richmond of 1724. In 1655 George Metcalfe of Askrigg, whose offence was forging a pass and counterfeiting the signatures of two Justices of the Peace, was ordered

> to stand in some public place in Bedale this day, in Richmond on Saturday next and in Middleham next Monday in time of market half an hour in each plase with the said words in his hat.

In January 1658 two men and a woman described as of a "roguish way of life" were branded on the left shoulder with the letter R, for rogue. The most horrendous of these punishments was that meted out at the same time as the above to Sarah Mitchell, "late of the City of York", who was

> indicted and arraigned and found guilty upon several indictments of felony for which she hath received judgment of death which is to be hanged by the neck until she be dead ..... but forasmuch as it appeareth upon search and tryall that she is conceived with quicke child, execution is to be respited till she shall be delivered ..... in the meantime the Sheriff is required to keep her in safe custody till execution be had, which is to be done at Richmond.

The names of the jury of 12 "grave matrons who sayd upon their oaths that she was with quicke child" are listed: most of them came from Richmond. We do not know whether the sentence was carried out. The gallows, also shown on Harman's Plan, were in Gallowgate, not far from the junction with the present Gallowfields Road.

The Richmond Parish Registers record the burials of two men as having been hanged, though whether by the gallows or as the result of suicide is not clear.

30 May 1609   Robert Hodgson hanged
12 January 1614   John Conyers bellman hanged

The bellman was employed to publicize important news and events by ringing a handbell and proclaiming them, and also to ring the town bells in the tower of Holy Trinity Chapel. The tower contains two medieval bells. The larger, which rings the Curfew and Apprentice bells, was also rung to indicate the death of an inhabitant, being tolled nine times for a man, six for a woman and three for a child. The smaller or Common Bell, once in St. James' Chapel, was rung to mark important events such as the election of Mayor, the town Sessions and also to alert the inhabitants to an outbreak of fire, when everyone was required to rush out and help extinguish it. The larger and smaller bells also rang the hours and quarters when the town clock was first installed in the tower some time in the early Stuart period. Holy Trinity Chapel was still used for some services at least and was the responsibility of the Borough, for the chamberlains' accounts show, as well as repairs to the clock, 7s. being paid each year "for washinge the sirpless [surplice] for Trinity Chapple" and 4s. 8d. was spent in December 1689 "for a seat in the Pulpit" there. Much of the Trinity building was, however, used for the consistory courts and their associated offices until, about 1710, all the records were packed up and transferred to Kendal, where the archdeaconry was based until it moved to Lancaster in 1718, before being brought back to Richmond in 1748.

The Hutton Monument was the most significant Stuart addition to St. Mary's Parish Church, but a clock was installed in its tower also. From 1611 all church services used the King James Authorized Version of the Bible and preaching, included in church worship since the Reformation, gained greater emphasis during the 17th century as the Puritans increased their influence. A tall pulpit was installed in the Parish Church, and carved oak panelling fitted around the walls, which helped to make it less draughty for the longer services. Many churches installed benches and, later, pews so that the congregation could sit during lengthy sermons, and initially these were free for all to use, but it became fashionable for families to install private pews and, later, elevated private galleries, in parish churches. Richmond church had many private pews carved with dates in the 1650s and 1660s and the initials of their owners, and when a house changed hands the pew was often included with the transaction. Boards painted with the Creed, Ten Commandments and Lord's Prayer were put up in 1660, and a new base made for the medieval font in 1661. The stalls from Easby Abbey, no longer used by a choir, were still in the chancel, and became the place where the Corporation sat for services from 16 June 1710. The church floor would less frequently be disturbed for interments as most burials took place in the churchyard during Stuart times.

Among the treasures of the Parish Church are two chalices, with their patens, made in 1642 and inscribed in Latin "the gift of William Lambert formerly Master of the Free School of Richmond". Lambert was Master 1613-17, and his most famous pupil was John Bathurst who became a physician whose patients included Oliver Cromwell. He also sat as a Member of Parliament for Richmond in 1656 and 1658, and married Elizabeth Willance, heiress of Clints near Marske-in-Swaledale, which estate thus passed to the Bathurst family. When Dr. John Bathurst died in 1659, he set up a charity to provide two exhibitions or scholarships for the maintenance of poor students at Cambridge and also the fee for binding a poor apprentice in Richmond. The endowment property included the site of what became, early in the 18th century, the King's Head Hotel, the name referring to the execution of King Charles I, although the sign seems always to have depicted a portrait of his restored son King Charles II. Richmond School still benefits from the Bathurst Charity. The Master when the Bathurst Charity first took effect was John Parvinge, Master 1648-96, his 48-year term in office being the longest in the School's history. On his eventual retirement due to old age and infirmity he was awarded a pension of £20 per year - the same as his salary when he became Master in 1648. He lived to receive seven years pension, dying in 1704 at the age of 79. It was during John Parvinge's Mastership that the Elizabethan school building was replaced in 1677 by a new school building slightly lower down the churchyard. Ironically, Parvinge's predecessor 1639-48 was also called John Bathurst, but was probably unrelated to the physician.

      Richmond was not directly affected by the Civil War itself, there were no local skirmishes and the Castle, being ruinous, was not used for either attack or defence, unlike Bolton Castle in Wensleydale where Richmondshire royalists were protractedly besieged by Parliamentarian troops. After the royalist defeat at the battle of Marston Moor on 2 July 1644 Prince Rupert, the royalist commander, retreated to Richmond and made his headquarters at the old Unicorn Inn, on the south side of the lower Market Place. He stayed some days, trying to rally his broken army. The consequences of this are implicit in two entries in the parish registers, both dated 7 July 1644, recording the burials in the churchyard of "a souldier" and "4 souldiers" respectively. There can be little doubt that these were unfortunate soldiers who had survived the battle and managed to get to Richmond, only to die there from their wounds soon afterwards.

      Following the battle of Marston Moor, the victorious Parliamentarians occupied the north of England with the various armies, which had constituted its forces. Richmondshire was for two years ruled by the Scottish army, which imposed much misery on the local inhabitants. The Scottish commanding officer, David Leslie, made his headquarters in Richmond, and chose as his base the ancient house of St. Nicholas, which had passed from the ownership of the Wray family to the Norton family of Thorpe Perrow. Related to the Nortons were the Wandesfords of Kirklington. Alice Wandesford, born in 1626, lived for some years after the death of her father in 1640 with her mother in the Wandesford dower house, Hipswell Hall near Richmond. During this time, and later after her marriage to William Thornton of East Newton near Helmsley, she often visited her relations at St. Nicholas. Her autobiography, written as Mrs. Alice Thornton, includes harrowing accounts of the hardships and indignities endured by residents of the Richmond area during those difficult years of the Scottish army's occupation. This is a paraphrased account of one incident at Hipswell.

> When the time came for the Scots to march back into Scotland, Captain Innes (a Scotsman), in boasting manner sent for his pay. At this time my mother was paying £25 or £30 a month to him. She sent what she owed him but he would not accept it and demanded double pay, which she would not or could not afford. So, on Sunday morning, he brought his company, and threatened to break in and smash up the house, using most vile and cruel oaths against her and me. He rounded up all her sheep and cattle and drove them off to Richmond. These cattle, of her own breeding, were my mother's special pride. I went up onto the leads on the roof to see him drive them off. He looked up and, mistaking me for my mother, cursed me bitterly.....
> So my mother gathered together the monies he had demanded and took it herself to General Leslie who lay at my Aunt Norton's house in Richmond and told him how Captain Innes had abused and worried her. By the mercy of God General Leslie listened to her complaint and took her money saying that Innes must accept it and return the cattle.

Further evidence of the damage the Scottish soldiers caused comes from a court case brought in 1652 for damages against the Alderman of Richmond and Constables of the Bailey, Frenchgate and Bargate, the town's three wards. The case related to events in 1645, a year which had seen Richmond severely affected by another severe plague, which probably also resulted from the Scottish soldiers' occupation. The parish registers for that year record the burials of 574 "infected people" between 26 March and 26 September, whereas the average for those same months over the previous five years was 40. At least 13 of the dead were buried in the Castle Yard, which implies that it was impossible to cope with them all in the churchyard. The distress among the Richmond poor was considerable, and Henry Bradrigg, Alderman in 1645, attempted to look after the sick out of his own pocket. Details of this, and of the damage wrought by the Scottish soldiers, have survived in evidence he gave to defend himself in the case.

Although many prosperous inhabitants had moved away from the town while the plague was raging, Bradrigg as Alderman had felt compelled to stay. He had commandeered empty houses and buildings on the outskirts of the town as 'pest houses', in order to isolate in them people who had become infected, and he and the Constables had taken food and drink to the sick there each day in an attempt to care for them. One of the houses Bradrigg used had belonged to Thomas Skaife, who had given Bradrigg permission to use it, but later tried to claim compensation for the use, which Bradrigg had refused to pay because of the deplorable condition it had been in. Skaife had since died, but William Browne, a neighbour and relative of Skaife, claimed to be the owner of the house and had brought the action. Bradrigg's defence included evidence about the condition of Skaife's house which had "lately before beene used for a Court of guard by certain officers and soldyers who lay in that towne and by that meanes was much defaced and was become very ruinous haveing neither any glasse left in or about it or any doore save the two out doores but all the in walls and divisions broken downe".

Bradrigg was arguing that the damage caused by the soldiers had already rendered it by normal standards uninhabitable before he had used it as a pest house. The outcome of the case is unknown, but we do know from the parish registers that Henry Bradrigg's own family and household were affected by the plague, for in less than a fortnight in July 1645 the burials are recorded of his wife, his maid and a grandson. He himself survived, remarried, and indeed served again as Alderman in 1662, continuing as a member of the Corporation until he resigned, probably due to old age, in 1672. He was then, uniquely, awarded an annual pension of £6 13s. 4d. for his services to the town all those years before in 1645. When he died in 1673 it would appear he was insolvent, perhaps he had never recovered from the expenditure during his first term as Alderman.

Following his defeat at the battle of Naseby on 14 June 1645, King Charles I was little more than a fugitive. The following year he threw himself on the mercy of the Scots who, after prolonged negotiations, handed him over to commissioners of the English Parliament at Newcastle-upon-Tyne early in February 1647. Treated as a prisoner, with a strong guard of horse and foot, he was taken to Holdenby House in Northamptonshire where he would be imprisoned for several months. The journey took ten wintry days, staying usually just one night at the various staging posts. The cavalcade travelled from Newcastle first to Durham, then to Bishop Auckland, and then Richmond where the party spent the night of 5 February, but it is not known where the King was lodged. Next they went to Ripon for two nights, then to Wakefield, Rotherham, Mansfield, Nottingham and Leicester to Holdenby.

Among the most vehement of those Puritans in the Long Parliament of 1640-52 who advocated the trial and deposition of Charles was one of Richmond's two Members. Thomas Chaloner, who sat in the Long Parliament of 1640-53, came from near Guisborough and his father had been tutor to Henry, Prince of Wales, the eldest son of King James I who had died, leaving Prince Charles as the heir to the throne. Thus it was somewhat ironic that Thomas Chaloner should be not only a radical republican, but even a regicide, for after having been one of the judges at the King's trial, he was also a signatory of the royal death warrant. This was in great contrast to Richmond's representation in the Short Parliament of 1640, when Sir William Pennyman and Sir Thomas Danby were among those most loyal to the King.

After the execution of King Charles I in 1649, the House of Commons required all those holding public positions to take fresh oaths of loyalty to the Commonwealth. Several of those on Richmond Corporation refused to do so, and were discharged from office. An Act of Parliament in 1653 changed the way marriages were to be solemnized in England. In Richmondshire the marriage ceremony itself had to be performed either by the Alderman of Richmond or some other Justice of the Peace in a public place other than a church. The banns still had to be called three times, but this could be done either in a church or some other public place, such as the Richmond Market Cross. Such marriages had to be entered in a special register by a properly appointed registrar. The Richmondshire register for the years 1653-60 has survived, and includes 328 marriages. A typical entry, for 14 May 1655, is as follows (with modernized spelling):

> Vincent Lambert of the parish of Coverham, widower and Margery Barnes of the parish of Aysgarth, widow. [The banns were] published three Lord's Days in the time of Divine prayers in the several weeks according to Act of Parliament provided in that case and married [by] Alderman John Kay. With the days of publishing the first day was April 29, the second time of publishing was the 6 of May, the third and last time of publishing was the 13th of May and [there was] no objection by anyone. Witnesses at the said marriage Edward Winnington, Percival Farmer, William Wynyard. The age of the man is 39, the age of the woman is 43. Henry Jackson, Registrar of Richmond.

Insisting on civil marriages was typical of the Commonwealth period, when many traditional celebrations and their associated feastings, which had lifted people's spirits in good times and bad, times of plenty and times of hunger, were banned and the cheer such events had provided were greatly missed. It was also forbidden to perform any kind of entertainment or acting, in either drama plays - called 'interludes', or even in traditional mumming plays. Travelling players were punished as rogues and vagabonds. In January 1652 four men, William Archer, Stephen Kirby, John Binckes (all from Richmond) and John Ripon, were arrested for "acting an interlude att Easby, Gilling, Masham and Well" and were brought before local magistrates in Richmond, who found them guilty and ordered that they be "striped to the middle and whipped till their bodyes be bloody for rogues". These unfortunate individuals were the forerunners of many distinguished actors who would perform in Richmond from the 18th century onwards.

It is not known whether Richmond Corporation was able to continue employing its waits, or town musicians, during the Commonwealth, as they had done earlier. The Richmond waits had been in demand throughout the north of England in the early part of the 17th century, there being records of them being paid to travel as far as Bolton Abbey in Wharfedale and Londesborough in the East Riding to play for the Earl of Cumberland at various times in 1611, 1612, 1621 and 1630. Either three or four of them made the journeys, and received sums ranging from 12d., 2s. 6d., 3s. 4d., or even 5s., perhaps depending on how long they stayed and provided entertainment. Sometimes they were referred to as pipers, so some may have played the bagpipes as well as the usual shawms and sackbuts. Later in the 17th century there are specific references to the waits among the Borough records waits, such as that dated 3 October 1670, when Richard King and Christopher Taylor were "admitted to be the musitinarii of the Burrough and have received ..... two cognizances or badges of silver haveing the armes of the said Burrough thereupon engraven". Later in the 17th century it is known that the waits were paid a small sum by the Company of Mercers, Grocers and Haberdashers to provide entertainment at their annual feast each November. The Borough's coat of arms, *gules, an orle argent, over all a bend ermine, crest a rose gules, crowned or* (a red shield with a silver border and an ermine diagonal band, and a red rose crest with a gold crown) were granted to the town by William Dugdale, Norroy King-at-arms, when he stayed in Richmond during an official visitation of Yorkshire in 1665.

After the eleven Commonwealth years of misery and repression, the Restoration of Charles II in 1660 was greeted in Richmond, as doubtless elsewhere, with unrestrained joy and boisterous celebrations. The following account of them is very typical of late-17th century public entertainment.

The entertainers processed into Richmond in solemn equipage as follows

1st   Three Antics before with bagpipes

2nd   The representatives of a Lord attended by trumpets, falconers, four pages, as many footmen and fifty attendants, all suited as became persons of quality

3rd   The representatives of a sheriff, with forty attendants in their liveries

4th   The Bishop of Hereford, with four pages and footmen, his chaplain and twenty other household officers, besides their attendants

5th   Two companies of Morris dancers, who acted their parts to the satisfaction of the spectators

6th   Sixty nymphs with music before them, following the Goddess Diana, all richly adorned in white and gorgeous apparel

7th   Three companies of foot soldiers, with a Captain and other officers in great magnificence

8th   Robin Hood in scarlet, with forty bowmen all clad in Lincoln green

They marched decently in good order round the Market Cross and came to the church where they offered their cordial prayers for our most gracious sovereign, a sermon being preached at the time

From thence my Lord invited all his attendants to his house to dinner

The Reverend Bishop did the same to his attendants inviting the Minister and other persons to his house where they were sumptuously entertained

The soldiers marched up to the Cross where they gave many vollies of shot, with push of pike and other martial feats

There were erected scaffolds and arbours, where the Morris Dancers and Nymphs acted their parts, many thousands of spectators having come from the country and villages adjacent

Two days were spent in acting Robin Hood. The Sheriff and Reverend Bishop sent bottles of sack to several officers acting in the play

Something more might have been expected from the Chief Magistrate of the Town, who permitted the conduit to run water all the time

The 'houses' where people were entertained were local inns. Robert Wilson was the Alderman of Richmond in 1660 who was, it seems, considered by some of his contemporaries to fail in his civic duties by not making the conduit run with wine! However, to commemorate the occasion more permanently he did give the town a fine silver-gilt mace, embossed with the crest of the arms of Richmond, a harp, and St. George's cross, and the quartered arms of France, England, Scotland and Ireland. The mace is inscribed *C II R* and *Robert Wilson, Alderman in that happy year of his Majesty's Restoration*, and is still carried in civic processions by the more 'junior' of the two serjeants-at-mace who are employed by the present successor body of the old Borough Corporation under its ancient charters.

The day of King Charles II's return to England in 1660, after fourteen years of exile on the continent, 29 May, was called Royal Oak Day. Two centuries later this event was still celebrated in Richmond by a two-hour peal of bells rung in the tower of the Parish Church. Even in the 1920s the boys of the Grammar School observed a bizarre custom linked with that day - any boy entering the school gates not displaying a sprig of oak leaves was set upon by his fellows who had armed themselves with stinging nettles, which were applied to his knees and other exposed parts of his body. As all boys at the school then wore short trousers, the experience was a painful one!

On 18 December 1661 five commissioners visited Richmond to 'regulate' the Corporation subsequent to the Restoration. Those former members and officers who had been dismissed during the Commonwealth were reinstated, and the charter of Queen Elizabeth I, which had also been suspended, came back into force. King Charles II issued a new charter in

1668 by which the corporate body was changed to consist of a leading citizen now renamed Mayor, plus twelve, now called Aldermen, who were all named in the charter. The Aldermen were to govern "with the consent and assent of the major part of the Free Burgesses". The term Free Burgesses - *liberi Burgenses* in Latin - was not defined, an omission, which gave rise to many disputes in subsequent years. The Mayor was to be elected for one year as before on St. Hilary's Day, 13 January, by the existing method whereby the Aldermen selected two of their number, usually the most senior, as 'lights' who presented themselves to "all the inhabitants of the Borough so the major part of them shall select one". The word 'inhabitants' was also subject to different interpretations, and before long the right to vote for the Mayor was vested in those freemen of the Borough who were members of one of the 13 trade companies or guilds. Each guild met so that its members could choose which 'light' they preferred to become Mayor.

The last Alderman of the old system, William Wetwang, was named as the first Mayor under the 1668 charter. To commemorate this he gave to the Corporation on 23 May 1668 a peg tankard, which is still in the collection of civic plate. The charter also named the Recorder, James Metcalfe, and the Town Clerk, James Close. The Recorder was to be "an honest and discreet man learned in the Common Laws of the Kingdom of England" and he was to advise the Corporation on all legal matters. The Corporation was to have a Common Seal of two pieces, which still exists. The larger part was to remain in the custody of the Mayor, the lesser piece in the hands of the Town Clerk, and both had to come together to make the sealing of any document official and legal. The 1668 charter also gave the inhabitants the highly cherished privileges of not sitting on any juries other than those within the bounds of the Borough and also of being free of all tolls throughout the length and breadth of England. Further, no Recorder or Town Clerk could take office until his appointment had been approved by the Crown.

The Corporation did not remain as a Mayor plus twelve Aldermen for long, because on 9 July 1684 King Charles II issued a second charter to the town, which named the mayor, John Metcalfe, the Recorder, Thomas Cradock, and eleven Aldermen, and added to the corporation a Common Council of twenty-four, who were also named. The Corporation continued in this form until 1835. Although the Mayor served only for one year at a time, the Aldermen and Common-Councilmen were elected for life. During his year of office the Mayor was a person of considerable authority in the town. He was Chief Magistrate, Coroner, Chairman of the Court of Record (held every Tuesday fortnight), Keeper of the Town Gaol, Clerk of the Market, enforced the Assizes of Bread and Ale and the other bye-laws, collected and disposed of all the tolls levied on all merchandise entering and leaving the town. He also chaired the Court of Pie Powder during the annual fairs, and was expected to attend meetings of the Select Vestry (responsible for Poor Relief and the maintenance of the highways). At the same time he had to uphold the dignity of his office on all civic and state occasions.

One of the most important civic occasions during each Mayor's year of office was the annual race meeting, the Richmond races being on a par with those in York and Doncaster for prestige. Horse races had been held in and around Richmond since Tudor times, and among the town's civic plate is the so-called Snow Tankard, inscribed *The gift of Sir Mark Milbanke, Bart., and John Hutton, sen. Esq., to the Corporation after a disputed Race in a great Snow at Easter.* The implication is that the two gentlemen, having put up the piece of plate as a rich prize, and the unseasonal weather having prevented independent witnesses from seeing the result, it was against their sense of sportsmanship for either to accept the trophy. Horses were in those days raced in several heats, of up to 4 miles in length, then the last two horses ran off to determine the winner. The precise date of this particular race is not recorded, the tankard is a fine piece of silver bearing the York hallmark for 1615 but from the genealogical information in the inscription it may have near the end of the 17th century.

From at least as early as the Restoration until the mid-18th century the races took place on the springy peat turf of the

Out Moor. Organization of the races fell on the town chamberlains, who had to order the trophies, record which horses were entered for which race, prepare the course and rope it off, set up starting and finishing posts, arrange for a weighing mechanism to be available and for the admission money to be collected from spectators. Richmond had to look its best for the races, and the liveried serjeants-at-mace had to look smart, often wearing new 'coates and trimming' for the occasion. The time of year when the races were held could vary, as the Snow Tankard shows, but September was usually chosen. Sometimes the races were added onto the Rood Fair, an advertisement in the *London Gazette* in August 1669 detailing that on 13 September beasts and sheep would be sold, with other commodities on 14th, and horses on 15th and 16th, while on 17th a horse race for a plate of £50 would be run, and on 18th a plate of £20 would be offered for 'lower prized horses'.

In general life returned to normal after the Restoration, not only with horse races being held again, but also with marriages once again taking place in the parish church, mumming plays and other entertainments being allowed again and people being allowed to enjoy religious festivals. Not everyone was, however, happy with membership of the Church of England. The mid-17th century was a turbulent period in religious terms, and in addition to the recusants mentioned in the last chapter, other groups of 'dissenters' arose. One of the best-known sects originating from the Stuart period were the Quakers, whose movement was founded by George Fox in 1647. The first Richmond Quaker known by name is Sarah Kirkby, who in October 1653 attended a Meeting of Friends at Bishop Auckland, which ended in a disturbance. It must be assumed that regular Meetings were being held in Richmond by 1660, because in that year three Friends purchased from Francis Smithson of Richmond a close of land on the north side of what became known as Quaker Lane, built a wall around it and used it as a burial ground for their co-religionists.

In the early days the Richmond Quakers were subjected to considerable persecution, largely for refusing to pay their equivalent of present-day local taxes because these were collected through the established church parish system. The Richmond Quakers' chief tormentor was a government informer called William Thornaby. In May 1670 he informed on one Jane Chaytor and her son John for holding a Meeting in their house, unauthorized gatherings of more than five non-conformists together being prohibited. However, when they were brought to trial the Richmond magistrates showed considerable leniency towards them. It was through the munificence of Robert Gosling, described as "of Richmond, gentleman", that the Quakers got their first and only Meeting House in the town. Gosling gave them a building in Friars Wynd adjoining the Town Wall, described by the early-19th century historian of Richmond Christopher Clarkson as "a very plain building characteristic of the simplicity and decency of that orderly Society". The Museum of the Georgian Theatre Royal now occupies the site. Clarkson says that by 1820 there being no Quakers in the town, their erstwhile Meeting House was being used as a schoolroom.

The Restoration gave a fillip to trade, and several of Richmond's thirteen craft guilds are shown by what survives of their records to have taken something of a new lease of life. Only the Company of Mercers, Grocers and Haberdashers, with surviving records going back to 1580, are known to have had documentary material of pre-Stuart date, and several guilds clearly started new minute books in the 1660s, 1670s and 1680s. It began to become a tradition in the 17th century for guilds to acquire silver table-pieces for their feasts, and the Fellmongers bought a silver tankard in 1613 but this was lost when their assets were dispersed when it ceased to function in the 19th century. A rare example of a fine piece of corporate silverware dating from before the Civil War was returned to Richmond in 1999 when the Cordwainers cup, given to that Company in 1642, was brought back to the town after a fund-raising appeal. A silver tumbler given to the Butchers in 1707 was given back to the town in 1925.

Although outside the scope of the town's thirteen trade guilds, the local knitting industry undoubtedly flourished in Stuart times, and it is known that many children were apprenticed as knitters, mainly orphans dependent on the parish who were put to a trade. From 1616 until after 1700 Richmond was the staple town for wool in transit from Northumberland and County Durham. This meant that every fleece sheared in this area had to come to Richmond to be "viewed, weighed and registered". Most of the wool was on its way to the West Riding.

A remarkable man associated with Stuart Richmond was Henry Jenkins who died at Ellerton-on-Swale, his birthplace, on 6 December 1670 at the age, so it was alleged, of 169. He was buried in Bolton-on-Swale churchyard where there is a monument to him, and there is another inside the church there. Jenkins must have been born about 1500, over thirty years before parish registers began. While the evidence for his astonishing longevity is admittedly circumstantial, it is not unconvincing. Being highly regarded for the extraordinary length of his memory he was frequently called as a witness in court cases, not only heard locally at the Archdeaconry Court in Richmond, but also at York Assizes. Antiquarians were interested in, and perhaps sceptical about, his memories but when educated people interrogated him their questions brought forth satisfactory answers, which it would have been difficult for an illiterate man to have learned from elsewhere. As a boy he had taken to Northallerton arrows which were destined for the battlefield of Flodden, and as a young man had worked as a butler for Lord Conyers at Hornby Castle, which he remembered the abbot of Fountains Abbey visiting.

An interesting account of Richmond at the end of the 17th century was provided by Celia Fiennes, the remarkable and independently-minded daughter of a Cromwellian colonel, who undertook two journeys by horseback through northern England 1697-8. She visited Richmond in 1698:

> Richmond town one cannot see till just upon it, being encompass'd with great high hills, I descended a very steep hill to it from whence saw the whole town which it self stands on a hill tho' not so high as these by it; its buildings are all stone the streetes are like rocks themselves, there is a very large space for the Markets

which are divided for the fish market flesh market and corn; there is a large Market Crosse a square space walled in with severall steps up, and its flatt on the top and of a good height; there is by it a large Church and the ruines of a Castle the pieces of the walls on a hill.

I walked round by the walls the river [Swale] running beneath, a great descent to it, its full of stones and rocks and soe very easye to make or keep up their weirs or falls of water, which in some places is naturall, that the water falls over rocks with great force which is convenient for catching Salmon by speare when they leap over those bayes; all rivers are low and dryer in the summer soe I saw them at the greatest disadvantage being in some places almost drye and the rocks and stones appear bare, but by those high and large stone bridges I pass'd, which lay across the rivers, shewd the great depth and breadth they used to be the winter tymes.

There was two good houses in the town, one was Mr. Darcy's, the Earle of Holderness' brother, the other was Mr. York's, both stood then and were chosen Parliament men; they had good gardens walled in all stone as in the whole town, though I must say it looks like a sad shatter'd town and fallen much to decay and like a disregarded place.

Celia Fiennes' mention of salmon in the river Swale is a reminder that they were still being caught in Richmond, and apparently by spear not just by netting. She was apparently taken with the cobbled streets, and her reference to stone buildings is interesting as it would seem the 'Great Rebuilding' had already started in Richmond. This term is applied to the replacing in stone or brick of older timber-framed houses, which were perhaps by the end of the 17th century looking run-down, if that is what her final comments mean. Most of Richmond's rebuilding was in stone, rather than brick, due to the availability of stone locally, although we know that some timber-framed buildings survived into the 19th century.

Of the two 'good' houses she singled out, "Mr. Darcy's, the Earl of Holderness' brother" was the late-16th century Hill House, and Mr. York's was Yorke House on the Green. Little is known of the garden then existing alongside Hill House, but much more has recently been researched on the garden of Yorke House. About 40 acres in 'Bargate Green', some of it formerly belonging to one of the medieval obits (endowments for an office to be said on the anniversary of a person's death) in the Parish Church, with the decayed Hudswell Pele, came into the ownership of the Yorke family in 1658 as part of the marriage settlement when John Yorke married Mary Norton, daughter of Maulger Norton of St. Nicholas. The Yorkes and the Nortons were old family friends, and John Yorke's half-sister Jane had married David Leslie, the commanding officer of the Scottish army of occupation based at the Nortons' St. Nicholas. John Yorke soon began building his mansion, a somewhat optimistic thing for a royalist to do in the time of the Commonwealth, but fortunately for him the Restoration was not far off. Both James D'Arcy and Thomas Yorke were Members of Parliament for Richmond, and both their kinsmen would play a part in the process by which Richmond became a 'pocket borough' in 18th century, as will be seen in the next chapter.

By the end of the Stuart period we can feel we 'know' more of Richmond's inhabitants, for some of their houses survive, and there is more detailed documentary material. Of the larger houses, St. Nicholas, Hill House and the Friary have already been mentioned and still exist. Yorke House was demolished in 1824 but there are many pictures of it, whereas another gentry house, Bowes Hall in Frenchgate, the town house of Sir Talbot Bowes of Aske, Alderman of Richmond in 1624 and for many years a Member of Parliament, was demolished about 1787 but there are no pictures of it. Oglethorpe House at the corner of Pottergate and Gallowgate was described as newly built in 1615, and its fabric is substantially original although it was altered in Georgian times. No. 39 Frenchgate was formerly called Cradock Hall, having been built about 1660 by Sir Joseph Cradock, first Commissary of the Archdeaconry of Richmond who held that post for 44 years. The building on the corner of Bridge Street and the Green is dated *1689* above its doorway, and its near neighbour No. 4 The Green is of only slightly later date having had mullioned-and-transomed windows. In the shop occupying No. 2 Finkle Street can be seen a ceiling dating from about 1647, with delicately ribbed panels of quatrefoiled Gothic pattern and small pendants. It was inserted into an older timber-framed building, once with overhanging jetties, encapsulated within the present building of Georgian appearance.

In addition to documentary evidence provided by the parish registers, Stuart records include a list of those Richmond residents who were assessed for Hearth Tax in 1673. This tells us not only the names of the 332 householders, but also how many fireplaces each house had. The tax was collected by the Constable of each ward. Bailey and Frenchgate wards were of similar size, with 94 and 99 houses respectively, and Bargate ward was larger with 139. A large number of houses only had 1 hearth, in both the Bailey and Bargate it was about 40% of the total, and slightly higher at 45% in Frenchgate, which might have been expected to be the most prosperous ward but apparently was not. The largest house in Richmond was Cradock Hall, with the amazing number of 20 hearths, followed by Hill House with 16, Yorke House and St. Nicholas both had 10, and Oglethorpe House had 7.

Complementary to this Hearth Tax list is the almost contemporary list, dating from 1679, of the people eligible to vote in Parliamentary elections by virtue of their owning a 'burgage house'. This was one which by ancient usage had the right to 'stint' or pasture cattle and horses on Whitcliffe Pasture, for the 'right' of a Parliamentary vote had been grafted on to other, older, privileges. Most houses in the town enjoyed those rights, a small proportion did not, and it is now difficult to understand how the differentiation was made. However, it was clearly becoming a hotly-debated issue in Richmond by the late 17th century, and so the first 'official' list, the equivalent of a modern electoral roll, was drawn up when an election was pending in 1679. Only if there was a contested election were lists drawn up later, two

View of the River Swale and Billy Banks Wood from the Castle Walk.

The Castle Keep and 19th Century cell block.

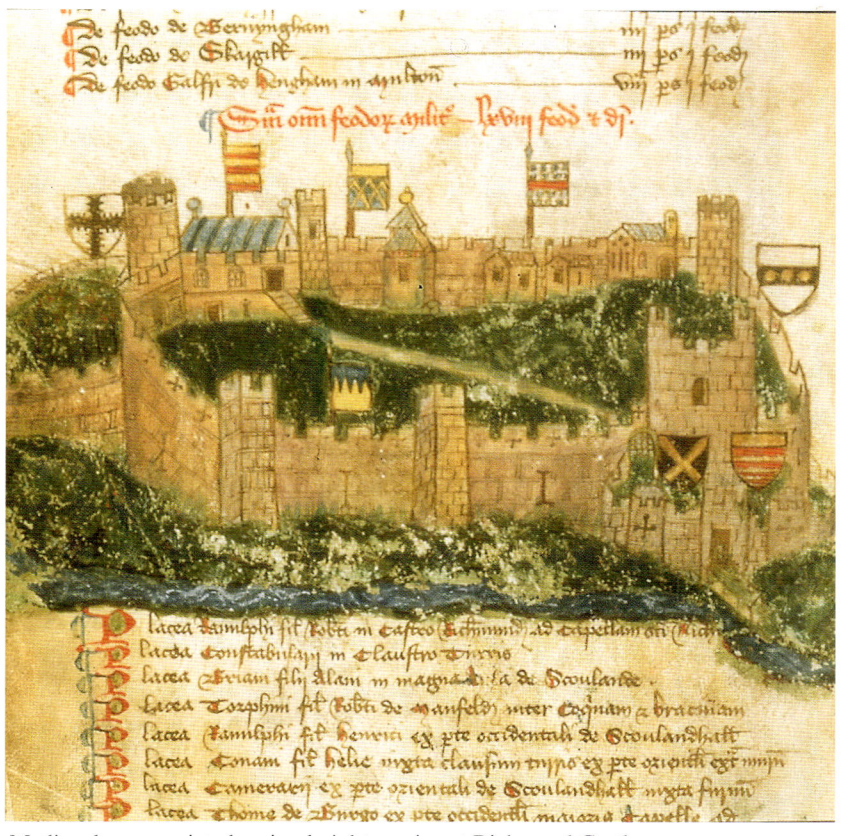

Medieval manuscript showing knight service at Richmond Castle.

Portrait of Queen Elizabeth I in Richmond Town Council Chamber.

The Hutton Monument in St Mary's Parish Church.

The first known picture of Richmond by Alexander Keirincx, 1639.

The interior of the Georgian Theatre Royal.

Richmond Market Place in Victorian times, painted by the local artist William Sanderson about the year 1900.

General view of the Market Place on Market Day, 1999, taken from the top of the castle keep.

The long lived Henry Jenkins

survive for 1773 and 1820, with the 'ghost' of a lost list from the early-18th century being implicit in the former. Another list of householders comparable to the 1673 Hearth Tax can be found in an unpublished memorandum of Window Tax collected in 1703.

On 21 July 1675 King Charles II had created one of his illegitimate children, the three-year-old Charles Lennox, the son of Louise de Kéroualle, Duchess of Portsmouth, as Baron Seathrington, Earl of March and Duke of Richmond. With the Richmond dukedom was granted Richmond Castle. In 1706 the Duke attempted to claim that over forty dwellings built up around the Castle were his also. The Town Clerk of Richmond took Counsel's Opinion, and was reassured that the Duke did not have the proverbial leg to stand on. Nevertheless, the disquiet which this matter must have caused those who thought they owned their homes in the area was still sufficient of a memory in 1724, when on Robert Harman's Plan of Richmond was drawn a black line around an area which includes many houses built near the Castle, and it is annotated The Duke of Richmond's Claim.

6

Georgian Richmond 1714-1837

The National History

    The reigns of four successive kings called George give us the term 'Georgian' which conveys a reassuring feeling of culture and quintessential Englishness, the irony being that George I (1714-27), the 54-year old Elector of Hanover, was unable to speak English when he ascended the throne in 1714. None of Queen Anne's 17 children having survived her, the country turned to a descendant of James I's daughter Princess Elizabeth, who had married the Elector of Palatine. It is hardly surprising that in 1715 the first Jacobite Rebellion attempted to put on the throne the 'Old Pretender' James Stuart, son of James II, and Queen Anne's half-brother. The frequent absence of George I in Hanover allowed his ministers to increase their power, the government being led by the first Prime Minister, Sir Robert Walpole

    Away from Parliament, Whig ministers spent their time building fine houses, filling them with pictures and statuary, and surrounding them with landscaped gardens, mostly inspired by an idealized image of Italy, Ancient Rome in particular. Thus the typical Georgian country house is classical in design with temples dotted in its grounds. Estate owners made money from investment at home and abroad, but many suffered a major loss when the South Sea 'Bubble' burst in 1720. King George II (1727-60) also spent much time in Germany, and had to fight off a second Jacobite Rebellion in 1745. The Hanoverian victory at

Culloden in 1746, when supporters of the exiled Stuarts were savagely put down by the Duke of ('Butcher') Cumberland, was commemorated in Richmond by the building of Culloden Tower.

George II was succeeded by his grandson, the young son of Frederick, Prince of Wales. King George III (1760-1820) had a very long reign but was afflicted by poor health which manifested itself in apparent madness. Known as 'Farmer George' because of his interest in the scientific improvement of agriculture, his was a time of dichotomy with slavery and children working in factories but also a great emphasis on elegance generally, including the architecture of Robert Adam and the pottery of Josiah Wedgwood. His reign saw the loss of the American colonies following the American War of Independence 1775-83, but there was no equivalent of the French Revolution of 1789, and Nelson and Wellington defeated Napoleon's imperial ambitions.

King George IV (1820-30), the Prince Regent during his father's illness, ruled in his own right only a relatively short time, having ruined his health with massive overindulgence, but he was a highly cultured man who encouraged both arts and sciences. The world's first passenger railway, the Stockton-Darlington line opened in 1825, and in 1829 Roman Catholics finally achieved Emancipation and so were no longer penalized and could at last hold public office. The reign of his younger brother King William IV (1830-37) saw passed many important Acts of Parliament which had been campaigned for long and hard, particularly in Richmond, such as the Poor Law and Reform in 1832, and Abolition of Slavery in 1833. Parliamentary reform was followed in 1835 by the Municipal Reform Act, which materially altered Richmond's local government, unchanged since the second charter of King Charles II.

The Georgian period saw Richmond rise to the peak of its historical importance, with the town becoming a provincial centre of social activities which brought with it prosperity and status. Richmond also gained an enviable reputation as a beautiful town with characterful topography, visited by artists, poets and topographical writers, a fame, which it still enjoys.

Richmond's two Members in the first Parliament of King George I's reign showed their loyalty to the new Hanoverian dynasty by presenting Richmond with a new ceremonial silver-gilt mace, the larger of the town's two maces still carried in front of the Mayor in civic processions and borne by the Senior Serjeant-at-Mace. A splendid piece of the goldsmith's craft, it is inscribed *The Gift of the Hon. Henry Mordaunt and Thomas Yorke, esq. the Representatives in Parliament for the Corporation of Richmond. Anno Domini 1714*, with their coats of arms as well as those of the Borough and the crown and arms of England. To accommodate the maces while the Mayor was attending church the Mayor in 1714, George Allen, placed holders for them, which are still used, on the Mayor's stall in the chancel. Above it he erected on a pole the small board painted with his name and the arms of King George I, which can still be seen. If all George I's subjects had been as content with Hanoverian rule as were those of Richmond, he might not have had to contend with the first Jacobite uprising of 1715. It was, however, mainly a Scottish rebellion, and much less a part of Richmond's history than its later counterpart of 1745.

Richmond is very fortunate in the wealth of its documentation, particularly for the Georgian period, when the importance of the town's history began to be appreciated in topographical descriptions, prospects, and maps. In 1722 the first book on Richmond, *Registrum Honoris de Richmond*, was published in London by R. Gosling, the author being Roger Gale of Scruton, M.P. for Northallerton 1705-13 and a commissioner of excise 1715-35. The son of the scholarly Thomas Gale, Dean of York 1697-1702, Roger Gale (1672-1744) was a noted antiquary, the first vice-president of the Society of Antiquaries, also a Fellow and treasurer of the Royal Society. His topographical papers were later published in 1781 as the *Bibliotheca Topographica Britannia*. Gale's *Registrum* contains many early Latin charters and similar documents relating to the Honour of Richmond, and also includes engravings of somewhat imaginative scenes associated with the Honour, such as William the Conqueror granting it to Alan Rufus, and the seals of the various holders of the Honour.

    A particularly important illustration in Gale's book is the Prospect of Richmond drawn by Henry Hulsbergh, a Dutch engraver who also made plates for Colen Campbell's *Vitruvius Britannicus* and Johannes Kip's *Britannia Illustrata*. Hulsbergh's Prospect shows the town in a somewhat general manner from the north-east, with some prominent features including the Castle, Parish Church and Grammar School, and a landscape background looking towards Downholme. The Prospect was dedicated to Francis Nicholson who was granted the Freedom of Richmond in 1725. Nicholson, almost certainly an illegitimate son of the Duke of Bolton, was born in 1665 at Downholme where the Nicholsons were a minor gentry family. After entering the army in his teens, he became within a few years one of the leading figures in colonial America, by 1688 being Lieutenant-General of the American colonies north of the Chesapeake Bay. He was Lieutenant-Governor of Virginia 1690-4, where he successfully established schools, being Visitor of the College of William and Mary. In 1694 he became Governor of Maryland, which had been founded by George Calvert of Kiplin Hall, and Nicholson laid out the town plan of Maryland's capital Annapolis, where a street was re-named in his honour in 1994. He was then Governor successively of Virginia from 1699, Arcadia 1713-15, South Carolina 1719 and Captain-General in 1725. Nicholson subscribed for four copies of Gale's *Registrum*, one he presented to Richmond Corporation, another to the Rector of Richmond and a third to Richmond School where he had presumably been educated. Of these last three, only the church has preserved its copy.

    Of much greater use as a documentary source is Robert Harman's Plan of Richmond, published in 1724, using a map-like format to show many historic features in a believable way matching other descriptions. It is reproduced as the front end paper of this book. Of particular interest is the picture of the Market Place, with the old Market Cross or 'the Great Cross', and a separate Barley Cross and Oat Cross, also an area to the south designated as the Leather Market near the Beast Market (or Shambles). He also shows the Conduit, as well as the Pillory, and at Clink Pool he shows the Ducking Stool. A few individual houses can be recognized although most streets are shown somewhat schematically. The Plan was dedicated to Sir Ralph Milbank of Halnaby near Croft, High Sheriff of Yorkshire in 1722. Nothing is known about Harman, who seems not to have been a local draughtsman, but he may have had some connection with another area where the Milbanks had estates.

A description of Richmond contemporary with Harman's Plan is provided by Daniel Defoe, the novelist and pamphleteer, who came here on one of his six journeys through Great Britain made between 1724 and 1726. Unlike many other visitors he was interested not in antiquarian remains but in economic matters, particularly the manufacturing industries which were then developing at the start of the Industrial Revolution.

> Richmond ..... is two or three miles wide of the Leeming Lane [the Great North Road], is a large market town, and gives name to this part of the country, which is called after it Richmondshire. Here you begin to find a manufacture on foot again, and, as before, all was cloathing, and all the people clothiers, here you see all the people, great and small, a knitting; and at Richmond you have a market for woollen or yarn stockings, which they make very coarse and ordinary, and they are sold accordingly for the smallest siz'd stockings for children are here sold at eighteen pence per dozen, or three half pence a pair, sometimes less...... The Swale is a noted river, though not extraordinary large for giving name to the lands which it runs through for some length, which are called Swale Dale .....

Defoe's account stresses the importance to Richmond's economy of knitted woollen 'stockings' - long socks worn by men wearing knee-length breeches rather than full-length trousers. The stockings were knitted on four needles, with one fitted into a sheath, which tucked under the belt, by men, women and children. This system enabled them to knit not only while sitting down but also walking, perhaps to market or to work in lead mines, for much of the knitting was done in Swaledale. Wool from local sheep was coarse but warm, hardwearing and, because of the oils it contained, also to some extent water-repellent, and so there developed an export trade to the Low Countries where many people worked on damp ground. Woollen caps were also knitted for the same market. Knitters were supplied with yarn by hosiers who also collected finished garments. Merchants oversaw their export, and arranged for goods from Europe, such as wines, to be imported along the same trade routes back into Richmond.

Daniel Defoe worked as a spy for Robert Harley, 1st Earl of Oxford and Tory chief minister under Queen Anne, famous antiquarian and collector of the Harleian manuscripts now in the British Library. It is therefore a remarkable coincidence that Defoe's account is exactly contemporary with that written by Harley's son Edward, later the 2nd Earl of Oxford. In 1725 Lord Harley was in his mid-30s but already a notable 'virtuoso' or great collector of fine paintings and books. He had travelled from his principal seat, Wimpole Hall near Cambridge, up to Scotland, where he also had property, by way of major cities such as Lincoln and York, as well as smaller towns like Pontefract, Tadcaster, Barnard Castle and Richmond, visited on the return journey. Lord Harley was accompanied by a gentleman friend, John Morley of Halstead in Essex, and his chaplain, Rev. T. Thompson who wrote the journal of their explorations. The party included ten servants, to look after not only the three gentlemen but also their 16 horses: six drew a massive coach, two were for the future Earl to ride, easier-paced horses carried Morley and Thompson, and the rest carried baggage!

The journal records the party's route after leaving Barnard Castle on the morning of 4 June 1725, crossing Gatherley Moor, passing through Gilling West, noting Lord Wharton's seat at Aske Hall and Lord D'Arcy's at Sedbury. Then

> We set out from Barnard Castle half after nine and in six hours, twenty minutes, came to a good inn at Richmond the "King's Head", kept by one Haslam. The way we were obliged to come with the coach is according to the Yorkshire manner of computation about fourteen miles. Being not to go any farther this day we had time to walk a little about the town, and accordingly went forth after dinner by a large open market place to the old Castle, which stands upon a very steep ascent towards the river Swale which washes the bottom of the rocky ground it stands upon. On this side of it which fronts the river, just by the walk that leads under the Castle wall, were some coins lately discovered by a labourer that was taking up some stones near the surface of the ground.
> There is no part of this Castle now inhabited, but there are sufficient ruins to bear testimony of its former glory both as to strength and magnificence. The situation is very pleasant, as is indeed that of the whole town, being surrounded by a fertile as well as delightful country, and having the Swale running just by on the south and east part of it. In this part of the county it is that the best horses are said to be bred, and everybody here is a born jockey, and any stranger may be soon furnished with all the cant and trick belonging to this way of trading by a little conversation and expense in dealing with these artists, who seem to be the most professed cheats in the world, in their calling, and yet are never deemed such, by a peculiar kind of courtesy of England.
> From the Castle ruin, we walked down towards the Swale, and so on to the church and school, in neither of which do I remember anything remarkable, except it be in the latter, if it may be accounted worth notice that the master of it is much troubled with a distemper called the "Hipp", which I always understood to be a malady to be prevented or most certainly

carried off by the brawlings of school boys, or those of an Ecclesiastic wife, both which it seems this unfortunate man has not found sufficient to expel it. It was now the dusk of the evening, when we returned to our inn, towards the back part of which stands an old tower, which made so pretty an appearance at a distance, that it invited us to a nearer visit; it formerly had a church adjoining to it ..... which now lies all in ruins and has only left this tower standing as some token of what itself might formerly have been, and if it was in all respects answerable to this relic, it must have been a very handsome and elegant piece of Gothic structure; and I think it a thousand pities that some kind hand from the neighbourhood should not stretch forth its munificence to prevent it from falling down ....

June 5. At five minutes after nine this morning we parted from Richmond, and for some way travelled very near the banks of the Swale, and it being market day at Richmond, and meeting many people on their way thither, we were confirmed in the truth of the report of this part of the country's producing notable horses of all kinds, for we saw none of the most ordinary people but what seemed to be better than ordinary.

Having left Richmond by the old road which ran alongside the river Swale to Easby, although he does not mention Easby Abbey, Lord Harley continued to Catterick Bridge and Hornby Castle, then to Snape Castle and later that day to Ripon. No wonder he would have liked the northern roads to have been better! His reference to the schoolmaster, Robert Close, suffering from the "Hipp" means that he was depressed, the word being an archaic abbreviation of hypochondrium. The Harleian antiquarian interest is shown in the reference to the discovery of the coin hoard in 1722. Harman's Plan is annotated with the quarry on the Castle Bank where the Roman coins had been found, just below what he describes as "a pleasant walk round the Castle", perfectly matching Lord Harley's "walk which leads under the Castle wall". Now called Castle Walk, it was formed by the Duke of

Richmond, as owner of Richmond Castle, as a Georgian promenade from which residents and visitors could enjoy views down into the valley of the Swale, with the bridge and Billy Banks Wood in one direction, and the Foss in the other. Successive Georgian Dukes substantially repaired the Castle over a long period of time, one of their agents, Mr. Wharton, even carrying out some early archaeological investigations in the area of the drawbridge. The references by both Harman and Lord Harley to Castle Walk show that it already existed in 1724/5, very early in the development of Richmond as a Georgian social centre.

  Lord Harley also gives us the first reference, in 1725, to the King's Head Hotel, the opening of which was a key event in that early development of Georgian Richmond. It replaced an older house, which had been acquired by Dr. John Bathurst when he was a Member of Parliament for Richmond in the 1650s. His grandson, Charles Bathurst, some time before 1720 built on the site a new town house, very different from anything then in Richmond, being much larger in scale than its neighbours with a front elevation three storeys high and eight bays long, in a symmetrical classical style. The building material was brick, very fashionable in Georgian times but probably unknown in Richmond then, and the bricks had to be burned in a specially constructed brick-kiln behind the site. Behind the house a large garden was made, landscaped with flower beds, groves of trees, a bowling green and a cockpit.

  As soon as he had completed this grand project, Charles Bathurst in 1720 began building another town house in York, which still exists as No. 86 Micklegate. The Richmond house became the King's Head Hotel and the garden, called Plasingdale by Harman, probably as a corruption of pleasing-dale, was a particularly useful amenity to the hotel. The name chosen, despite the town's Hanoverian loyalties, implicitly remembers the executed Stuart, King Charles I. The inn-sign, however, portrays the head of Charles II. The name must have been very confusing because the building's immediate neighbour to the west was a much older inn called the King's Arms. The demolition of most of the King's Arms in 1813, to make way for a new street, gave that new street the name King Street, rather than it being named after the King's Head.

Both Charles Bathurst and his wife Frances died in 1724, leaving three daughters and a son to inherit the family fortune, based largely on the Bathurst lead mines in Arkengarthdale. This son, also Charles, was High Sheriff of Yorkshire in 1727 and was in that same year involved in a Richmond controversy. Queen Elizabeth I's charter had given the right of voting for the Members of Parliament to the Alderman and Burgesses, but the term 'burgess' had not been defined. The first Richmond representatives had been local men living in or near Richmond, but as it became more prestigious to be a Member of Parliament, those with social and economic ambitions sought election more energetically. Dissatisfaction with the tradition that the right to vote was limited to the owners (not occupiers) of Richmond's ancient 'burgage houses' had been growing.

When an election was called following the death of King George I in 1727, the sitting Members, Sir Conyers D'Arcy and John Yorke, were opposed by Bathurst and Sir Marmaduke Wyvill of Constable Burton. The Mayor, William Daville, as returning officer for the election, was responsible for vetting the claims of those attending the hustings to vote over the three-day period that the poll was open. There must have been some chaotic scenes as people argued over who had the right to vote, for Daville, in collusion with Bathurst and Wyvill, allowed many of his friends who were not burgage owners to vote, and disallowed others who were. The result of the voting was

Charles Bathurst	298
Sir Marmaduke Wyvill	253
John Yorke	146
Sir Conyers D'Arcy	126

The total of 823 votes cast implied that 412 houses were franchised! Daville declared Bathurst and Wyvill to be duly elected: D'Arcy and Yorke and 30 other burgage owners petitioned the House of Commons that the election had been invalid. A House of Commons committee upheld the complaint, quashed Bathurst's and Wyvill's election, reinstated D'Arcy and Yorke, and confirmed that "The Right of Election of Burgesses to serve in Parliament for the Borough of Richmond in the County of York is in such persons only as are owners of ancient Burgages in the said Borough, having a Right of Pasture in a common field called Whitcliffe Pasture". This definition that only the owners of the burgage houses, of which there were 273, could vote for Richmond's Parliamentary representatives remained in force until the 1832 Reform Act. As there were no further contested elections until 1820 the ruling might have seemed academic, but was in fact to change the course of Richmond's history and see it become a 'Pocket Borough', as will be seen later in this chapter.

The year 1727 was also particularly memorable for one Roger Strickland, who moved into Oglethorpe House, the large and handsome house at the junction of Pottergate and Gallowgate on 15 May of that year. His was a remarkable life story. He was born on 22 April 1680 at St. James' Palace in London, where his parents were courtiers to the future King James II and Queen Mary Beatrice of Modena, his father being Mary's Vice-Chamberlain. The Stricklands went with the Stuarts into exile in 1685, taking with them their eldest son Roger and his two younger brothers Mannoch and Francis. Young Roger was sent to the Roman Catholic college at St. Omer, becoming a page at the Versailles court of King Louis XIV of France then a captain of horse in the French army. From 1706-18 he was in St. Germain and Avignon at the court of the exiled Stuarts, headed after James II's death in 1701 by the Old Pretender, initially with both parents but after the death in 1709 of his father Robert, just with his mother Bridget.

In 1717 Roger Strickland's unmarried uncle, also Roger, died and left him a small estate of twelve farms at Catterick, inherited from the mother of Robert and the elder Roger. This Catterick estate was Roger Strickland's only potential source of income, for the Stuart court was in increasingly dire financial straits. As a Roman Catholic he was debarred from holding any public office or becoming a member of a profession, and with his Stuart associations his position was politically precarious. He was, however, successful in negotiating with the Hanoverian authorities permission to take up his inheritance, and returned to England late in 1718. Seeking a suitable, Roman Catholic and preferably comfortably-off, lady he married Catherine Scrope of Danby Hall in Wensleydale early in 1725, and looked around for somewhere for them to live. It needed to be within reasonable distance of Catherine's family and of his Catterick property, and where there was a social environment compatible with their status as a gentleman and his wife. Richmond was ideal, and having little money he rented Oglethorpe House, where he lived until he died there on 22 July 1749. Catherine continued to live there for a time after his death and then in a smaller house in Newbiggin until her death in 1777.

Their story might never have been known but for the survival, among the Scrope family archives, of the account book of their every household expense from 20 May 1727 until 1750, after Roger's Strickland's death. The account book, which has been published, provides an intimate insight into the lives of Roger and Catherine and their sixteen children, mostly girls, in Oglethorpe House, and also implicitly mirrors life in Georgian Richmond during the second quarter of the 18th century. It tells us the books and newspapers Roger Strickland read, shows us the furniture and other household items purchased, including that for the family chapel set up in the house in 1737, describes fashionable clothes bought for the girls, details the accoutrements provided for the children such as shoes and hair-brushes, gives us the wages of various servants, even the cost of sickness and death.

Other documentary sources detail how the second Jacobite rebellion of 1745 affected Richmond in general and Roger Strickland in particular. It would have been no secret that he had Jacobite sympathies, the question was whether he had actively supported that cause. This was further complicated by the fact that his younger brother Francis was one of the 'Seven Men of Moidart', that small band of supporters who had landed at Eriskay with the Young Pretender, 'Bonny Prince Charlie'.

Roger Strickland was subject to two interrogations, firstly in October 1745 when his house was searched and his papers examined by the King's messenger, and secondly in June 1746 shortly after the Battle of Culloden, fought on 16 April, following the arrest in Newcastle-upon-Tyne of a Stuart messenger, John Hickson, whose wife came from Richmond. No evidence of any treasonable activity was found on either occasion, and he was allowed to live out the remainder of his life with his reputation unstained. He did, however, purchase a portrait of 'the Prince' in 1747 and also send 12 shillings to 'the poor Scotch prisoners'.

The account book does not say where those Scottish prisoners were, but they were probably at some distant location for the only evidence for Jacobite prisoners being in Richmond is earlier than 1747. The temporary imprisonment of prisoners captured during the Jacobite campaign was an unwelcome responsibility forced on many towns. Christopher Clarkson in his *History of Richmond* published in 1821 says

> The only inconvenience experienced here, was from the custody of the Scotch prisoners, on their removal to the north, many of whom were confined in the Grammar School, and others in Trinity Chapel, and from an expence of 1*l*. 10*s*. upon the Corporation for impressing carriages, providing candles &c. for soldiers on their march through the town, and for horsehire for the lame and sick.

Another list of the costs incurred by the town in putting up 193 'rebels' on their journey from Carlisle to York Castle is dated 15 January 1746, suggesting that they were captured after the Jacobites were forced to retreat from Derby on 6 December 1745. The document shows that on this occasion rebel officers were housed in the Grammar School, and the men in the Common [or Town] Hall, the former being supplied with white bread, the latter with brown. Meat was purchased from local butchers and other food from innkeepers; women were paid for cooking and washing up. Saddle horses for the officers were hired from within the town and also from surrounding villages, and carts were used to transport the sick and wounded for their journey to Bedale.

Richmond seems to have been pleased with the Hanoverian victory at Culloden. Certainly its Members of Parliament, as Whigs, were relieved that their seats were safe. One of the two, John Yorke, commemorated the event by building a belvedere originally called Cumberland Temple, now known as Culloden Tower, on a vantage point on his estate once the site of the old Hudswell Pele Tower. Above a plain base, in the form of a cube, a tall octagonal tower contains two beautiful rooms, exquisitely detailed inside with woodcarving and plasterwork of the highest quality, the first room of Gothick character, the top room more Rococo. As well as forming a prominent landmark when seen from Richmond, it offers stunning views of the town and of Billy Banks Wood. The architect was almost certainly Daniel Garrett of County Durham, who had recently designed a similar Temple at Aske for John Yorke's fellow Member, Sir Conyers D'Arcy. Yorke was married to Conyers D'Arcy's half-cousin Anne.

This handsome Gothick folly was part of Yorkes' elaborate landscaping of the hillside above Yorke House, his mansion on the Green which they had also Georgianized. The grounds had previously been laid out with the late-17th century gardens noted by Celia Fiennes and shown on Harman's Plan, formal lawned gardens to east and west of the mansion, and a walled garden containing an elaborately geometric pattern of parterres. In the 1730s and 1740s John and Anne Yorke transformed their gardens, replacing the parterres in the walled garden with a lawned area with viewing tower, fruit beds and a glass-house. Tree-lined terraces led to Culloden Tower and also to the river Swale, from which the hanging woods on Billy Banks formed a visual continuation in the picturesque manner. In 1769 the Yorke family added another folly, a menagerie now called Temple Lodge and used as the house of the estate since the demolition of Yorke House, and at the bottom of the hill a handsome stable block designed by John Carr of York about 1772, which was converted into cottages called Yorke Square and was demolished in 1958. Lady Harley, wife of the 2nd Earl of Oxford, who visited Richmond on 1 May 1745, on a similar perambulation around the country to that made by her husband just over twenty years earlier, said of Richmond:

Culloden Tower after its restoration by the
Landmark Trust in 1982

a pretty market town situated very romantically on the top of a hill. Lay at the "King's Head", a tolerable inn. Mr. Yorke, their representative, has a good house here with hanging gardens on the side of the hill.

This picturesque phase of the gardens, and also Yorke House itself, is shown on Samuel and Nathaniel Buck's South-West Prospect of Richmond published in 1749 which, with its pair, the North-East Prospect, gives a detailed picture of the town as its Georgian fame was growing. These are reproduced on the end paper at the back of this book. The original sketches made by Samuel Buck in 1718 were intended for a volume of engravings of gentry seats planned by the antiquarian John Warburton, but this publication did not materialize. The Bucks' text on the North-East Prospect gives their interpretation of Richmond's history and other attractions to potential purchasers of their engravings:

> Richmond is a Considerable Town in the North Riding of Yorkshire, pleasantly situated on the River Swale (so named from the rich Mountains about it). Alan Rufus, Earl of Britain, who came into England with William the Conqueror, built here a Castle and Fortification, to which Conon, Grandson to Stephen Earl of Britain, Brother to the said Alan, added the Beautiful Tower which is yet standing. Richmond hath given the titles of Earl and Duke to many Illustrious persons of the Blood Royal successively, particularly that of Earl to King Henry IV and Henry VII, as it now does to his Grace the Duke of Richmond. This Town is the capital of a large District call'd from it Richmondshire ..... Richmond, in Virtue of several Grants from the Crown and the ancient Earls, was very early erected into a free Borough with very Considerable priviledges to the Burghers, amongst others that of being Toll free throughout the Kingdom. Formerly it was governed by an Alderman and twelve Capital Burgesses, but by a charter granted by King Charles II, the Corporation now consists of a Mayor, a Recorder and twelve Aldermen with twenty four Common Council men, Elected by the Mayor and Aldermen for the time being. Richmond is also the Capital of the Archdeaconry of Richmond, and the place where the Consistory Court and publick Register for that peculiar jurisdiction have been kept from time immemorial ... It is a place of good Trade which is daily improving by reason of the late Encouragement given by the Corporation to Industrious and Ingenious Tradesmen and Mechanicks of all sorts and

from all parts to settle among them. The Air is extremely Healthful, and the Town generally admired; as well for its Delightful situation and great variety of Beautiful and Extensive Prospects, as the many remaining Monuments of the Grandeur and Magnificence of the Ancient Nobility who took their Titles from it. The Market is kept on Saturday, which besides affording great plenty of all kinds of provisions, is one of the best Corn Markets in the North of England. The Fairs are three, viz. Palm Sunday Eve, the Saturday before Thomas a Beckett, and Holy Rood Day; with these Advantages it is the less to be wonder'd that the Neighbourhood of Richmond should abound with so many Noblemen's and Gentlemen's Seats. The present Members of Parliament are the Earl of Ancram and John York Esquire.

Prominently central in the North-East Prospect is the Parish Church, the Grammar School, and the Rectory which had been rebuilt in 1716 after the medieval building had fallen into disrepair. The Parish Church was improved internally to reflect the early Georgian liturgical emphasis on preaching, notably a new pulpit and reading desk paid for in 1738 by the Earl of Holderness of Hornby Castle, who held several prominent public offices in Richmondshire, and the Borough's two Members, John Yorke and Sir Conyers D'Arcy. The following year the Corporation repaired the Easby choir stalls. In the mid-18th century some of the leading families of the town constructed private galleries in the church, and some also formed private burial vaults below various parts of the building, such as that of the Yorke family below the chancel.

The Rector of Richmond for almost half a century from 1739 until his death in 1787 was Rev. Francis Blackburne. He was a scion of the town, being born there in 1705, and his grandfather of the same name was an Alderman and merchant of some standing who lived at St. Nicholas. Rev. Francis Blackburne was a remarkable man, he held radical political views, supporting the movement which led to the French Revolution, and was the author of several controversial theological publications, notably the *Confessional* first published in 1766, which went through two further editions in 1767 and 1770. In particular he was unable to accept the doctrine of the Trinity, becoming leader of the Unitarians within the Church of England, and both his daughter Jane and step-daughter Hannah married clergymen who held Unitarian views. Despite his unorthodoxy he not only retained the rectory of Richmond but was also appointed Archdeacon of Cleveland and a Canon of York.

Blackburne was a renowned preacher, and as well as preaching regularly in St. Mary's Parish Church he also lectured on the Scriptures on Wednesday evenings in winter in Holy Trinity Chapel, which through his influence was brought back into use as a place of worship, becoming a perpetual curacy from 1755 with the financial assistance of Queen Anne's Bounty. The Corporation had the building renovated and pewed, with the help of a voluntary subscription, in 1744. At about the same time they also repaired and altered the north aisle in order to bring back to Richmond in 1748 the courts and offices of the Archdeaconry, the secular Georgian Gothick appearance of which is recorded in many old paintings and prints. From 1740 the Corporation encouraged the building of houses around Holy Trinity Chapel to form Trinity Church Square, the south side being built largely in 1761. The Toll Booth was built to the south-west of the Chapel in 1744, a large building with shops for rent on the ground floor, to encourage the town's increasing commercial success. Above were the offices of the Chamberlains who collected the tolls, and here were kept the town's standard weights and measures. Mounted on the roof of the Toll Booth was a bell, which was rung to indicate the opening and closing of the market. The Toll Booth was demolished in 1948. To serve the town's growing population better, and also to enhance its image with prosperous residents and visitors, the Corporation constructed a new Shambles for the butchers in 1764, near where the Market Hall now stands. The Wool House, also on the south side but further west, seems to have gone out of use in the mid-18th century.

The new Town Hall was built in 1756 at a cost of £600 on the site of the old guildhall of the religious fraternity of St. John. By providing this handsome facility suitable for balls and assemblies, Richmond Corporation was following a trend set by other towns in deliberately encouraging fashionable and monied patronage. A gracious external staircase, enclosed in stonework in1759, led up from the Market Place to the first-floor assembly room, lighted by four crown-glass chandeliers, at one end of which was a room for card games - gambling being a popular Georgian leisure activity - and at the other a supper room. A later extension housed the Court of Record, into which fine early-Georgian court furniture was brought from an unrecorded location, perhaps the Consistory Court although this does not entirely fit with the date 1732 on the royal coat of arms surrounded by the coats of arms of the thirteen guilds of Richmond, painted by John Baker, over the mayor's seat. The card room was from 1759 also used as the Council Chamber, the Corporation having met for some years in the Consistory Courtroom. The need for a licence and catering facilities led to part of the building becoming the present Town Hall Hotel. The assembly room, sometimes called the Common Hall, of what is always now known as the Town Hall, still hosts many social functions in Richmond today, and despite its later alterations is a reminder of the town's gracious Georgian past.

The assemblies were intended to be exclusive gatherings, and only subscribers could obtain tickets. The annual subscription was two guineas in the 1740s, and was paid quarterly, the first instalment of twelve shillings in January, with ten shillings payable in April, June and October. The older generations gossiped, played cards and watched the younger folk dancing. Meeting potential marriage partners was an important function of the assemblies, which were eagerly anticipated by young men and women of prosperous local families, dancing masters coming to Richmond to teach them the latest dances in advance of the annual 'season'. Although assemblies were sometimes also held at other times of the year, Richmond's main 'season' was usually a week in early September, particularly after the resumption of horse racing in 1753, which seems to have lapsed about twenty years earlier.

Richmond Corporation organized the annual race meeting, with two local gentlemen being appointed as stewards each year. Further to increase the status of the Richmond 'season', the Corporation increased the value of the trophy for the principal race to 100 guineas, inaugurating the Richmond Gold Cup on 10 September 1759. The first winner was Dainty Davy owned by the Duke of Cleveland, which also took the cup on the next four occasions, so becoming a legend in Richmond turf history. An oil painting of the horse, signed T. Smith and dated 1758, together with a list of the races it won, still proudly hangs at Raby Castle, and for a time there was a Dainty Davy public house in Rosemary Lane. The 1764 Gold Cup winner was Silvio, owned by Mr. John Hutton of Marske, and ridden by Charles Dawson, who a few years later set up as a trainer in Richmond, building premises in Hurgill Road still called Silvio House. Later in the 18th century a Geordie jockey, Billy Peirse, developed a famous racehorse training establishment at Belleisle, then an old inn serving the 'jaggers' or leaders of trains of pack-ponies which brought lead from the Swaledale mines down the old road from Marske.

Silvio's success was in the last season when Richmond races were run on the open stretches of the Out Moor, for in 1765 the Corporation, at great expence, set out a new racecourse on another section of Whitcliffe Pasture, not as far away from the town and on the north side of the old road to Marske. This new course, more formal in concept, consisting of an oval-shaped mile-long track, continued in use until 1891. On the highest point in the centre of the track, a grandstand was in 1775 erected at a cost of £1,200, which was defrayed by public subscription, the purchasers of £5 shares receiving a transferable metal ticket which admitted the holder free into the stand during all race meetings. Designed by John Carr, architect of many other racecourse grandstands including a larger one at York, the Richmond grandstand was a very fine piece of architecture, which greatly improved the standard of elegance and amenity of the racecourse, and it is very sad that only its ruined remains can be seen today. It consisted of a colonnaded lower storey and an upper storey with large glazed doors, which opened onto a stepped balcony, an even better view being afforded by the flat roof. In front of the building was a betting ring enclosed by curving walls with gates.

At about the same time a smaller private stand was erected next to the main grandstand by the Dundas family who came to Aske in 1762. Sir Lawrence Dundas (1713-81), the second son of successful Edinburgh merchant Thomas Dundas, for a time shared the family drapery business with his elder brother Thomas before branching out on his own as a merchant contractor. Securing lucrative army contracts for the Hanoverian campaign to crush the Jacobite rebellion in Scotland in 1745-6, and on the outbreak of the Seven Years War in 1756 to supply allied armies on the Continent with uniforms, weapons, ammunition, horses and provender, he became very wealthy. The fortune he amassed made him almost a millionaire even in the 18th century, enabling him to add to the property he already owned in Scotland, land in Ireland and the West Indies, and also to buy several estates in England including a fashionable house in London's Arlington Street. In 1762 he bought two estates in Yorkshire - that of Marske-by-the-Sea (from the Lowther family) and Aske (from Lord Holderness, nephew of Sir Conyers D'Arcy).

Sir Lawrence injected money not only into the Aske estate itself but also into many aspects of Richmond life. Several institutions benefited from his patronage, particularly those which suited his tastes, for example it is no coincidence that Richmond racecourse was relocated shortly after his arrival and acquired its fine grandstand only a little while later. Indeed the Richmond Gold Cup won by Silvio is now among the collection of the Museum of Fine Arts in Boston, Massachusetts as a fine example of the silver-gilt race cups made by the leading silversmith partnership of Daniel Smith and Robert Sharp, and designed by the famous architect Robert Adam who enjoyed considerable Dundas patronage at some of his other properties.

What attracted Sir Lawrence here was not only the Aske estate itself and Richmond's social activities, but the Borough's two Parliamentary seats. Since the 1727 ruling that the votes were vested in the owners of the 273 burgage houses, it had become apparent that anyone owning 137 of them would hold the majority and could therefore nominate the candidates, indeed the Members, of his choice. This would make Richmond a Borough in their 'pocket', a situation that several families eyed longingly. The Yorkes were long-established as Members, and did buy up a handful of burgage houses, but seem not to have had either the capital or the political will to take it further. Lord Wharton, who owned Aske first as Marquess and then as Duke, made strenuous attempts to accumulate burgages, eventually owning 65. In 1727 Aske was purchased by Sir Conyers D'Arcy, a courtier who represented Richmond in several Georgian Parliaments and whose family's main seat was Hornby Castle near Catterick. He improved Aske Hall and its parkland and buildings, most conspicuously erecting the prominently sited folly Olliver Ducket, probably on the site of an old lookout tower, which may have become used as a dovecote, for 'ducket' is a corruption of that word.

By the time he died in 1758, Sir Conyers had doubled the number of Richmond burgages he owned, and Sir Lawrence bought 131 burgage houses from the Earl of Holderness for £30,000 in 1760, before he had purchased the Aske estate. Within a short time the Dundas family owned 163 burgages, and Richmond was a Pocket Borough in their nomination until 1832. Sir Lawrence's policy for acquiring burgage houses is well documented in 'A Plan of the Borough of Richmond in Yorkshire', which he commissioned in 1773 to show every house in the town. The draughtsman George Jackson not only drew a scaled map of great historical interest, but coloured the houses in four categories. Those houses which Sir Lawrence already owned were coloured black, those which the Yorke family owned were coloured brown, those owned by miscellaneous other people, and which it might therefore be possible to acquire, were coloured red, and those which did not have burgage rights, and which consequently were of little interest to Sir Lawrence were coloured blue. An accompanying document described each building's owner and occupier.

Richmond was greatly improved in the mid-late 18th century. Not only were public buildings rebuilt, but most of the private houses were either 'Georgianized' or rebuilt. These typically have at the front an imposing door-case, derived from the classical orders, and vertically sliding sash windows with classically proportioned panes of crown glass, and panelled shutters inside. Other internal features usually include six-panelled doors, a gracious staircase with expensively turned balusters, and sometimes decorative plaster ceilings and cornices. Among the older houses improved were Hill House, which was re-fenestrated with elegant Venetian windows, and Oglethorpe House, which was given a handsome staircase.

New houses included The Grove near the lower end of Frenchgate, built about 1750 by Caleb Readshaw, "an opulent and eminent merchant, and one of the first who established in this town the lucrative trade of exporting knit yarn stockings and woollen nightcaps to Holland and the Netherlands", according to Christopher Clarkson. The Grove was built in brick, then fashionable and a more expensive material than local stone, and took its name from the avenue of trees in its rear garden, since built over. The house is sited so as to have splendid views down the Swale valley towards the ruins of Easby Abbey, such spectacular views being a newly fashionable luxury in Georgian times. A few years later Caleb's son Cuthbert created pleasant walks in picturesque Billy Banks Wood and built on the top of Round Howe "an elegant summer-house in the form of a Chinese Temple", below which on the pool above the weir of Whitcliffe Mill he kept a "pleasure-boat". Also of about 1750 is No. 15 Bridge Street, built by John Elsworth, a prosperous fellmonger, and another Georgian town house, No. 47 Newbiggin, built in a more eccentric Gothick style of architecture by Leonard Raw of Reeth, who had made money from lead-mining. Of about 1785 is Prior House, built by Richmond banker Francis Winn (1742-1809), Mayor of Richmond in 1790. The house was later the home of Thomas I'Anson, brother of the 'Lass of Richmond Hill' who will feature in the next chapter, who kept in the house a notable collection of paintings which visitors were sometimes allowed to see.

An unlucky tradesman was John Moore, a brazier or worker in brass who was murdered while travelling home to Gilling West from Richmond market in 1758. His body was found alongside the Gilling road near the Borough boundary. It was at first assumed he had met his sudden death within the jurisdiction of the Richmond coroner, the Mayor, who held an inquest, and Moore was buried in Gilling churchyard. It was then realized that he had died just outside the Richmond boundary, and so his body was exhumed so that another inquest could be held by the North Riding County Coroner, and he was re-buried in the same grave. His murderer was never caught, despite such strenuous efforts that Moore's relatives gave the town a commemorative cup, which is still in the town's collection of civic plate. Moore's tombstone can still be seen in Gilling Churchyard, inscribed with a lengthy poem describing his unfortunate end.

As Defoe and the Buck brothers suggest, Georgian Richmond was prosperous commercially as well as socially and politically. A link with the town's erstwhile textile industry is still provided by the name of the Bishop Blaize Inn, for St. Blazius was the patron saint of wool-combers, and on his feast day, 3 February, wool towns mounted a carnival procession similar to that described in Chapter 5 for the Restoration of King Charles II. Another source of Richmond's trade was lead-mining in Swaledale, much of the smelted lead being brought by packhorse train down Hurgill Road to a depot at the Nag's Head Inn, now called Wellington House. Copper was also mined, particularly in Billy Banks Wood, and the Yorke family tried to find the same vein on their side of the river, but without much success and the adits were eventually converted into grottoes as an additional feature of the landscaped garden.

To facilitate trade and industry, and also to improve communications with the western part of the Archdeaconry of

Richmond, the Richmond-Lancaster turnpike road was built from 1751. Work began at the Richmond end with the construction of a new road up Sleegill, taking a gentler ascent up the steep hill than had the older road, Boggy Lonnen. A gate and toll house was constructed at the top of Sleegill, at Holly Hill, where the tolls were collected on behalf of the turnpike trust, and Cravengate was widened and re-aligned to take traffic up from the Green. The surveyor of this turnpike road was Alexander Fothergill, a Quaker who had a remarkable capacity for work. One of his unenviable tasks was the collection of Highways Rates or boon days work from the citizens, who dodged if they could! Surviving fragments of Fothergill's diary have been published which demonstrate his frenetic activity, travelling between Richmond, Askrigg and his home near Semerwater. Typical extracts from his diary are:

> 4th May 1754. Paid William Hodgson for leading stones from Swale to repair some places ruined by the watter in Sleegill, 5 days, 15s.
> 22nd August 1754. Paid William Branson and John Carleton for removeing earth and makeing new wall to widen the road in the low end of Cravengate, £2 2s.
> 9th April 1755. Paid Edward Carter for leading 219 cart loads of gravill out of Swale to repair the road up Cravengate at 21/2d. per load. Paid.... for leading rubbish fallen down into the road in Cravengate.
> 29th April 1755. Paid Stephen Farmer for 42 square yards of land taken into the road in the low end of Cravengate.
> 24th October 1755. I then went to Holyhillgate to desire Thomas Metcalfe to .....order the piles and garsill [brushwood, to form a raft over the top of the boggy land onto which the metalling of the road could be laid] for Sleegill to be ready

The new road crossed the Swale by the narrow four-arched medieval bridge but this, already in need of repair, was severely damaged by an immense flood in November 1771. It was temporarily patched up but it was clear that a major rebuilding was necessary, not only to replace the bridge but to increase its capacity. As the boundary between the Borough of Richmond and the North Riding of Yorkshire ran down the middle of the river, responsibility for the bridge was shared between the two authorities and bureaucracy got in the way of a speedy resolution of the problem. The old bridge became increasingly unsafe, but eventually both authorities accepted the design drawn up by the Bridgemaster of the North Riding, York architect John Carr and reconstruction began in 1788. However, two separate contracts were let, one by each authority, and two building firms worked on the new bridge, Messrs. Bennison and Walsh being appointed to build the Richmond half at a cost of £888, while John Parkin of Aysgarth built the North Riding half for £899. Nevertheless the project was completed successfully, except for the unfortunate death by drowning of Thomas Dunn, one of the labourers employed, and the new bridge opened in 1789, the year of the French Revolution.

The Green Bridge as it is called because of its proximity to the Green, is typical of John Carr's high standard of bridge design. The stone came from quarries on Gatherley Moor. A milestone on the bridge gave the distances along the Richmond-Lancaster Turnpike Road *To Askrigg 18 To Lancaster 56*, and another stone commemorated the rebuilding and the two Mayors of Richmond during the time it took to complete the work *Rebuilt 1788 H[enry] Blegborough 1789 T[ristram] Hogg MAYORS*. Both these inscriptions were re-cut in 1978 and 1979 respectively. When the river is low the bases of the three piers which carried the old bridge can be seen in the river bed immediately upstream of the present bridge.

Richmond's continued growth in social importance and commercial prosperity during the Georgian period resulted in both residents and visitors increasing their expectations of the facilities available in the town. For example, the small quantity of drinking water available from the Elizabethan conduit was considered inadequate, and the old steep streets caused difficulties for the carriages and sedan chairs, which became fashionable in Georgian times. The first change to the street pattern, prompted by the new bridge and turnpike road, was the improvement of the tortuous alleyway called Carter's Lane leading from Bargate to the Market Place to form New Road in 1774. The elevated path on the north side of Quaker Lane from its junction with Hurgill Road, extending along Pottergate, Frenchgate Head, and Maison Dieu past St. Nicholas to the limit of the Richmond Borough Boundary near the entrance to Sandford House, was made at the same time, to segregate pedestrians from the horses and horse-drawn vehicles increasingly using these busy thoroughfares. Many other streets were resurfaced with cobbles at this time, confusingly referred to as 'paving' in the old records.

A new supply of drinking water was brought from springs at Aislabeck to feed a reservoir constructed on the site of the old Market Cross, which was demolished to make way for it. The water then flowed by gravity to four collection points, called pants in local dialect. Part of one of these can be seen in Bridge Street at the bottom of Cornforth Hill. To assist those collecting water from it on dark winter evenings, an oil lamp was lighted, the wrought-iron lamp holder for which survives. Above the Market Place reservoir was erected the present market Obelisk, which is inscribed *Rebuilt A.D. 1771, Christopher Wayne, Esq., Mayor*. Wayne was an apothecary. Unlike a traditional market cross, it may have been intended to resemble London's Adelphi Water Tower built about 1745 some 200 yards below Westminster Bridge on the south bank of the river Thames.

The Richmond obelisk was designed by Robert Plummer and built by George Branson, both local stonemasons. The agreement between Branson, and the Corporation who bore the cost, can be summarized thus:

> Branson is to have all the stonework of the old Cross "except the dogs cut in stone placed at each corner" and the stone column in the centre. He is to construct beneath the new Cross a cistern 40 feet in length, 8 feet wide and 4 feet deep to hold 8,544 gallons of water. To the north-east of the new Cross he is to construct another small cistern to hold not less than 400 gallons of water to be connected to "the Great

Reservoir" by a pipe 2 inches in diameter with a stopcock. The walls of the large reservoir are to be 18 inches thick, cramped with iron and "laid in terras" [stepped]. The base is to be composed of ashlar stones 8-12 inches thick "rabbited" [rebated] one into another, on a clay base 12 inches thick. The reservoir is to be covered with "an arch of stone neatly pointed and set in terras two inches thick". At the bottom is to be a plug "for the letting water .... so as the same may be cleaned as often as necessary". A door giving access to the interior is to be placed in one of the recesses in the "pedistal" above ground "with stone steps down unto the great cistern ..... The pedistal part of the obelisk to be arched over on the inside in a Gothick manner with bricks to spring a little above the door". The smaller reservoir is to be connected to "pants" in various parts of the town. The whole is to be completed by 10th October 1771. Branson is to "uphold the whole building for the term of 7 years" and is to receive £180 10s. for the work.

The obelisk was constructed as planned, but the main reservoir beneath it does not exactly follow the contract details, being circular in plan, perhaps geological conditions necessitated amendments. It is not known if there was a second reservoir nearby. The cross originally surmounting the obelisk was damaged by lightning and was replaced in 1902 by the present cone-shaped finial, the stone of which has never weathered to match the rest of the structure. Further improvements to the town's water supply included the building of a reservoir at the Aislabeck spring in 1812.

Another feature of Richmond's social 'season' was the annual muster of the North York Militia, part-time soldiers who undertook regular training, rather as Territorial troops do today, and who could be called up if necessary. A Richmondshire battalion was raised in 1759, and training took place on the moorland around Richmond, with officers drawn from local gentry. The men were billeted on local innkeepers, mainly being put up in the stables and out-houses, in numbers varying with the size of the inn, from perhaps 8 to 70. Apart from bringing a vast amount of trade into the town, the effect of the Militia can be seen in the parish registers with many local girls marrying militiamen, just as occurs with the soldiers at Catterick Garrison today. The parish registers also record the children subsequently born and, due to the high levels of infant mortality of the time, in many cases dying. In 1819 a new depot and arsenal of the North York Militia was built at the top of Cravengate in 1819, at a cost to the North Riding of £1,500. The buildings survive and are now used as cottages, called Temple Square.

It was not only the ordinary soldiers who attracted the attentions of local girls, the handsome red-coated officers aroused the interest of young ladies as in a Jane Austen novel, particularly at the assemblies, balls and supper parties, and the races. One of the North York Militia officers was Ralph Milbank of Halnaby near Croft. In a letter written on 2 July 1776 to his future wife Judith Noel-Wentworth, he said of his annual session with the Militia "We play at Soldiers in the Morning and drink bad wine in the Evening". Ralph and Judith were eventually married on the 9th January 1777, with an extremely long and complicated marriage settlement drawn up by lawyers acting for both families, and in October 1783 they leased from the Dundas family Hill House, to have a town house in Richmond convenient for hosting social events connected with the season generally and the Militia in particular.

In a letter dated 27 October 1787 Judith describes her social engagements over the past few days - on Sunday she had entertained Lord Faucenberg (of Newburgh Priory near Coxwold) when he came to inspect the Militia, on Monday evening she had hosted a dinner for all the officers, on Tuesday she went for tea and supper to Sedbury Park near Scotch Corner, and on Wednesday she had a small dinner party and then "we went all to the Play". The reference to the "Play" is particularly interesting, for the date is almost a year before the present purpose-built theatre opened. We know from diary entries that travelling companies of players were visiting Richmond for the 'season' by at least 1765, and the parish registers show that the Butler company came regularly from at least 1774. Before the purpose-built theatre was available, the players must have improvised an auditorium, perhaps sometimes using the Town Hall assembly room. There are also a number of documentary references to theatrical performances being held in the Bishop Blaize Inn in the Market Place, in the 'long room', or public dining room occupying the whole width of the front of the first floor of the building.

Samuel Butler, the actor-manager of the company of players whose circuit included Richmond, wrote formally to ask the Corporation for permission to build a theatre on 26 October 1787. He was in the town for a somewhat later-than-usual 'season' that year, as was shown by Judith Milbank's letter dated the following day. Butler was granted a lease to run from the following May for the site, adjoining the disused Quaker Meeting House, and the new theatre was put up and fitted out in double-quick time ready for the September 'season' the following year. The building is externally very plain, as was generally then the case, and also because it could not be seen to effect, being built on 'back land' behind the Market Place. Victoria Road not as yet being in existence, the entrance was down the narrow Friars Wynd, which also did not allow a distant view. The paybox just inside the door served all three floors, the pit, boxes and gallery, of the tiny but elegant auditorium. The stage, which is steeply raked, occupied half the plan of the building, originally extending forward beyond the start of the boxes, so that the players and the audience could interact. The acoustics in the building are exceptionally good, Butler clearly knew a great deal about successful theatre design. *[see plate 6]*

Samuel Butler was altogether a remarkable man. His was a precarious existence, yet he managed to find the capital to construct several theatres across his widespread circuit which also covered Beverley, Harrogate, Kendal, Northallerton, Ulverston, Whitby and Ripon. The Richmond theatre is the best-preserved Georgian theatre surviving in an unaltered form anywhere in the country. The shell also remains of the Northallerton theatre, but otherwise all vestiges of Butler's others have disappeared. The players in the company were highly respectable people, many related to clergymen, who sacrificed much for what they believed in, not only concerning their dramatic presentations, but also the political campaigns, which were implicit in many performances. Two plays were performed on the opening night of the Richmond theatre on 2 September 1788, the younger George Colman comic opera *Inkle and Yarico*, which highlighted the problems of slavery, and Mrs. Inchbald's comedy *The Midnight Hour*, which addressed the position of women in society. Butler's prologue was written by the actor James Field Stanfield, who would name his son Clarkson after Rev. Thomas Clarkson, one of the leaders of the anti-slavery movement. Clarkson Stanfield became a well-known marine and landscape painter.

Many of the players in the company were related, either directly or by marriage. Samuel Butler became the third, and much younger, husband of Tryphosa Brockell whose previous husbands had been an actor in and the actor-manager of the company, and she had run the company after the death of the second. Another of the actors was Fielding Wallis, the son of an Irish clergyman, whose elder daughter became the actress Jane Wallis, a favourite at Bath, and his younger daughter, Margaret, married James Tate, who will feature shortly in this chapter. Samuel Butler continued acting into old age, and died in 1812 while at Beverley, the memorial marking his burial in St. Mary's Church quoting from Shakespeare's Scottish play: *A poor player that struts and frets his hour upon the stage, and then is heard no more!* His second wife continued to manage the company, as later did his son, the actor Samuel Butler junior. Constantly moving from town to town, the players endured a very hard life, particularly the actresses, who worked during pregnancy, moved on soon after giving birth, then acted alongside a carrycot in the wings. Many players were freemasons, and gratefully received considerable support and hospitality from fellow freemasons in towns visited, including those of the Richmond lodge which had been founded in 1763 as yet another example of the innovations influenced at least partly by the newly-arrived Sir Lawrence Dundas.

The only surviving record of the opening night of the Richmond theatre was provided by a Richmond schoolboy of 17 who wrote in his journal:

> The New Theatre opened. A Prologue by Stanfield spoken by Butler. Inkle and Yarico and the midnight hour. Side scenes etc. by Cuit and Coatsworth. The Theatre was very elegant. Earl Fitzwilliam, Sir. Thos. Dundas, etc. etc.

Sir Thomas Dundas was the eldest son of Sir Lawrence. The painters of the scenery were local decorative painter Robert Coatsworth, and a more famous artist, the elder George Cuit (1743-1818), born at Moulton and educated at Richmond School, who in 1769 went to Rome to study art, generously sponsored by Sir Lawrence Dundas. On his return from Italy in 1776, Cuit intended to pursue his career as a painter in London, but finding that 'the smoke' suited his health less well than his native heath, he instead settled in Richmond and spent the rest of his life in the town. For over forty years he worked as an artist, using watercolours, gouache and oils, painting landscapes, portraits, even pictures of race-horses and cattle if one of his best patrons so wished. These included not only Sir Lawrence Dundas, but also John Yorke, John Hutton of Marske and his brother Timothy Hutton of Clifton Castle, and Sir John Lawson of Brough Hall.

Many of Cuit's landscapes contain one of the local country 'seats', and favourite views included Easby Abbey, and distant views of Richmond. His technique often involved a "bird's eye" viewpoint, with a correct representation of a vista impossible to see from the ground. Even on his distant views, the detail is minutely correct, and his paintings constitute a useful documentary source of historical information. He became quite a local character, a favourite of his fellow citizens as well as the local gentry, and many important visitors intent on buying one of his scenes of Richmond or Easby beat a path to the door of his house in Frenchgate, where he was frequently to be found giving art classes. A schoolboy contemporary of Cuit's was Thomas Harrison, the son of a Richmond carpenter, and Harrison accompanied Cuit on his 'Grand Tour', then later became a distinguished classical architect in Lancaster and Chester. Thomas Harrison was also, indirectly, responsible for the Elgin Marbles coming to England, for in 1799, while working on Lord Elgin's house at Broomhall in Fife, he suggested that his Lordship should prepare casts of the "remains of Athens" as these would be of particular value to English architectural students. This sparked off a succession of events, which ultimately resulted in "the Marbles" being brought to this country.

The schoolboy writer of the description of the opening night of the Georgian theatre was James Tate (1771-1843), a future Master of Richmond School and later a Canon of St. Paul's Cathedral in London. Of very humble origins - his father was an itinerant maltster who went around the local farms making malt from barley - he was born in Bank Yard off the Market Place on 11 June 1771, and his intellectual ability soon becoming apparent he was admitted to the Grammar School at just under seven years of age. He went up to Sidney Sussex College, Cambridge and later was ordained, the priesthood being then the usual route to an academic career. His appointment as Master of the School in 1796 followed a protracted squabble among members of the Corporation who, as governors of the School, had the right of appointment. His rival candidate Rev. Caleb Readshaw, nephew of the builder of The Grove, had to be content with being appointed Vicar of Easby, a sinecure usually held by the Schoolmaster.

On his appointment as Master, James Tate married actor Fielding Wallis' daughter Margaret. He remained Master until 1833, the school gaining a high reputation for academic success as Tate became a famed classical scholar, particular of Greek. In addition to the free places for town boys, he was able to educate boys whose parents sent them privately from a wide area. He sent 99 boys to Oxford and Cambridge, mostly to Trinity College, Cambridge, where they took so many prizes that they were dubbed "Tate's Invincibles". Among Tate's *alumni* were several who later held high office, particularly in the Church, two becoming archbishops. Tate's versatility as a classical scholar was such that when, in 1825, the Stockton and Darlington Railway Company was founded, he was approached by the directors to suggest a motto for the new enterprise. He offered them a choice of several, but the one they chose was *Periculum privatum utilitas publica* - The risk is to the few, the benefit to the many.

James Tate (1771 - 1843) Master of Richmond School, Yorkshire 1796 - 1833

Among those pupils of Tate's who went up to Trinity College, Cambridge was the son of the future Prime Minister, Earl Grey, and when Grey became the first Whig Premier after the Reform Act of 1832 Grey offered Tate preferment, as a Canon of St. Paul's Cathedral. Thus Tate spent the last ten years of his life in London, where one of his fellow canons was the famous wit Sidney Smith. Tate was succeeded at Richmond School by his eldest son, also James Tate, who will feature in Chapter 7. The elder Tate's success was largely due to the ability of his own headmaster, Rev. Anthony Temple, Master 1750-95, who himself sent 29 boys to Oxford and Cambridge. One of his most famous pupils, apart from George Cuit and James Tate, was Fletcher Norton, Speaker of the House of Commons 1769-82. The School's high reputation during the Masterships of Anthony Temple and both James Tates brought many distinguished parents to Richmond, which continued to attract important visitors.

John Wesley, an indefatigable traveller, records in his journals three visits to the town:

Friday 3rd June 1768. I rode to Richmond, intending to preach near the home of one of our friends; but some of the chief of the town sent to desire me to preach in the Market-place. The Yorkshire Militia were all there, just returned from their exercise: and a more rude rabble-rout I never saw; without sense, decency or good manners.
Tuesday 14th June 1774. Hence [from Redmire in Wensleydale] we hastened to Richmond, where I preached in a kind of square. All the Yorkshire Militia were there; and so were their officers, who kept them in awe, so that they behaved with decency.
Tuesday 9th May 1786. I went on [from Thirsk] to Richmond. I alighted according to his own desire, at Archdeacon Blackburne's house. How lively and active he was some years ago! I find he is two years younger than me; but he is now a mere old man, being both blind and deaf, and lame. Who maketh thee to differ? He durst not ask me to preach in his church 'for fear somebody should be offended'.

> So I preached at the head of the street, to a numerous congregation, all of whom stood as still (although it rained all the time) and behaved so well, as if we had been in the church.

According to tradition, the "kind of square" mentioned by Wesley on his second visit was at the east end of Newbiggin. One of Wesley's preachers in Richmond was the 'Reverend' Joseph Sager. Born severely handicapped, the son of a Canon of Salisbury Cathedral, after graduating at Oxford he indulged in a life of debauchery in London which alienated him from his respectable family, and they gave him a small annuity on the understanding that he kept well away from them. He came to Richmond where earlier generations of his family had lived, and kept a private school noted for his ill-temper and floggings, augmenting his income by writing for illiterate townspeople. Known as a raconteur, many of his stories concerning his misspent youth, he was a familiar figure in Richmond, riding on a donkey, dressed like a clergyman with a wide-brimmed hat over a large powdered wig, singing lustily as he headed Methodist funeral processions to the graveside. He died in September 1806 at the age of 71. His tombstone in the churchyard is inscribed with a Latin epitaph which he composed himself, translated as *Salisbury was my birthplace, Oxford taught me, London ruined me. Alas! what a little soil is needed to cover a man however learned!* Despite his disabilities he had married successively three young women, by two of whom he had children, and the tombstone also commemorates them - Sarah (died aged 25), Mary (aged 25) and another Mary (aged 26), and his two sons, Pemberton and Bristow, "who died infants".

Another visitor was Viscount Torrington, in 1792:

> Richmond stands most romantically; the noble Castle; the bridge; the River Swale: all catch and charm the eye. A sharp ascent leads to the market place, which is spacious, and handsomely built; and in it, at the King's Head, I secured my quarters, but in a newly painted room. In this town are now

assembled, for their annual exercise, the North York Militia, composed of much good stuff ....

At the back of the inn, in a garden, are the ruins of the Monastery of Grey-Friars; now call'd The Friaredge.

I, next, made a walk around the Castle and a noble walk it is; with the hanging bank over the River Swale; and the views of the utmost beauty towards the bridge, and the backing wood. Returning from these gratifying sceneries, to another of hope - dinner, I was not so highly gratify'd with stale salmon; and butter'd chops that did not make my chops water; but I feasted upon my letters, my wine, here was good: so I take another bumper ....

My evening saunter was thro' the churchyard; stopping frequently to survey the river, the waterfall, and the Castle, with its lofty tower, reminding me of Ludlow Castle.

The path twining by the river side, under a wood; whereon two jolly anglers walk'd with me to their sport; and could I have spared time I had made a third.

From this Vale there is a super-abundant enjoyment for the sight; - the town - the Castle; the Churches; the river; - and in my first view - the Abbey of Easby or St. Agatha, to which I eagerly bent my steps; and enjoy'd it at full stretch. There cannot be a more complete, a more perfect ruin: about every part of it did I crawl; and every part could I trace; adjoining is a small church, sprung from the ruins an old gateway, one of the former approaches is left. .....There cannot be a nicer ruin, (An antiquaries phrase) or one of happier situation. In my way I observ'd to my left, insulated by the River Swale, the remains of St. Martins, of which but little is standing; and that little I could sufficiently view from the opposite bank.....

Having tasted, (sweetly) of one walk, I was eager, after coffee, to try a second, when I took another ring (like a hare) over the bridge, and thro' the wood over the river, and Mr. York's seat; now this wood might be made a little Hackfall, and the views from it are delightful; the river foams at bottom, and the bank rivulets might be open'd; which should always be done in side, steep hills. My wearied legs obey'd my curiosity, and I trail'd a long journey here; and then about the market place, and to a civil shop thereon, half perfumer, half bookseller; who was really informant.....

Tuesday June 12. Time must not be thrown away; and so to business. I rise, now, to a moment; and, today, to a fresh morning. Then paced about the market place for 1/2 an hour, till my coffee, and hot roll were ready.

The North York Militia is a fine body of men..... The Adjutant one can distinguish at a distance by his red face, and old sergeant-like appearance .....

Then I resorted to my friend the bookseller ..... he recommended me to seek a Mr. Cuit, a painter of merit, who took sketches of this country; and I found him, at his house, with two young ladies, the scholars, a poor, civil, kind of man; but his art did not enchant me so much, as the view from his back window, over the vale, the River Swale, and Easby Abbey. I advised the young ladies "Not to stoop over their drawings; but should that pain their bosoms, might it be the only pain they ever felt therein". Looking into the larder, (a good larder it was) at my return, I took thence, (that is the right way) a cold shoulder of lamb, &c. and a gooseberry pye "Now for your good bottle of port, waiter"; spread quickly; I never dealt better....

Butter sells, here, for 5 pence the pound, and a fowl for 10d.; - and coals are very cheap, house good and at easy rent, walks charming, and fly-fishing excellent, Richmond becomes one of the best retiring towns in England.

The bookseller Lord Torrington visited was almost certainly Isabella Tinkler, who had a shop in Finkle Street. George Cuit made an aquatint of her just before she died in 1794 at the age of 92, sitting heavily on a low stool, sucking a clay pipe, her stock of tomes on shelves behind her, a stocking half-knitted on its four needles near by. Another local character was stonemason and architect John Foss (1745-1827), Mayor of Richmond in 1805 and 1825, who constructed many local buildings, including about 1806 his own house, No. 32

Frenchgate, later named Minden House, which has a remarkable semi-elliptical cantilevered stone staircase. One of the buildings he constructed was the Workhouse, at the junction of Cravengate with what was later Reeth Road, demolished in 1961. Richmond House now stands on the site.

Nearly contemporary with Viscount Torrington's description of Richmond are the records made in a different format by the artist Joseph Mallord William Turner (1775-1851), who made at least three visits to the town, in 1797, 1799 and 1818. Engravings made of scenes captured on his last visit were commissioned to illustrate Whitaker's *History of Richmondshire* published in two volumes in 1822. There are four prints of local scenes, two of Richmond, one of Easby Abbey and another of Aske Hall, all beautifully composed pictures, emphasizing the point that Richmond was a "must-see" location, but as documentary records they are not reliable. Whitaker's history was followed by Christopher Clarkson's epic *History of Richmond* published by Thomas Bowman in Richmond in 1821, which followed his shorter history published anonymously in 1814. Clarkson was the son of a Richmond butcher, and after a brief military career had hoped to enter the Church, but involvement in a duel put paid to that ambition. A copy of the 1821 volume, copiously annotated by its owner, James Arrowsmith, who lived at the corner of Millgate and the Market Place, which is now in York Minster Library, provides a great deal of information and gossip about Richmond and its more colourful and characterful residents in the Regency era.

James Arrowsmith was an upholsterer, an occupation of some status, slightly higher than that of the several cabinet-makers who also found a lucrative living from the well-to-do residents who settled in the still-fashionable town, many of them gentlefolk who retired here, as Viscount Torrington observed. For the same reason the town acquired a number of doctors and apothecaries, also a few surgeons but they were of inferior status in those days. Richmond Corporation occasionally granted a special dispensation for 'foreign' tradesmen to settle and work in Richmond, such as William Terry, 'clockmaker, watchmaker and silversmith' granted his freedom in 1806. Other occupations indicative of the status of late-Georgian Richmond include gunsmiths, dressmakers, staymakers, hairdressers and perukemakers. A Georgian wig-curler made of pipe-clay was discovered during an archaeological excavation near Holy Trinity Chapel in 1991.

At the beginning of the 19th century, Richmond was still in its Georgian heyday. The demand for social activities was still sufficient for a new function room to be added to the rear of the King's Head Hotel when the formation of King Street, in 1813, made it possible to have large sash windows overlooking the new street, rather than the smelly stableyard of the old King's Arms Inn on the site before. Intended as an additional assembly room, it is now called the Ballroom, and is accessed by the elegant Regency staircase added at the same time. Archery was a favourite recreation for Regency gentlemen, who practised on the Batts. A Society of Richmond Archers had been founded in 1755, it had a livery of Lincoln green with yellow buttons, and two of their silver trophies, a gorget and bugle came to light in 1993.

Several new educational establishments came into being in the early-19th century. A Scientific Society was founded in 1810, followed by a Mechanics' Institute in 1820, and as well as providing young men with technical education these bodies provided lending libraries, amalgamated in 1910 to became the town's public library. The parish church had in 1791 established a Sunday School, supported by private donations, which instructed children in reading as well as the Catechism and Scriptures. More day schools were also started, notably the Corporation School in 1812, with a master employed at a salary of £50 per annum, the first being George Wade, a portly, disfigured character known for his practical jokes, who continued there until his death in 1830. The number of boys, aged between 8 and 14, was limited to 40, and the teaching was conducted on the Lancasterian or monitorial system. The Corporation School closed in 1902, and its building in Tower Street became the Territorial Army Drill Hall, demolished about 1960 when old people's bungalows were built on the site. In 1825 the National School, or Church of England Elementary School, was built in Lombards Wynd, the building now being called Kimber House since the school moved to modern premises. Its Infants Department was built in 1834 in the predecessor of Dundas Street, the narrow Burley's or Hutchinson's Wynd leading westwards off Frenchgate. Here had stood the old Bowes Hall, demolished by Lord Dundas who replaced it with a terrace of four houses, Nos. 47, 49, 51 and 53 Frenchgate, about 1785.

The town's population rose from about 2,800 in 1800, when about 500 houses were occupied by about 600 families, to 3,542 in 1821, when 738 houses housed 760 families. The increase was accommodated not by the town spreading outwards, but by its becoming more densely populated, with houses being sub-divided and the infilling of land behind frontage properties with houses. An example of this is Bank Yard, west of the High Row of the Market Place, although few of its once-handsome Georgian cottages now remain. Bank Yard took its name from the bank established at its Market Place end in 1792, known as the Old Bank after the opening of the New Bank of Hutton, Other and Simpson at the Millgate corner of the Market Place in 1806. A rare survival of backyard development is Carter's Yard off the south side of Newbiggin, with cottages of one and two storeys, restored in 1981.

The evocatively-named Waterloo Street was backland development of about 1815 in the area near Bank Yard formerly called Thornhill Dykes, but only a few cottages survive there now as most were demolished in 1963. The British victory at Waterloo clearly inspired the town to give that name to the new area of housing. The town has another link with the campaign in that among the many fascinating tombstones in Richmond Churchyard are those of Augustus Blytheman and William Watson, both veterans of the battle. Neither of them were natives of the town, but after distinguished army careers following their having survived Waterloo, both ended their days in the area, Watson retiring to Richmond, Blytheman as a servant to Thomas Taylor Worsley who lived at St. Trinians. An earlier phase of the

French wars had touched the hearts of Richmond people when in 1798 they raised a public subscription for the disabled sailors and widows and children of those killed in Nelson's victory of the Nile.

The old open fields of Richmond had long since ceased to be farmed in the medieval system, and parts, particularly of the East Field, had effectively passed into private hands. Attempts to regularize this by planned Enclosure were made in the 1760s, and detailed maps were drawn of the three fields, but there was local opposition and the idea was dropped in 1776. After further attempts, an Act of Parliament was passed in 1802 authorizing the enclosure of West Field, Gallow Field and East Field, together with Whitcliffe Pasture and the Outmoor but further opposition delayed implementation until 1810. Most of the original West Field, together with that part of Whitcliffe Pasture, which had become the Racecourse, were left as large open spaces, but the rest was enclosed with fences, hedges or stone walls to form irregularly shaped fields. Before the land was allocated to individual owners, access roads, a bridge, paths, stiles and "watering places" were laid down, most of which are still recognizable today.

Richmond was relatively unaffected by the 'Industrial Revolution', but nevertheless there were some changes. The Green Mill was closed in 1765 when Thomas Yorke bought it out to avoid commercial users passing through his landscaped garden, and about 1780 Church Mill was rebuilt, on a new site slightly upstream of the old, on a much larger scale to run three pairs of millstones. It continued to grind corn into the 20th century, a sawmill being added in the 19th century. The ancient dye house closed about 1778, fulling having ceased at local watermills as the production of woollen cloth became concentrated in the West Riding. Whitcliffe Mill was from 1784 leased by the Corporation to various tenants for a succession of textile uses, none of them, it would seem, very successful. Several local watermills, such as St. Martin's Mill, found a new use more suited to Richmond's intellectual prominence in the late-18th century, that of paper making. After much heart-ache caused by the river Swale several times washing away the dam, a large papermill was established at Whitcliffe Mill by Henry Cooke from 1823, using Fourdrinier machines. This enterprise succeeded and became a large employer, particularly of women working as rag sorters, many of them from Ireland.

In 1820 one of the first gasworks in Europe was opened at the Foss-Head, near the site of the ancient Castle Mill. Operated by a private company, its purpose was to improve the fashionable Georgian town's street lighting, the old oil lamps which stood at such important locations as the corner of Friars Wynd to light the way for patrons going to the theatre, being replaced by gas lights. About 1830 a brewery was built at the west end of the Green, which lasted until early in the 20th century. In 1836, to facilitate the still-important trade in lead, a new turnpike road was made from Richmond to Reeth, leaving Richmond by 'Long Hill' near the top of Cravengate, and proceeding by Lownethwaite, where a new bridge had to be constructed across the river Swale, and then by Ellerton and Grinton to Reeth. Toll houses were sited on the Richmond side of Lownethwaite Bridge and at Hegs Gill just east of Grinton. A branch road connected the Richmond-Reeth turnpike road to Marske. The surveyor for the whole work was Thomas Bradley of Richmond.

The Whig sympathies of Richmond led to its support for the movement calling for the Reform of Parliament. By the early 1830s there were many new towns, particularly in the industrial West Riding, which had no representation in Parliament except for those with wealth who could vote in county elections. Leading citizens in Richmond, such as James Tate and John Hutton of Marske, strongly advocated changes giving more people a democratic say in the selection of the country's government. So there was much rejoicing when the Reform Bill was finally passed, giving the vote to male occupiers of houses valued an annual rental of £10 or more. On Thursday 21 June 1832 there was a procession through Richmond with banners and music, followed by a Reform Celebration Dinner held in the Market Place, much enjoyed by the 1,000 men present, who after dinner drank 20 toasts! The 'dinner' seems to have taken place at lunch time, for there was "tea afterwards in the Town's Hall for above 500 women", according to James Tate - the recipient of toast no. 15.

The government official who recommended that Richmond should keep its two Members of Parliament made the following report on the town:

> The general appearance of the Town of Richmond is that of a wealthy and substantial town; it is situated in the midst of an agricultural district, has no manufactures, but an extensive market, both for corn and fruit; of the former, 300 quarters upon average are brought to sale each market day; and with the latter it supplies the manufacturing districts of the West Riding. The town is increasing rather than decaying; the higher class of its population appears to be composed in a great measure of persons who, wishing to live a retired life, are attracted to it by the beauty of its situation and of the surrounding country, the cheapness of provisions arising from the excellence of its market and the immunities and privileges which its inhabitants enjoy.
>
> For the Corporation of this Town possessing an annual income arising from landed estates of nearly £1,000 this sum is expended for the public benefit in lighting, watching and paving the town, and supplying the same with water; so that the inhabitants are subject to no rates in respect of these various items of public expenditure; they are also, by charter, exempt from the payment of county rates, and are not liable to serve upon juries for the County or Riding; they have also the privilege of educating their sons free of expense at a celebrated Grammar School in the Town, which has an endowment arising from real estates of nearly £300 a year. There are also three Hospitals for aged persons, and many other charitable institutions. The Shops in this Town also, within the last twenty years, have greatly increased in number and respectability. Capital and Business have also much increased within the same period. No buildings are now in

the course of erection in any part of the Town, nor are any improvements in progress; yet within the last two years five fifteen-pound Houses have been erected on entirely new sites; and within the last ten years 55 additional Houses have been built. Richmond, moreover, is the Capital of a district called Richmondshire; and it has a very respectable Constituency; in fact, the amount of its Population but inadequately represents its real importance; and all the circumstances attending its present condition, its situation, and resources, being taken into consideration, there seems to be little probability of its retrograding in importance.

The next item on the Whig agenda was the reform of local government, and the Municipal Reform Act followed in 1835. This changed the constitution of the Richmond Corporation from what it had remained since the second charter of King Charles II, the new Corporation consisting of a Mayor, four Aldermen and twelve Councillors, which it remained until 1974, with the vote being vested in all ratepayers. The town had been divided into those in favour of Municipal Reform, and those against. Both sides presented their case to the public in a series of sometimes vitriolic pamphlets, those of the reformists being printed by Thomas Bowman, and those on the aldermanic side by Matthew Bell. Stalwarts of the Municipal Reform Association were the brothers George and Christopher Croft, and George Croft was elected the first Mayor of the reformed Corporation. A portrait of George Croft was bought to hang in the Council Chamber of the Town Hall in 1987.

Much is known about many of the town's individual late-Georgian residents from a number of sources. A source which has already been mentioned is the 700 inscribed tombstones in Richmond Churchyard. One of the most intriguing inscriptions is the following:

Here are deposited / the remains of the / Revd. Peter Delaire, Rector / and Prior of Bazouges la / Perouze in the diocese of Rennes / in Brittany. He departed this / life on the 16th

Febry. 1800, aged 82. / He was a clergyman of the most / irreproachable manners, of true / piety and devotion and one of the / many thousands of the French / ecclesiastics, who / sought and found asylum in this kingdom when / they were reduced to the necessity / of emigrating from their own. / R.I.P.

As a result of the French Revolution more than 5,000 French clergy sought refuge in England, being, in general, well received. Relief committees were set up in many places, some of which received government aid, one of these being at Catterick, near the Roman Catholic stronghold of Brough Hall. Presumably the cost of Peter Delaire's tombstone was met by local people who thought well of him.

Another churchyard memorial which masks an amazing story is the table tomb of Estcourt Sackville Cresswell, "a scholar of the Free Grammar School of this Town who died after an illness of ten days" on 30 October 1836, erected "as a testimony of their affection and esteem ..... by his sorrowing school fellows". In 1836 there was a gunsmith's shop at the junction of Friars Wynd and the Market Place. One lunchtime when the owner of the shop had gone home and left his apprentice in charge, the lad was joined by another teenage boy. The two started experimenting with a tinder-box in close proximity to an open barrel of gunpowder. A spark dropped into the barrel and the resulting explosion broke every pane of glass in the upper part of the Market Place, and blew the two boys across the cobbles to the Market Obelisk, where they picked themselves up and ran home apparently unharmed. In the apartment above the shop lived the Reverend Mr. Cresswell, a nonconformist minister, with his family and servants. No one was killed at the time, but within a fortnight two members of his family and one servant were dead, presumably of shock, Estcourt being one. The year 1836 also saw the creation of the Diocese of Ripon, and thus of the title Bishop of Ripon, a reorganization which led to the closure of the Archdeaconry of Richmond courts in Holy Trinity Chapel.

To conclude this chapter, it seems fitting to summarize the importance of Richmond during its Georgian heyday by quoting parts of a doggerel poem written about 1800. It is of no poetic merit, but it seems to capture the whimsical appeal of Richmond. It was written by an unidentified elderly but spirited lady, who was trying to persuade her cousin, Colonel, later Lord, George Harris (1746-1829), to become one of the many who retired to Richmond. He had just returned to England after his victory over Tippoo Sahib, Sultan of Mysore. Her pleas were unsuccessful, as he bought Belmont Park in Kent. The spelling of the poem has been retained:

> Dear Colonel, in London, I beg you won't stay,
> But to Richmond, post haste, with all speed come away;
> Nor sigh with regret when you leave the great city,
> For here, I can promise you many things pretty.
>
> Without door, the prospects are fine, all allow;
> And why they are so, I will just tell you how;
> But, ere I proceed, I'll convince you they're fine,
> On the strength of a judgment superior to mine;
> When Lord Newark was here, he declared in a hurry,
> That Richmond in Yorkshire, beat Richmond in Surry.
>
> Here are Hills for high-minded, and vallies for low,
> Thro' which old Swale's waters delightfully flow;
> Here are forces and mills, and meadows so green,
> And the finest of Cattle that ever were seen, -
> I should like 'em much more, if I fear'd not their horns.
> Here are Streets, but not pleasant to those who have corns.
>
> On the top of a mount, stands a Castle sublime,
> Though 't has suffer'd indeed, from the teeth of old time.
> Three abbeys from thence you may see with your eyes,
> In a state which all true Antiquarians most prize,
> For in many parts, not a stone stands on another,
> And one turret nods round in vain for a brother.

A most beautiful Steeple, ('twas built for the Friars,)
Which no one e'er sees, but he greatly admires:
Two Churches, a Church Yard, a Parsonage,
a School House,
Where the boys study latin, and how they may rule us.
Here's a Play-house, a Bowling-green, Assemblies, Card Meeting,
Horse Races, Militia, and a Club for Tripe eating;
And some people say, you'll not taste better Ale,
'Twixt the banks of the Ganges and those of the Swale.

For Companions here's people of various conditions;
Parsons, Lawyers, Apothecaries, Priests and Physicians:
Here are Gentlemen too, which some say the best trade is,
And plenty of every description of Ladies.
Here's a Widow of ninety, will give you a hugging,
And Ringers who long at the ropes to be tugging.

7

Victorian Richmond 1837-1901

The National History

Neither King George IV nor King William IV left a surviving child, so the throne passed to the young daughter of another, younger, son of King George III, the Duke of Kent. The Duke of Kent was not well-off, and had not expected to be so close to the throne, but when it became clear that his daughter would succeed, his poverty was a potential source of embarrassment and so he was very grateful to Sir Thomas Dundas for advancing him £2,500. The young Queen Victoria was only 18 at her accession, and she needed a husband. She married Prince Albert in 1840 and had nine children. The 1840s saw most towns connected to the railway network. In the same year as the Queen's marriage, the Penny Post was introduced, making the post accessible to a wider cross-section of society. Prince Albert took a great interest in manufacturing and was responsible for organizing the Great Exhibition of 1851 in the amazing cast-iron and glass Crystal Palace. Prince Albert died unexpectedly in 1861, from typhoid fever caught from the drains of Windsor Castle, and Queen Victoria mourned his loss for the rest of her life, setting a fashion for lengthy periods of mourning and elaborate funeral and mourning rituals.

Queen Victoria's first Prime Minister, Lord Melbourne, was inherited from her predecessor, he was followed by Sir Robert Peel, 1841-6. The Great Potato Famine in Ireland of 1845-6 saw many Irish people move to England, including some to Richmond. The Crimean War of 1854-6 saw an increase in military activity in the town. Other foreign affairs included the Indian Mutiny of 1857. During William Gladstone's first term as Prime Minister 1868-74 Forster's Education Act made elementary education compulsory for all children. Benjamin Disraeli became the Queen's favourite Prime Minister in 1874. Queen Victoria was declared Empress of India in 1877 and in 1887 celebrated her Golden Jubiliee. In 1888 the Local Government Act set up elected county councils, with civil parish councils in rural areas. The remarkably long reign of Queen Victoria saw her Diamond Jubilee in 1897. The Boer War, which began in 1899, lasted until 1902, after the Queen's death in 1901.

Richmond's 'New' Corporation elected after the Municipal Reform Act of 1835 made much of the improvements it had quickly achieved. One of these was a new water supply, needed by the growing population to augment that from Aislabeck, which was good in quality but inadequate in quantity, despite the 1812 reservoir. A new reservoir was built in Gallowgate, where Alexandra Way now stands, its since destroyed commemorative tablet reading:

> Victoria Waterworks / The supply of water was brought from Coalsgarth / by the first Council of / the Borough of Richmond / elected under the Municipal Corporation Reform Act. / The Right Honourable Lawrence Lord Dundas / having granted to the council a lease of the spring for 999 years. / The work commenced 12th January 1836 / was opened the 14th May 1837 / being the 18th anniversary of the birth of / Her Royal Highness the Princess Victoria / and in the successive mayoralties of / George Croft Esquire.

The inscription includes two titles, which changed shortly afterwards. Princess Victoria became Queen on 20 June 1837, and in April 1838 she offered Lord Dundas (Lawrence, the grandson of the first Sir Lawrence and son of Thomas, who had become a baron) an earldom in recognition of his father's generosity to her father, the Duke of Kent. The title Dundas chose was Zetland, an archaic form of Shetland where the family owned property. A town house owned by the Dundas family at the top of Frenchgate was rebuilt about 1840 and given the name Zetland House. It was also one of the first houses in Richmond to be built with gas lighting, the town gas works having expanded in order to supply private householders as well as street lighting. The Queen's marriage to Prince Albert in 1840 was marked by the naming of a new group of houses near the old Pinfold as Albert Place - the name plaque with its characteral lettering of the period can still be seen from the later Victoria Road.

The prosperity of Richmond's Saturday Market as described in the government report of 1832 is described in greater detail by William Wise, the "old Richmond lad" later of Northallerton who much later in the 19th century set down his childhood recollections of the town in the 1830s and 1840s.

> Hundreds of stalls in every available place fill the ample area, stalls for broad and narrow cloth, corduroy and fustian, spice and gingerbread cut and moulded into the shapes of men and animals and even tipped with gold. Stalls for fresh juicy garden produce, for fish of various kinds and rows of carts pressed into service as stalls. A double row of carts of great length sells nothing but potatoes, two other great rows stretching the length of High Row offer grain. Crowds of millers and their men banter good-naturedly with their customers and acquaintances. The grain is all home grown from within a radius of twenty miles of Richmond. It had a freshness, sweetness in smell and handling lacking in the present-day foreign imported corn.

Around the Market Cross, standing in their scores on bits of straw without shelter or covering of any kind, are the farmers' rosy cheeked wives and daughters bearing heavy baskets covered over and lined with spotless white linen, containing the sweetest, richest and creamiest butter in long rolls each of twenty-four ounces weight. Others had baskets of fresh laid eggs. These were quite unlike the small bantam-looking foreigners we see in the shops today. There were fine and rich looking, as large as a fair-sized cricket ball, real "home-rulers" full of meat and fragrance. You did not have to hold them up to the light to see if they were fresh. You had the good wife's word that they were gathered that very day at dawn. Each basket was itself a nest lined with sweet smelling vernal hay. Others had baskets of the creamiest, tastiest cheeses: Swaledale and Wensleydale were famed for these.

And then the farmers' wives. Clean, warmly clad, homely, healthy, ruddy, lean, red-handed, motherly, matter-of-fact women who well knew what care, economy and hard work were. Never grumbling, they faced life and its problems with stout hearts and a simple homely faith. To the bonny lasses beside them they passed on the simple philosophy of thrift, good management and hard work, the teaching they had received from their mothers before them.

Among these stalls the inhabitants of Richmond and the villages around threaded their thoughtful ways, delicately tasting the butter and cheese - traditionally proffered on a well-scrubbed shilling - and slowly and deliberately making their purchases, checking and re-checking their change after each transaction.

On one side of the Cross were rows and rows of baskets containing poultry of every kind. Live ducks and geese, chickens and occasionally turkeys. All had their legs tied and were laid on the cobbles in rucks in the straw. Poultry in those days was rarely bought ready trussed for cooking as at present. They were purchased alive with the feathers - used in pillows, cushions and mattresses - as much sought after as the flesh itself. You killed the bird in your own home. A favourite trick among the juveniles was for two of them to approach a farmer's wife selling these birds. While one of them distracted her attention the other loosed the bonds around the birds' legs. The chase and pandemonium which ensued in the crowded Market Place was a talking point for days afterwards.

Spread on the ground near the front door of Trinity church was an array of all kinds of ropes, halters, baskets, tubs, pails, buckets, churns, garden and hay rakes, spades, forks and the like. Lower down the Market Place as far as the Coal Hill were all kinds of earthenware, glass and china. The pottery sellers were famous for their repartee, back-chat and rivalry and this part of the market always drew large numbers of the adult and juvenile males who had nothing to do but stand around and gape. The anxiously awaited climax to each bout of salesmanship was when the potter in apparent exasperation at the reluctance of his customers to make a purchase hurled a cup, saucer or plate on to the cobbles in mock despair and woefully watched it disintegrate. But trade in earthenware was invariably good; in the best regulated household pots invariably get broken! ....

But the finest sight in the market were the butchers' shambles. I believe that nowhere in the North Riding was there such a show of meat as at Richmond. Prime home-fed beef, mutton, veal and pork was displayed on clean white cloths in covered stalls provided by the Corporation at a small rental. The well-dressed, well-fed, red-faced butchers, all in clean white aprons and sleeves, brandishing their sharpened, flashing knives and cleavers, had a busy time for a few hours supplying their numerous customers from town and country with the joints they required.

These butchers' stalls were of wood, well-built, covered over but open back and front. They were set up on the Friday night in the area from the Toll Booth between the Town Hall and the back of Trinity Church right down to the bottom of the Market Place. They were taken down and stored away when the market was over. They numbered over a hundred and were occupied by the best butchers in a circuit of twelve to sixteen miles. There was none of your American or Canadian frozen beef, your Iceland, New Zealand, Buenos Aires or Australian mutton, but real Yorkshire beef and half-bred mutton and lamb, fed on good swedes and home grown meal. And the bacon! Rich and sweet from pigs fed on nothing but acorns and oatmeal...... The pigs were fed on the best and the curing was done with nothing but oak chippings.

A lady crosses Newbiggin in about 1870

The continuing perception of Richmond as a fashionable and quality town affected the way in which the railway was brought to Richmond. The importance of the town meant that it was to have quite an early railway line, but there also seems to have been a deliberate concern that it should not harm the town aesthetically. For two years there was controversy as to where the station should be - Ryder's Wynd, and Clark Green near Clink Bank were among the locations suggested. In the end it was decided to terminate the line on the St. Martin's side of the river, because of the engineering difficulties of bringing the railway across the river Swale into the town. As it was, the nine-mile long branch railway from Eryholme on the main East Coast line necessitated building the Iron Bridge near Easby. The Great Northern Railway Company, of which George Hudson was Chairman, used the York architect George Townsend Andrews for the buildings along the line, which were among his many great feats of railway architecture. The architectural style chosen was a Victorian version of Tudor/Elizabethan architecture.

The passenger station has a glazed roof supported on cast and wrought ironwork, some of the columns being signed *JOHN WALKER, YORK*, the ironfounder to Queen Victoria 1847-53, who made the railings and gates for the British Museum. The Richmond railway complex included a goods station, engine shed, gas house, houses for the station master and the goods manager, and a terrace of cottages for lesser staff, plus the new road bridge which provided access to the station site across the river Swale. The old Low Church Wynd was widened and upgraded into Station Road, and the King's Head ran a horse-drawn omnibus to meet every train arriving in Richmond. The station complex subsumed the site of St. Martin's Mill, as the land had to be made up to a great depth from the level of the river.

The building of the railway line, particularly the major earthworks involved to achieve the necessary levels, required the employment of vast numbers of raw, brawny 'navvies', the likes of which Richmond had not seen before. Here is a contemporary account of their behaviour:

The town was full of navvies. Between pay-days they were quiet enough, but pay-day was an orgie, and the orgie concentrated in the market-place. Drinking, of course, was immediate and heavy. So was the fighting. Men lay about senseless, partly from liquor and partly from blows, over a good area of the market-place. I seem to remember seeing ten or a dozen so lying at one time, and not without blood about, while the market-place was filled with reeling and quarrelsome giants. Well might the Corporation be scared. They appealed to London. The Chief Commissioner of the Metropolitan Police sent them one of his best men of the renowned A Division.

Manning [sic] the new constable was tall, gaunt, in high training, but did not look strong. He was most positive in his Scotland Yard ideas. He wounded local sentiment by adhering to the London police uniform, then a body coat with tails, tight trousers, and a tall hat with a glazed crown. In the tail-pocket was the poor fellow's truncheon, and from the pocket it was soon drawn if the peace had to be asserted ....

The A Division Londoner was a splendid fellow - knew no fear - scorned to turn tail or avoid a disturbance. It was really fine heroism. He knew he had been sent for to keep that market-place in order on navvies' pay-day. Keep it in order he would. But he did not. With unflinching mien he walked into the midst of the half-drunken throng, interfered with their combats, ordered them about as if he had been in Palace Yard. They set about him. I saw that man flung five feet above his height into the air, and allowed to come down on the flat of his back on to the cobble-stones. But on the next pay-day he was there again as if nothing had happened, with the old determination in his face. It was a hopeless task. The navvies said they would kill him. They did. It did not take long. He went into a swift decline. He died at his post.

Charles Manley was buried on 2 January 1845 and the town, greatly embarrassed by the tragedy, raised a subscription for his widow. The first uniformed police force had been established in London by the Home Secretary, Sir Robert Peel, in 1829, hence the nickname 'peelers'. Its success meant that other places wished to follow suit, and the Municipal Reform Act of 1835 permitted towns to establish police forces. Richmond Corporation decided to do so in 1838, and the first uniformed officer in the town took up his post in January 1839. He was James Whiting, who came from Liverpool, and he was paid one guinea a week. It was Whiting's successor, Galliers, who was unable to cope on his own with the navvies, hence the appeal to London for assistance. The town police were initially based in the Town Hall, but when the Borough Gaol in Newbiggin was rebuilt a police station for the Borough Force was incorporated into it. This served as the town police station until the 1960s, and the inscription *POLICE STATION* above the doorway used by the public can still just be read. Meanwhile the Gilling Division of the North Riding County Constabulary was also based in Richmond, and a new county police station was built 1873-4 as the headquarters of that division. Now a private house, No. 29 Victoria Road, it remained the administrative base of that division after the absorption into the county constabulary of the borough police force in 1889.

The formation of Station Road enabled a new Grammar School building to replace the old churchyard school. The new building was erected as the 'Tate Testimonial', as the result of a public subscription in memory of the elder James Tate, and the architect was G.T. Andrews of York who had designed the railway station complex. The new school was opened on the 27th of September 1850, during the time that the younger James Tate was Master, 1833-63. Sadly, the younger Tate had none of the drive and powerful personality of his father, and when he died in 1863 after a long period of illness, the School had declined in fame and in numbers to a mere 15 boys. However, his mastership was notable for a particularly famous pupil. On 1 August 1844 Charles Lutwidge Dodgson, later to become famous the world over as Lewis Carroll, started his schooling at Richmond school, while his father was Rector of Croft. Two years later he went on to Rugby School, and from there to Oxford, where he later became a mathematics don.

The west end of Victoria Road about 1870, with the town Pinder who rounded up stray animals and kept rights of way clear of undergrowth. Notice the horse droppings!

All the boarding pupils of both the elder and younger James Tate lived with them in their family home, in the northern half of what is now called Swale House and is the main offices of Richmondshire District Council. A range of studies for the older boys to work in had been built in the back garden about 1815 by the elder Tate, who had nicknamed the house *Cloaca Maxima*, after the Great Drain of Ancient Rome, for the house stood in what was then known as Great Channel, because a lot of water drained into it, but it is now simply an extension of Frenchgate. The younger James Tate had married Anne Elizabeth Simpson, who was literally "the girl next door", for her father Thomas Simpson and his family lived in the other half of Swale House. James and Anne Tate were friendly with the family of Mark James Pattison, Rector of Hauxwell. The Pattisons owned Prior House, for Mrs. Pattison was Jane Winn, daughter of the banker who had built the house. Through the friendship of the two families, James and Anne Tate's eldest son, another James, became close to Dorothy Wyndlow Pattison and they became unofficially engaged, but the romance was broken off due to bitter opposition from Dorothy's father. If they had married, the history of nursing might have taken a different course, for Dorothy became the famous 'Sister Dora' (1821-78) of Walsall.

Although as the 19th century progressed towards its midway point Richmond was losing its pre-eminence as a provincial social centre, some important cultural traditions nevertheless continued. Franz Lizst gave a piano recital in the ballroom of the King's Head Hotel on 27 January 1841 during a British tour, and the poet laureate, Alfred Lord Tennyson visited Richmond during a tour of Yorkshire with the poet Francis Turner Palgrave at the end of July 1853. Lady Tennyson, who had a year-old son and was pregnant again, was taken ill in Yorkshire and had to stay longer than intended to recuperate. There were still dancing masters in Richmond in the 1850s, and also music teachers, some apparently of Italian origins judging by their names. There is a tombstone in the Churchyard to Rica Taschella, who died about 1860, whose husband was a music teacher. Theatres, however, were becoming established in the burgeoning industrial towns, generally more of the more down-market music hall variety, and the Richmond Theatre closed in the 1840s having been used less regularly since the Butler company disbanded in the 1830s. In 1848 the pit was leased to the wine merchant Croft and converted into wine vaults.

A number of changes took place in the 1850s. In 1853 the Richmond (Yorkshire) Burgage Pastures Act extinguished the rights of individual burgage owners to claim grazing stints on the racecourse area, and vested the land in a committee of management consisting of nine burgage owners. This Pastures Committee still meets annually to let the land, which has been used for training racehorses. In 1854 the Corporation replaced the old shambles by an indoor Market Hall, with a glazed roof supported on cast-iron columns, rather like a railway station, which is still used and has in recent years been open more and more days per week.

The military importance of Richmond was increased when, in addition to the annual training of the North York Militia, plus that of the Richmond Forester Yeomanry Cavalry, Richmond Castle was leased by the Duke of Richmond to the Militia in 1855, shortly before the outbreak of the Crimean War. The area inside the bailey was levelled as a parade ground, and a row of houses was erected there to accommodate the families of the permanent staff. At the same time the ruinous entrance to the Castle was rebuilt, and adjoining this a block of cells was provided for military prisoners. In 1858 a captured Russian cannon was placed in the Castle grounds, being dragged up from the Railway Station by willing volunteers, enthusiastically cheered on by watching schoolboys. The cannon was removed during World War II, and its present whereabouts is unknown. In 1875 Richmond was designated as the headquarters of the 19th Regimental District, comprising the North Riding of Yorkshire, and during the next three years a new Barracks was erected at the top of Gallowgate to accommodate 10 officers and 340 men. There was also a hospital, canteen, library, officers' and sergeants' messes, stables, stores etc. The whole complex covered some 15 acres and was surrounded by a substantial wall pierced with mock firing slits and flanked with towers. This became the training quarters of the XIXth Regiment of Foot (the Green Howards) until 1967 when the Barracks ceased to be used for military purposes.

Throughout the 19th century regular troops were stationed in and around Richmond, and they must have heard with some disquiet of the Indian Mutiny of 1857. One wonders if they knew of a Richmond link with that far-away event, for among the British heroes of it was John Laird Mair, First Lord Lawrence of the Punjab, who had been born in Richmond on 4 March 1811, while his father, Lt. Col. Alexander Lawrence of the XIXth Regiment of Foot, was stationed here, lodging with his wife in what is now No. 1 Millgate. Lord Lawrence died in 1879 and was buried in Westminster Abbey, where an inscription beneath his marble bust gives a short account of his distinguished career. On 19 December 1909 a memorial to him was unveiled in the south aisle of Richmond Parish Church.

St. Mary's Parish Church was extensively restored 1858-62 under the direction of Sir George Gilbert Scott, the architect of many Victorian churches and later to design the Albert Memorial and St. Pancras Station in London. The whole of the west tower, the outer walls of the east end and some other sections of the outer walls of St. Mary's were retained, but the interior was totally reconstructed, with lofty new arcades supporting a taller and more steeply-pitched roof. The nave was extended eastwards into what had been the first bay of the chancel, and the floor levels, which in the old church had dropped down various sets of steps towards the east end because of the steep slope of the site, were levelled up. All the old pews and Georgian galleries were removed, although the Easby choir stalls and most of the old monuments were put back, though not necessarily in their old positions. The organ, which had stood in a gallery at the west end of the church since 1809, was moved to its present position in the north chancel aisle, and was incorporated into a larger instrument in 1883. Some fragments of medieval stained glass, heraldic shields which had escaped Puritan pick-axes and survived the ravages of time, were gathered together into the tracery of the south aisle windows. Victorian stained glass was inserted into some windows following Scott's restoration, notably the brightly coloured but not garish east window by O'Connor.

In 1864 Holy Trinity Chapel was also heavily restored by Scott, who replaced the largely Georgian appearance it had had with a more Gothic character. The ground floor of the north aisle, where the Consistory Court had been, became a row of shops, which seemed appropriate at the time as other shops surrounded the building. The interior was re-fitted as a Victorian church, and this became the Grammar School Chapel when the then headmaster, Rev. Thomas Henry Stokoe, became also perpetual curate of Holy Trinity, and the schoolboys formed a choir. Richmond School's fortunes were restored by Dr. Stokoe, master 1863-71, who was followed by James Snowden 1871-84 and Jean Rougier Cohu 1884-90. It again attracted boarders from all parts of England, being dubbed "A Great Yorkshire School", enjoying sporting as well as academic success. The Tate Testimonial building was extended in 1867 by the addition of what boys of "R.S.Y." (Richmond School, Yorkshire) called 'Big School'. The first lay headmaster was Douglas Rucker Smith in 1895, and during his time the School purchased the Friary as a house for the headmaster, and a purpose-built boarding house, designed by Darlington architects Clark and Moscrop, was added on to it, it no longer being acceptable for masters to have to accommodate boarders in their own homes. W. J. Moscrop had been educated at the School, having grown up at Olliver on the Aske estate.

Although 19th-century Richmond grew only in proportion to the increase in the national population, this was still enough to be reflected in a considerable increase in the accommodation available for religious worship. In addition to the restoration of the buildings of the established church, the nonconformists also built and rebuilt chapels. The Roman Catholics, whose small chapel in Newbiggin had been built in 1809 by Sir John Lawson of Brough Hall, was rebuilt on a larger scale in 1855. This eventually became the chancel of the church completed by 1868 to the design of London architect George Goldie, with an adjacent new presbytery, which bears the datestone 1869. The Roman Catholic Church contains some interesting memorials, including one erected to the memory of the Reverend Father Robert Johnson who died in 1865, having been the officiating priest for over half a century, and a stained glass window commemorates banker Peter Constable Maxwell who died in 1851 and his wife Helena Bruno. They lived at The Grove in Frenchgate, where they succeeded the Stapleton family, another Roman Catholic family who had made a private chapel in the house, complete with a stained glass window.

The Roman Catholics also, under the patronage of Louisa Catherine Caton, 7th Duchess of Leeds of Hornby Castle, established a convent for the Religious of the Assumption in 1849/50. The sisters ran an orphanage and a school for poor children and also set up a night school for the Irish women working as rag pickers in Henry Cooke's paper mill. At first the convent consisted only of a house called the Hermitage on Reeth Road, then new buildings designed by leading Roman Catholic architect George Goldie were opened in 1869. Buildings for a girls' boarding school, designed by Clark and Moscrop, were added later, and remained in use until the school closed in 1993.

The Wesleyan Methodists built a large new chapel opened in 1841, having been begun in 1839, the centenary year of Methodism. Costing £2,200 and seating 650, it was accessed from a passage leading off the Market Place, being built on 'back land' extending down to Ryder's Wynd, on the opposite side of which had been their first chapel since 1807, a three storey building also housing a Sunday School, demolished in 1985. The 1841 chapel survives, currently called the Chapel Gallery, having closed when the present Methodist Church was built in 1939 at the junction of Dundas Street and Queens Road. The Primitive Methodists, who had a following in Bargate and the Green, in 1861 opened their new Ebenezer chapel in Bargate, which cost £500 and seated 260, it too had a Sunday School attached. After the union of Wesleyan and Primitive Methodists in 1932, the Bargate chapel closed in 1934 and is now the headquarters of Richmond Operatic Society.

A new Congregational Church and Sunday School was built in Dundas Street in 1883 on land leased from the Earl of Zetland, it was a handsome Gothic Revival building with an octagonal belfry, designed by Clark and Moscrop, accommodating 320 worshippers, and closed almost a century later in 1982. It replaced the Independents Chapel of 1835 in Tower Street, now converted into flats, which became the town's first Museum. This housed the important geological collection amassed by Edward Wood, a Richmond draper and Fellow of the Geological Society. A fossil, the *Woodocrinus*, was named after him, of a crinoid organism related to the starfish found in sedimentary rocks in Swaledale. In 1894 this museum was taken over by the North Riding Naturalists Field Club, and Wood's geological collection is now in the Yorkshire Museum in York. The Richmond museum was, of course, on a much smaller scale than the famous Smithsonian Institution founded in Washington, U.S.A., in 1846 by James Smithson, the natural son of Hugh Smithson, the Duke of Northumberland of Stanwick near Richmond. A noted scientist in his day, he lived mainly on the Continent but never visited America. However he bequeathed his fortune "to the United States, to found at Washington, under the name of the Smithsonian Institution, an establishment for the increase and diffusion of knowledge".

Richmond's two cultural bodies flourished through Queen Victoria's reign, in 1864 the Scientific Society had 103 members and the Mechanics Institute 260. The first local newspaper also came into existence in the mid-19th century, when in 1855 the *Ripon and Richmond Chronicle* was established by John Bell, one of the sons of Matthew Bell, the bookseller and stationer in Finkle Street. The *Ripon and Richmond Chronicle* was eventually merged in 1895 with the slightly older *Darlington and Stockton Times*, founded in 1847. The 'D and S' continues to be an institution in the life of Richmondians, its Richmond and Dales edition providing a valued source of information. It continued to be published on a Saturday, still with advertisements on the front page, until 1997 when publication day was changed to Friday, and news appeared on the front page.

A Richmond printer of the later-19th century was Thomas Spencer, who had premises at the corner of Finkle Street and the Market Place. His shop attracted much custom from the visitors now coming to the town by railway, and he published a large number of postcards of local views, and also pamphlets on such topics as *Robert Willance: His Miraculous Escape from Death while Hunting on Whitcliffe Scar*, and it was he who was largely responsible for creating the myth, now much cherished in Richmond, that the song 'Sweet Lass of Richmond Hill' related to Hill House in Richmond.

The ballad, written by Leonard MacNally (1752-1820), a successful playwright and Dublin lawyer, was published in 1789, with music by James Hook (1746-1827), a famous organist and composer. The song became a great success, being a particular favourite at the fashionable Vauxhall Gardens in London, where it was a 'hit' for the popular tenor Charles Benjamin Incledon (1763-1826). On 16 January 1787 MacNally had married Frances I'Anson (1766-95), at the fashionable St. George's Church, Hanover Square in London. Frances was married there because the I'Anson home was then in Bedford Row, but her father, lawyer William I'Anson, came of a Wensleydale family, and Frances had been born at the I'Anson home in Leyburn High Street. Leonard and Frances MacNally spent the first five years of their married life in London at No. 5 Pump Court in the Temple, and they had two daughters, Frances and Elizabeth. In 1792 the family moved to Dublin, where Frances died aged less than thirty on 30 September 1795. Leonard, looking after his two small daughters, married again in 1797, and continued to live in Dublin until his death in 1820. Sometimes the two girls visited their maternal uncle, Thomas I'Anson, who lived at Prior House in Richmond.

However, there seems to be no substance whatsoever to the tradition that Frances I'Anson lived at Hill House and was wooed there, or under a walnut tree in the garden, by Leonard MacNally. Her maternal grandparents, Ralph and Martha Hutchinson, tenanted Hill House 1750-68, so it is possible that as a baby or a toddler Frances was taken to see them there, but they did not live there when she was at an age to be wooed by MacNally. That the song was written for his wife is a romantic possibility, although it is more likely that the words refer to Richmond-upon-Thames, which was much closer to the

MacNallys' lives than the Yorkshire Richmond, and also was well-known to the London audience the song was aimed at. Nevertheless, that there was, and sometimes still is, heated debate particularly in newspaper columns about the origins of 'the Lass', is largely due to Thomas Spencer, and he pressed the claims of Richmond, Yorkshire to 'the Lass' to enhance its tourist reputation. Spencer was aided and abetted by various members of the extended I'Anson family and, somewhat surprisingly, by James Louis Garvin, a journalist on the staff of the *Newcastle Chronicle* 1891-99 and editor of the *Observer* newspaper 1908-42. While in Newcastle, Garvin was employed by William Arthur I'Anson, the last direct male descendant of the Leyburn branch of the I'Anson family to write a memoir of 'the Lass', which it was hoped Spencer would publish, but its length proved over-ambitious.

Thomas Spencer was a prominent freemason, and his house, on Maison Dieu, was called Lennox House after the freemasons' lodge. There were many characterful shopkeepers of his generation. Leonard Cooke, a prosperous grocer, who had purchased the advowson, or right to appoint clergy, of Holy Trinity Chapel from Richmond Corporation when that body was prevented from continuing to hold it by the Municipal Reform Act, in 1854 built himself Terrace House, named from the Georgian promenade along Maison Dieu which provided a splendid panorama of the town. A grand villa in the Italianate style, it later became a hotel, and is now a nursing home. Many Victorian houses were constructed using a new roofing material, Welsh slates, which were cheaply available once the railway had opened.

Another shopkeeper of note was Robert Spence, an ironmonger who claimed his business had been founded in 1788. He constructed iron tram-lines to assist the transport of heavy goods such as cast-iron fireplaces, which were brought to Richmond by rail, and then laboriously hauled by horse and cart up Station Road and into the Market Place, between his large shop in the Market Place and its supplementary warehouses in Friars Wynd. Among the vast range of goods he sold were early bicycles, and indeed he was one of the leading lights of the Velocipede Contests organized in the town from 1868-70! The drapers' shop of geologist Edward Wood was Robson Wood and Co. in Finkle Street, which also had a long history, being founded in 1820. A name of more significance to shoppers further afield was John James Fenwick, who eventually founded Fenwick's, the group of large department stores based in Newcastle-upon-Tyne. He was born at No. 83 Frenchgate, the Victorian shop front of which was where he started his shop keeping career.

A passage beside No. 83 Frenchgate leads through to Flints Terrace, which takes its name from ironfounder James Flint, who lived in the house the other side of the passage. About 1835 he took over the house and business, which had been built up since about 1790 by Joseph Bradwell. The foundry was in the continuation of that Frenchgate plot towards Pottergate, which became known as Flints Yard, more exposed since the demolition of Lile Cottage to make way for old persons' flats. A versatile craftsman, James Flint even described himself also as an architect, and built himself a fine house at Brompton-on-Swale. He was also an engraver, one of his pictures providing a rare view of the interior of the pavilion erected and handsomely decorated for a dinner of the Municipal Reform Association, which was dated 2 November 1843.

The 19th century saw a great increase in the use of horse-drawn carriages, and there was a need to form an approach to the town centre, which was more level and suitable for such vehicles. As a continuation of King Street, Queen Road was formed about 1887, and named for the Golden Jubilee, replacing the old backland area known as Back-of-the-Friars, and at the same time Victoria Road replaced the late-Georgian promenade known as Back Flags. Thus there was at last a fairly level approach into the Market Place from Reeth Road, Hurgill Road, and also Pottergate, which took traffic from the Whashton, Gilling, Darlington and Brompton-on-Swale directions. The increased use of wheeled vehicles resulted in the establishment of several businesses making the sprung carriages, which were then fashionable.

Horse-drawn carriages and hearses were particularly used for funerals as part of the elaborate mourning rituals, which developed in Victorian times after the death of Prince Albert. This trend is reflected in monuments in Richmond Churchyard. Very prominent beside the path leading up to the south porch of the church is a tall Corinthian column, which bears on its plinth symbols of freemasonry. It is a monument to Matthew Greathead who died on 31 December 1871 at the remarkable age of 101 years and 8 months. Having been initiated into freemasonry on 27 December 1797, he had been a member for 74 years, and he was given a masonic funeral on 5 January 1872. The brethren marched to the church in procession, after his body had rested overnight in the newly-built Masonic Hall in Newbiggin. Previously the lodge had met in various inns around the town, including the Freemasons' Arms in Bargate, the Blue Bell at the bottom of the Market Place where Woolworths is now, and the Black Bull on the south side of the Market Place between the present Golden Lion and the Bishop Blaize. In 1868 the lodge had appointed a committee to investigate how to provide a meeting room, and it came forward with two suggestions. One was to convert the old Theatre, and the other was to construct a new building in Newbiggin on land belonging to the Earl of Zetland. The latter option was the one chosen, and the new hall became operational on 5 May 1870, a special Provincial Grand Lodge being held in it on 23 September presided over by the Provincial Grand Master - the Earl of Zetland.

The churchyard was used for burials until the new cemetery in Reeth Road opened in 1886, and the majority of the tombstones in the churchyard are of 19th century date. There are in excess of 700 inscribed stones recording details of about 1,700 individuals. An obelisk below the east end of the church commemorates James Brown Simpson, attorney-at-law and the first Town Clerk of Richmond after the Municipal Reform Act, who died in 1855. A Cottage Hospital was erected in Gallowgate in 1876 in memory of his son of the same name who became James Brown Lestor. One tombstone mentions 24 members of the Thompson family who lived on Cornforth Hill. A famous member of that family was Francis 'Matabele' Thompson who, in association with Cecil Rhodes and with much bloodshed, added Matabeleland to the British Empire, and named the farmstead he established Cornforth Hill. Another member of the family, Alderman Thomas Thompson, in 1872 gave to the town the chain of office which the Mayor of Richmond still wears, and his portrait, wearing the chain, hangs in the present Council Chamber. The chain was made by a Richmond goldsmith, W. S. Robinson, and has in addition to the badge depicting the arms of the Borough, medallions showing the coats of arms of the medieval trade guilds.

Several tombstones commemorate the various artists who continued to be attracted to Richmond. The tombstone with the most striking name must be that of Julius Caesar Ibbetson, who died in 1825 at the age of 42, the son of the better-known painter of the same name who ended his days in Masham and died there in 1817. Ibbetson junior was also an artist, and taught drawing classes in the town. He married the landlady of the Fleece Inn, which stood at the north end of Friars Wynd on the site of the present pub, rebuilt after a fire in 1897, facing Victoria Road, in Scottish Baronial style to a design by the Darlington architect George Hoskins. Another artist was William Ripley Robinson, who also had a bookshop, and in 1833 he had published Robinson's *Guide to Richmond* illustrated with prints of his own pictures. A simple tombstone in the churchyard commemorates Jessey Margretta Joy, a fine watercolour artist who lived in Frenchgate, and who died in 1883 aged 69. The late-Victorian Tyneside painter Ralph Hedley was born at Gilling West in 1848.

To the list of books about Richmond by Gale, Whitaker, Clarkson and Robinson was added Harry Speight's *Romantic Richmondshire* in 1897, and the *History of Yorkshire, Wapentake of Gilling West* published in 1885 as the first volume of an intended series by the imaginatively-named Marshal-General Plantagenet-Harrison. Born George Henry Harrison at Whashton in 1817, he adopted the name George Henry De Straboglie Neville Plantagenet-Harrison in 1843, and was mainly interested in the pedigrees of local families. Early in the 20th century another writer, Edmund Bogg, would add slightly cheaper topographical works to the range available. By the late-19th century there were also journals produced by county antiquarian societies, such as County Durham's Surtees Society, and Yorkshire's Archaeological and Topographical. Society, the latter's journal including, for example, a report on Sir William St. John Hope's excavation of Easby Abbey in 1886. Brief local histories were also included in the various trades directories which appeared during the 19th century, the most helpful one being Thomas Bulmer's *History, Topography and Directory of North Yorkshire* for 1890.

    Directories provide useful historical information on tradesmen and residents of some standing, though shed no light on lesser individuals and employees. The Census returns from 1851, however, reveal every person regardless of standing, gender, age etc. A Census was taken from 1801, but those before 1851 only provided a head count. Richmond's population rose from just under 3,000 in 1801 to a 19th-century peak of 4,500 in 1881. From the mid-19th century there are photographs, which provide records of both individuals and the local townscape. Richmond had a succession of resident studio photographers starting in the second half of the 19th century, one of the most interesting being William Sanderson (1854-1930). He worked as a photographer in partnership with his younger brother Herbert, as well as being himself an accomplished artist. *[see plate 7]* Their shop in the Great Channel sold artists' materials. In the 1980s it became fashionable to publish books of old postcards and photographs, and Richmond has had its share of these. One of them includes a selection from the 'Hunton Portfolio', a number of glass negatives, which were given to the Richmondshire Museum and were identified by the detective work of the Honorary Curator, Peter Wenham, as relating to the family of Wensley Hunton, a local solicitor whose firm still continues as Hunton and Garget. The photographs show the family, their house, their doings, in the last decade of Queen Victoria's reign and also into early Edwardian times.

Some early photographs of the town show crowds eagerly gathering to hear election polls. In 1867 the number of Richmond Members of Parliament was reduced from two to one, and the constituency was further enlarged by the addition of the parishes of St. Martin's and Sleegill, the extensive Easby parish having been added in 1832. The population of this large area totalled 5,134, but the electorate, of £10 householders, numbered just 316. The 1872 Ballot Act brought in the secret poll, and Richmond had to get a polished oak ballot box, which was used for the first time in the general election on 7 November of that year. The *Northern Echo* estimated that 10% of the electorate were illiterate, but considered they had nevertheless had little difficulty coping with the new secret voting system. The report ended with an extraordinary comment: "I am exceedingly happy to report that the men of Richmond have profited by the hint I gave them the other day about personal cleanliness. Nearly everybody was clean washed today, a result highly satisfactory from a sanitary point of view."

The last borough election was held in 1880, the Redistribution Act of 1885 removing the town's independent representation, and Richmond was merged into the Richmondshire Division of the North Riding of Yorkshire, which had a population of 58,839. The name of the seat was, however, retained, and still remains, and the tradition of declaring the Richmondshire Division poll in Richmond itself continued until 1982 when it was moved to Northallerton. The Dundas family continued to represent the town in Parliament until their Pocket Borough seat was no more. Thomas the second Earl of Zetland had no children and his nephew Lawrence became the third Earl in 1873. He was created Marquess of Zetland in 1892 having been Lord Lieutenant of Ireland 1889-92.

Other changes were brought about by the forces of nature. On 29 January 1883 a great flood destroyed the Castle Paper Mills, which James Cooke had established beside the Foss Head in 1865. The artist and photographer William Sanderson recorded their destruction in a sketch in oils taken on the spot between 11am and 1pm that day - presumably setting up a camera was too difficult out of doors at that time. The siting of a 'factory' at the Foss Head had incurred the wrath of various topographical writers, who considered it to spoil a Richmond beauty spot egg John Ruskin in 1880:

..... Alas! the entire scene is now destroyed by a complete inferno of manufactory at the base of the Castle .... There is no more lovely rendering of old English life; the scarcely altered sweetness of hill and stream, the baronial ruins on their crag, the old-fashioned town with the little gardens behind each house, the winding walks for pleasure along the rive shore - all now ...... devastated by the hell-blasts of avarice and luxury.

James Cooke had increased the power of the watermill on the old site by raising the height of the natural waterfall with a brick weir. This attracted this rebuke from Mrs. Alfred Hunt in her introduction to a later edition of Turner's *Richmondshire:*

.... all the grandeur of Richmond is gone - it has been sacrificed to the profit that could be made out of the water power of the river ..... the papermaker prospered, the business increased, and went on increasing and now half the river is encumbered by an unsightly growth of huge factories and works of all kinds. That is by no means all. Having bought the field on the other side he acquired the right to increase the flow of water through the mill by building a wall across the stream. This is immediately behind the force which flows over a mill-dam, which indeed it is. In dry seasons the whole body of water passes through the old mill race.

Nature took its revenge on Richmond again on 8 July 1893. A contemporary newspaper described it thus:

Shortly after two o'clock on Saturday afternoon, Richmond and district was visited by a thunderstorm the violence of which has had no equal within the memory of the oldest inhabitant. ..... Raindrops as large as a crown piece fell at first. These were succeeded by small hail-stones, which rapidly increased in size until they became as large as bantam's eggs. A wind rose at the same time and these large missiles fell in a perfect deluge. A scene of the wildest confusion followed in the Market Place, for the market folk had not then started on their homeward journey. Women and children screamed with fright, and ran into the nearest shops for shelter; but these did not afford them much protection, for the enormous pieces of ice shot through the windows like cannon balls. With such force did they fall that pots and ornaments on the opposite walls were smashed to pieces. The rattling of falling glass and pots, with vivid flashes of lightning combined with the screams.... and the heavy peals of thunder formed a scene, which will never be forgotten by those who witnessed it. .....

The damage done is enormous, and very few houses in the town escaped without broken windows, while in many of the large houses not a single window remains unbroken. .... The bulk of the damage was done in Frenchgate, Millgate, Market Place and Newbiggin. ..... In the King's Head Hotel, no less than 175 panes of glass were smashed ... and at the Wesleyan Chapel there were 135 broken.... The sky-light over the magisterial quarters of the Town Hall, which is of very thick glass, was smashed in pieces. The large one over the billiard room at the same hotel was also broken. When the room was entered after the storm abated, water was standing to a depth of two inches on the billiard table. ..... Hundreds of people turned out to view the ruins in the evening. Mr Sanderson photographed the Market Place, which had the appearance of having been bombarded. All this damage was wrought within a space of ten minutes. ..... A piece of ice measuring 5½ inches in circumference was picked up in Major John Smurthwaite's dining room at the Temple, and long after the storm abated perfectly round balls of ice, measuring seven inches in circumference, were found in the gardens. ... It is estimated that .... in the town some 100,000 panes of glass have been broken. The storm seems to have been confined to a very small area. At Catterick Bridge and Leyburn in Wensleydale there was only a heavy downpour of rain.

There was a military camp on the Racecourse at the time, and some unfortunate soldiers were injured, though not fatally. The long tradition of horse-racing in Richmond had come to an end two years earlier. The last meeting was on Thursday and Friday 6 and 7 August 1891, and the last race was won by a 3-year old horse called Undecimus owned by Mr. S. Petrie and ridden by S. Chandley. The course had been condemned as dangerous by the Jockey Club because horses, now more finely bred, were running at much faster speeds than when the racecourse had first been used, and its bends were too sharp for the greater speed. Attendances had also decreased because there were now other racecourses with better rail access, such as that at Catterick Bridge, and it was a long uphill walk from Richmond Railway Station.

However, there was soon a new annual event, which attracted many people to Richmond. In the 1880s and early 1890s cycling clubs from Northumberland, Durham and Teesside held an annual get-together, or 'Meet', every Whitsuntide at Barnard Castle. In 1892 the clubs located in the Teesside area broke away and instituted their own gathering (called the North Yorkshire and South Durham Meet) at Richmond. A race track was made around the Cricket Field in Victoria Road for the cycle races. The Meet has been held annually ever since 1892 (except for breaks during the two World Wars), and the set pattern which evolved has always included a church parade, carnival procession, and a fairground in the Market Place, with a programme of dances, concerts and band competitions which has varied somewhat over the years. The date has been transferred from the Whitsuntide weekend to that of the Late Spring Bank Holiday. Every year a President of the Meet is elected who chooses a badge of his own design incorporating his monogram. A complete set of these is proudly worn by each year's President. The cycling element disappeared for a time but has since been reintroduced.

The re-assembled Victoria Fountain

During her long widowhood Queen Victoria travelled around the country little, her public engagements being undertaken by various of her children, particularly the Prince of Wales, later King Edward VII. He and his consort, the Princess Alexandra, visited Richmond in 1889, the arrival and departure of the royal party from Richmond Station being marked by the planting on the triangle of land to the west of the Station of five sycamore trees and one horse chestnut, which were named Alexandra, Albert Edward, Stanley, Prince George, Victoria and Albert the Good. Queen Victoria's long reign was marked by two permanent commemorations in Richmond. A cottage hospital established in 1899 was named the Victoria Hospital (in honour of her Diamond Jubilee), the fund-raising committee being energetically led by the Marchioness of Zetland. This served the community for exactly a century, closing in 1999. A replacement for the old water point in the lower Market Place was commissioned on the death of the Queen Victoria, to be called the Victoria Fountain, but was not completed until three years after her death on 22 January 1901 after a reign of 63 years, being erected in 1904. It was then removed as a hazard to the growing quantity of traffic in 1958, to be mislaid by the Borough Corporation and only relocated in 1985. It was eventually re-erected outside the Richmondshire Museum in 1987.

8

Twentieth Century Richmond 1901 – 2000

The National History

King Edward VII (1901-10) came to the throne as the new century had just begun, after an adult life in waiting, spent in the pursuit of pleasure. The Edwardian era was a time of opulence, but also saw the first old age pensions for those over 70 introduced in 1909 by the Chancellor, David Lloyd-George. The reign of King George V (1910-36) was a troubled time. The country's traditional way of life was shattered forever by the outbreak of World War I (1914-18), usually referred to as the Great War, which caused atrocities and slaughter on an unimaginable scale. With such a high proportion of their menfolk absent from home and workplace, women moved into hitherto unheard of realms of activity, and thus in 1918 women over 30 achieved the right to vote. Such profound social and economic changes were to continue for the rest of the century, the voting age for women being brought down to 21, the same as for men, in 1929.

Social and economic unrest erupted in 1926, when the ten-day General Strike brought everything to a halt, and the major economic slump of 1929-33 led to the Jarrow Hunger Marches. King George V's Silver Jubilee in 1935 was intended to raise the spirits of a nation which until 1939 marked 24 May, Queen Victoria's birthday, as Empire Day with solemn ceremonies around the Union Jack and children's sports. George V's death in 1936 was followed by the Abdication Crisis when his eldest son, who would have reigned as Edward VIII, chose instead to marry the twice-divorced American Wallis Simpson. His next brother, the Duke of York, succeeded the throne as King George VI (1936-52), his reign witnessing another major conflict, World War II (1939-45), after Prime Minister Neville Chamberlain's ill-judged treaty with Adolf Hitler at Munich in 1938. The immense effort to achieve victory in the Second World War was spearheaded by the bulldog-like qualities of Winston Churchill, who was ousted as Prime Minister in the landslide election success won by the Labour Party in 1945. That post-war government saw the introduction of the Welfare State, with the establishment of economist Sir William Beveridge's National Health Service and National Insurance Scheme, and oversaw the nationalization of the country's basic industries, including coal, electricity, transport and steel. King George VI's Queen, Elizabeth, survived to celebrate her 100th birthday in the year 2000. Her namesake, Queen Elizabeth II, reigned for the rest of the century and beyond.

The second half of the twentieth century saw a gradual increase in general prosperity, most famously observed by Prime Minister Harold Macmillan's quip in 1957 "You've never had it so good". Harold Wilson, famous for his pipe and Gannex raincoat, was Prime Minister during the Swinging Sixties, when the pace of social change quickened, as homosexuality was legalized, the death penalty abolished, the birth control pill became available, and divorce and abortion were made easier to obtain. In 1975 Great Britain joined the European Union. The first British woman Prime Minister was Margaret Thatcher from 1979, who curbed the powers of the trades unions and de-nationalized the major industries. Her successor, John Major, was in office for the opening of the long-awaited Channel Tunnel in 1994, the same year which saw the introduction of the National Lottery which changed the funding system of worthy causes to a form of voluntary taxation proffered most willingly by the least well-off. The Prime Minister at the end of the century was one of the youngest ever, New Labour's Tony Blair.

The universal adoption of, and eventual dependence on, the internal combustion engine resulted in many social changes, including road improvement, the building of motorways from 1969 and the creation of extensive car parks, as well as the culling of the railway network under Lord Beeching in 1963. The twentieth century also saw powered flight, space travel, and the use of atomic and nuclear power for both peaceful and aggressive purposes. Oil and gas were extracted from under the North Sea, leading to the virtual extinction of the coal industry. During the century working hours, and years, became shorter, allowing more time for recreation. This led to people taking holidays both at home and abroad, and tourism becoming an important national industry. Related to this has been the increasing interest in and appreciation of the country's heritage.

The Edwardian era in Richmond began with events linked with Victorian political and military activities. A silver two-handled cup bearing the London hallmark for 1900 was given to the town with the inscription *Presented to the Corporation of Richmond, Yorks., by the Mayor (Captain Gerald Walker), as a memorial of their safe return from South Africa of the Volunteers of that Borough, 1901.* There were five volunteers. There was also much rejoicing in the town when the end of the Boer War was declared in 1903. That year saw the town's first telephone exchange, installed in the new Post Office building in King Street, now the Kleer-Vu shop. From here the first Old Age Pension was paid in 1909 by the Postmaster since 1900, Albert Morton. In 1906 the first Marquess of Zetland, a generous benefactor to the town, leased to the Corporation of Richmond for 999 years at a yearly rent of one shilling, land on the south side of Quaker Lane for use as a public amenity. It was to be called the Ronaldshay Recreation Ground after the courtesy title of his eldest son. Written into the lease was the proviso that the Corporation "will not at any time permit public meetings for the discussion of political, religious, trade or social questions or other matters of controversy to be held or religious services to be conducted or lectures or addresses delivered". The Park was opened at Easter 1907 and is still a much-used local amenity. As was fashionable in Edwardian times, a bandstand was soon added; this was demolished in 1983.

The following year, 1908, the Marquess of Zetland leased the ancient house called St. Nicholas to a new tenant, the Hon. Robert James, the youngest son of Walter Henry, 2nd Baron Northbourne. The gardens of the house then consisted merely of a lawn in front of the house with a few flower beds and a large greenhouse on it, a kitchen garden and a small tennis court. 'Bobby' James began creating for St. Nicholas a new garden, based not on the then fashionable concept of formal carpet-bedding, but instead innovatively constructed 'rooms' walled in with yew hedges, to form a series of micro-climates. Early on the garden at St. Nicholas was visited by Lawrence Johnson, who used this idea as the basis for his Gloucestershire garden at Hidcote, now owned by the National Trust. The Hidcote garden has been highly influential in English garden history, as it has been much copied elsewhere, but the concept originated at St. Nicholas.

Further away from the house, Robert James planted rocky outcrops with rhododendrons, some of which he himself brought back from plant-hunting expeditions to the Himalayas. After the death in 1922 at the age of 48 of his first wife, Evelyn Kathleen Wellesley, daughter of the 4th Duke of Wellington, he married Lady Serena Lumley, the 10th Earl of Scarbrough's young daughter. Lady Serena James has continued to live at St. Nicholas during her long widowhood, lovingly tending and keeping open to the public daily the famous garden her late husband created, and saw in the Millennium at the age of 98. A leading character of 20th-century Richmond, she is held in such great affection for her long service to the town, particularly during the Second World War, that she was made a Freeman of Richmond in 1987.

From 1908 until he retired from the army two years later, Lord Robert Baden-Powell was General Officer Commanding the Northumbrian Division of the Territorial Army. Richmond was the headquarters of this Division, and the General stayed first in the King's Head Hotel, and then in a suite of rooms prepared for him in the old Militia building in the Castle Yard, from which he had a superb view overlooking the Green Bridge and Billy Banks wood. The artist Harold Speed painted this scene and gave the picture to Lord and Lady Baden-Powell in 1912 as a wedding gift. After her husband died in 1941, Lady Baden-Powell gave this picture to Richmond Corporation, and it now hangs in the Mayor's Parlour in the Town Hall. With this gift was a sketch, also by Speed, of Lord Baden-Powell, together with some pages from the latter's diary, which had particularly relevance to Richmond. Shortly before he arrived in Richmond, Baden-Powell had published his *Scouting for Boys* and founded the Boy Scouts in 1908, and it was here in Richmond that one of his first Scout troops was raised. In 1910 he also founded the Girl Guides. In 1953, while Frank Dickinson was Mayor, a plaque was put on a wall in the Castle Yard near to where Baden-Powell had his quarters, replaced in 1981 by the present plaque, which has this inscription:

Robert Baden-Powell
Founder of the Scout and Guide Movements
Lived from 1908-1910 in the Barracks
which formerly stood on this site

The extraction of copper ore from Billy Banks Wood finally ceased in 1912, having last been worked by the Yorkshire Minerals Company. The Boulder Flint Company, attracted here by a vein of chert in the hillside of Billy Banks Wood, re-activated the mine about 1906, and constructed the stone adit, which can still be seen on the riverside. In 1907, 379 tons of ore were extracted which yielded 20 tons of refined copper. The ore was brought out of the adit and tipped into hand-pushed tubs running along a narrow-gauge railway mounted on a causeway, carefully constructed of large blocks of chert similar to those used for railway station platforms, extending to the Green Bridge. From here it was taken by horse-drawn carts to Richmond Station for transportation for smelting elsewhere. The causeway was built literally at the river's edge, and most of it has now been either swept away or at least considerably disturbed by the turbulent river Swale. Another Edwardian industrial initiative was a planned extension of the railway line to Reeth, to revitalize the declining lead industry of Swaledale by avoiding bringing down by road to the rail-head in Richmond the cumbersome lead. Difficulties in devising a suitable route for the line were finally overcome in 1913, and detailed plans were made for its building, but construction was scuppered by the outbreak of World War I.

Market Day in July 1912

One of Lord Baden-Powell's duties while in Richmond was to determine where a new army camp should be located. He suggested it should be in the Hipswell/Colburn area, but nothing was done until the outbreak of World War I greatly increased the need for additional military training facilities. Work began in the Spring of 1915 on what became known as Catterick Camp, the first troops moving into barracks there in very unfinished and primitive conditions in October of that year. In 1916 some 5,000 German prisoners of war of non-commissioned rank housed there were employed on camp construction and road making. One of the roads they built ran from Richmond Railway Station, past St. Martin's Priory, to join up with the old Hipswell-Hudswell road not far from West Wood, thus creating a direct link between the Camp and Richmond Station. The new road was named Rimington Avenue, after Major-General M.F. Rimington, Catterick Camp's first Commandant. Uncovered during construction of the road was a large glacial erratic rock, which was placed on the roadside next to Station House and inscribed with the initials of the War Department, the date 1917-1918, and a Latin text which can be translated as *O powerful one, move me if you can!* Having become partly buried as the road was gradually raised, the bottom part of the inscription was re-cut at the army's expense in 1995. Catterick Camp has grown dramatically since its crude and muddy beginnings. Renamed Catterick Garrison on 1st January 1973, it became the largest military base in Europe following the government's Strategic Defence Review of 1997, which earmarked it for expansion, and now has a population of 15,000, considerably larger than that of its older neighbour, Richmond.

The horrors of World War I affected every family, either directly or indirectly. A list of men from Richmond already in uniform by 1915 was drawn up by the Red Cross, it gives 396 names, of whom 14 had already died or been killed, plus several others wounded. Letters have been published from one young officer in the Green Howards written to his family back home in Richmond. Randal William Shuckburgh Croft was the son of Christopher George Croft, Town Clerk of Richmond 1898-1919 and a descendant of the Croft family much involved in early-19th century Reform in Richmond. Randal Croft was wounded on the first day of the Battle of the Somme on 1st July 1916, when 13 officers and over 300 other ranks fell as casualties in the first three minutes of the attack. He recovered and saw further action, before being killed during the Battle of Arras on 12 May 1917.

Early in 1916, shortly before the Somme, the government brought in the Military Service Act which legalized conscription for single men aged 18-41, but allowed those opposed to military service on conscience grounds to appeal to local tribunals for exemption. The military leaders were desperate for more troops, the British Expeditionary Force having suffered dreadful casualties in France, and as they were hoping to extend conscription to include married men also, they particularly wanted to prevent single men evading service as Conscientious Objectors. Many men were opposed to conscription, for a number of reasons, some of which were religious, political or philosophical, and a Non-Combatant Corps had been formed into which those who refused to fight could be drafted to undertake non-aggressive manual tasks. Richmond Castle was re-opened as a base for them in May 1916. Those with the strongest convictions refused to accept military orders, such as to wear military uniform, and could thus be court-martialled.

Determined to make examples of the most troublesome 'conchies', the military authorities secretly transported sixteen from Richmond Castle to France where, as it was an active war zone, it was permissible to put them before a firing squad if they disobeyed an order, however fatuous. In the end, events including Lord Kitchener's death early in June intervened, and they were not shot, but they were subjected to torturous punishments, which were a disgrace to Britain. Although it was a time of national crisis, these events were so shameful that records of them have been hushed up by successive government and military authorities. Probably the most important surviving documentation survives in the block of punishment cells, beside the gatehouse in Richmond Castle, in which the 'prisoners of conscience' were held. On the limewashed walls of those eight small cells they wrote in pencil details of their thoughts and what happened to them when and where. The graffiti is very fragile, and has only survived by default for, apart from a brief similar use at the beginning of World War II, the cells have been used only for storage of such things as grass mowers. Attempts failed to have them opened to scholars, let alone the public, partly on the legitimate grounds that people entering such small spaces would create both physical wear and tear and also environmental damage. Only after a harrowing television programme made by Tyne Tees Television and broadcast in January 1995, was English Heritage persuaded to pursue a method of presentation, and modern computer technology allowed a 'virtual reality' touch-screen machine showing details of the cells finally to be installed in the Castle in 1999.

A Voluntary Aid Detachment was formed in Richmond late in 1914, and several of the town's larger houses served as convalescent hospitals for the war wounded. Frenchgate House, vacant after the deaths in 1913 of the Misses Ryder, was used as a 36-bed hospital, and Swale House provided additional hospital facilities from 1916. Bonfires were lit in the Market Place to celebrate the end of the Great War in 1918. Many maimed and wounded men returned home to Richmond, as to other settlements: many others did not return. A War Memorial, bearing 101 names, with a Garden of Remembrance for the town's fallen, was created in 1920 where there had been wartime allotments next to the Friary. This work necessitated the lowering of the ground in the ruins of the Grey Friars' choir, but sadly no record was made of any archaeological discoveries. The appearance of Queens Road was further changed by the construction of the row of semi-detached houses in 1920.

In 1921 a separate memorial to the fallen of the Green Howards Regiment was created at Frenchgate Head, opposite the bottom of Gallowgate where it would be seen by all those going to and from the Barracks. The names of those members of the Green Howards who were killed are kept in a book of remembrance in the Regimental Chapel formed in the south chancel aisle of St. Mary's Parish Church. The furniture there was made by Robert Thompson of Kilburn, each piece having on it his distinctive mark - a mouse. During the work of creating the memorial chapel, the sedilia, piscina and aumbry associated with the chantry of St. Katherine were uncovered, together with traces of wall paintings, indicating that in medieval times this church, like that at Easby, had frescoes. In 1923 the church bells were re-tuned and re-hung, there are eight bells, and the same fine peal is still rung for weddings and Sunday morning services. The Victorian galleries had been removed from the church in 1921.

Later in the century a new high altar and reredos were installed as a memorial to the Second World War, and later still a freestanding altar was made for the nave in accordance with changes in liturgical fashion. Towards the end of the century, a further major restoration was carried out, and while the church was closed in 1989 the congregation was welcomed in great ecumenical spirit into a temporary home in the Roman Catholic church. Redecoration in 1993 was followed by the removal of the baptistery to the north aisle and the creation of new social facilities at the west end in 1997. Other changes have included the interment of ashes in the churchyard as many people opted for cremation rather than burial, the introduction of lay readers, the Alternative Service Book and, controversially, the ordaining of women. The trail-blazer in the Richmond Rural Deanery was Rev. Jennifer Williamson, first curate in the Easby group of parishes and then priest-in-charge of Gilling West and Kirkby Ravensworth. By the end of the century the religious denominations of the town were co-operating in holding joint services for special occasions under the heading Churches Together in Richmond - Church of England, Methodist and Roman Catholic, and the Pentecostal Church which was established in the 1950s. There is also the Kingdom Hall of the Jehovah's Witnesses in Castle Wynd.

In 1921 the title of Bishop of Richmond ceased to be used for a suffragan bishop in the Diocese of Ripon. There were two Bishops of Richmond, John James Pulleine 1888-1913 and Francis Charles Kilner 1913-21. Another memorial to the Great War was the opening in the Market Place in 1920 of a Young Men's Christian Association meeting place for soldiers at Catterick Camp. The funding for this was contributed largely by the Richmond Meet. A leisure facility much supported during

World War I was the showing of cinema films. The first moving picture show had come to Richmond in 1909 in the form of Randall Williams Travelling Movies, which were shown in a marquee erected in the Market Place outside the King's Head Hotel. Music was supplied by a portable organ. The front seats cost 3d. while standing room on a ramp behind was 2d. The next year two enterprising Richmond men built a wooden building near the Cricket Field in Victoria Road where they showed films alternating with music hall turns. The third and most ambitious attempt came in 1911 when Thomas Pinder rented the Market Hall from the Corporation and started a twice-nightly show. The screen was just inside the present entrance and was lowered a few minutes before the performances began at 7pm and 9pm. The projector was situated on a platform at the other end of the hall. Power to operate it and to light the hall was supplied from a belt-driven dynamo powered by a petrol engine, Richmond not having electricity until 1926. Music was supplied by a foot-operated pianola playing musical rolls. Mrs. Pinder took the money at a portable pay box at the entrance. Then in 1915 a purpose-built cinema was built by a Darlington man, Robert Hastwell, at the corner of Ryder's Wynd and Queens Road. The manager was Joe French, who appeared each evening in immaculate evening dress. Hastwell's new enterprise developed various teething troubles, and Pinder took advantage of this by circulating throughout the town playbills pointedly headed "Pinder's Perfect Pictures". Pinder competed in another way, by building his own cinema of wood and asbestos at West Wood, about half way between Richmond and the fast developing Catterick Camp. He called it Westwood Palace, and the site is now marked only by part of the concrete base alongside the road. Pinder's Market Hall cinema came to an end as a result of a fire in 1923, but the Queens Road building survives as Rodber's hardware shop, having become a Bingo Hall after closing as a cinema. In 1938 a second cinema, the Zetland, was built in Victoria Road by the Darlington firm of Messrs. Dougills, it lasted until the late 1970s, and then in 1982 was converted by the Pentecostal Church into the Zetland Christian Community Centre.

Richmond had from the beginning of the 20th century a number of sports facilities. Football was played, there was even a Zetland League, and in Victoria Road there was the present cricket ground, around which was an athletics track, while a golf course was created at Bend Hagg Farm. The river Swale, however, provided many local leisure facilities. The pool above Whicliffe Mill weir was used as a lido, with steps and primitive changing rooms, and the paper mill's large dams were used for skating in winter. The smooth sheet of water above the Easby Mill weir was used for rowing boats in Edwardian times, and the small cottage at Backhouse Ings came to be called Boat House Cottage. An angling society was formed in 1912, one of its founders being Charles Spencer the gunmaker, and its Honorary Secretary from then until his death in 1963 was the historian (Leslie) Peter Wenham's father, Peter Charles Wenham, who had then just come to Richmond as assistant to the Town Clerk, from a similar position at Hythe in Kent.

The river Swale was also the inspiration, which caused a Richmond man to feature for a short time in the national press. Robert Hey (1875-1954) was born in Middlesbrough but lived in Richmond for most of his life, where he became known for his inventive mind and skill at healing sick animals. Greatly disturbed at the appalling loss of life in British and American submarine disasters of 1925 and 1927, he invented a device - which unfortunately he never patented - for "saving crews from sunken submarines". He experimented successfully with his apparatus in the deep pool of the river Swale just above the copper mine in Billy Banks Wood, near where he lived on the Green. He wrote to the naval powers of the time - Britain, France, Germany, Italy, Japan and the U.S.A., but was chagrined when an American inventor received both financial reward and personal recognition for an invention very similar to his own. Feeling that he had been cheated, he took a horse-drawn caravan round various cities in the Midlands and North of England, and held meetings advocating his claim, but to no avail. Robert Hey's sense of injustice was exacerbated by hardship, for it was a time of little work, and there was a shortage of coal during the General

Strike of 1926, despite the town's proximity to the coalfields of County Durham. Mothers took their children and prams to forage and fetch wood from the surrounding countryside for the kitchen fires on which they were dependent for cooking, baking and heating water.

In 1927 Richmond was on the centre line of totality of an eclipse of the sun. The Royal Observatory and other scientific institutions took up vantage points at such places as Olliver Ducket and the Grandstand to view this rare phenomenon. A few minutes before totality occurred clouds obscured the sun and the visible eclipse was, sadly lost, but the onset of near darkness and a dramatic drop in the temperature were vividly remembered by those who were there. A reminder of that eclipse still remains in Richmond in the form of an old AA sign on a wall near the junction of West Terrace and Quaker Lane, and there was consternation when the sign disappeared in 1996, but it turned out that it had been removed only temporarily because it had become loose. The mayor in 1927, James Eyles, acted as host to several days of events over the period when vast crowds flocked to Richmond, and he raised money for the repair of the tower of Holy Trinity Chapel, which had recently been exposed by the demolition of some of the properties clinging around it. The restoration of the tower was supervized by Mr. Rutherford, the eminent architect of York's new Deanery. The removal of some of the shops attached to Holy Trinity Chapel had been begun in 1923.

In 1929 there were celebrations to mark the sex-centenary of the granting to Richmond of a charter by King Edward III in 1329. The main event was an elaborate pageant illustrating the town's history, written by Avalon Collard who was involved with light opera productions in Darlington, and performed by a large cast of local residents. The stage was set up in Temple Grounds, in front of the natural auditorium of Tenter Bank, the hillside adjoining the Culloden Tower. The inspiration for putting on the pageant came from W.W. Foster, the Town Clerk, whose daughter Marjory played Frances I'Anson, the Lass of Richmond Hill. An ox was roasted in the Market Place by the town's butchers, slices of the meat being sold for 1s. 6d. on commemorative plates, now collectors' items, naming the mayor, George Wade, a builder who lived at Ronaldshay House in Wellington Place.

The musical life of Richmond took a new direction in 1929 when Dr. Arthur James Bull moved to the town to take up the post of music master at Richmond Grammar School. He also taught at the Girls' High School, and became organist and choir-master at St. Mary's Parish Church. He gave music lessons to countless children, taught adult education classes, worked as County Music Organiser for the North Riding and led various orchestras and choirs. Having a long working life, which lasted until he died at the age of 90 in 1991, he nurtured a love of music and high standards of musicianship on several generations of people. During World War II he recruited for his orchestras several distinguished musicians who found themselves posted to Catterick Camp. His daughter and son-in-law, Katherine and Tom Carr, have also continued his musical legacy by continuing to organize and support numerous activities such as the Richmond Subscription Concerts and the Swaledale Festival for the rest of the century. Dr. Bull was an ardent Socialist, and was in Richmond during the Depression years in the early 1930s. In 1931 some of the Jarrow Marchers spent a night in the Market Hall on their way to London. A Richmond haulier, George Henry Firby, supplied them with bales of straw on which they slept.

Katherine Carr has several times served as Mayor of Richmond and as Chairman of Richmondshire District Council, following a succession of women who have held public office in the town since the 1930s. The first woman mayor was Mrs Mary (Minnie) Hodgson, who held the office for three consecutive years 1932-34. She was followed by Miss Ruth Roper who likewise served for three years 1934-37. The 1930s also witnessed one of the heaviest falls of snow ever experienced in the town, when several feet of snow fell on the night of 25/26 February 1933. The pattern of having regularly to increase the volume of water supplied to the town continued, with a new reservoir being created beside the Whashton road to store water from the Coalsgarth spring. It was opened in the year of King George V's Silver Jubilee in 1935. The Coronation of King George VI in 1937 is commemorated by the name in Reeth Road of Coronation Place for a new street of council houses built in that year. The town had built its first twenty council houses in Fontenay Road in 1923.

In 1938 a young architect, Denis Clarke Hall, won a national competition set by the *News Chronicle* to design an ideal school. Shortly afterwards, he was commissioned by the Board of Education for the North Riding to design new buildings for Richmond High School for Girls, established in 1920 with 57 girls to provide grammar school education for girls, its first headmistress being Miss D.O. Shepherd, and its motto "Quest Conquest". In 1940 the school moved from its old building in Frenchgate, now St. Agatha's, into its new buildings, the design of which was based on the principles of the Modern Movement in architecture. Load-bearing walls built of local stone were blended with flat-roofed buildings constructed of cast in-situ concrete frames. The effect of the whole was not only pleasing and popular with girls and teachers, but it was so highly regarded by the architectural profession that it became a model for many post-war schools.

The outbreak of World War II in 1939 brought yet more soldiers to Richmond. They filled up Catterick Camp, the Barracks in Gallowgate, and also the new camp of utilitarian brick buildings put up to the north of Green Howards Road. The top of the Castle keep made a useful fire-watching post. Richmond men were again called up for military service, in even greater numbers than during the Great War. The published roll-call just of Old Boys of Richmond Grammar School who had been called up by 1945 numbered 353, of whom 29 were killed. The most highly decorated was Alan Broadley, DSO, DFC, DFM, an RAF navigator killed while on a secret mission over France in 1944. A vivid memory of all those in Richmond during the war years was the noise and vibration caused by the explosion of an ammunitions train at Catterick Bridge Railway Station in 1944. Twelve people were killed, both civilian and army personnel, including the Station Master, a number were injured and the Railway Hotel next door was ruined.

    The Mayor for all the war years was a veteran of the Great War, having served at Gallipoli, William Robinson, who worked at Robson Wood and Co, the old-established drapers in Finkle Street. He and his wife, Dolly, served the town devotedly, particularly during those six hard years. During the weeks of 1-7 August 1943 and 6-13 August 1944 the town participated in a Holidays at Home scheme intended to cheer people up in the darkest days of the war. For the 1943 event there was a theme based on a celebration of the 850th anniversary of the town's alleged first charter. It may have been mistaken but the intention was typical of the man behind it, David Brooks, Town Clerk of Richmond 1941-56, who left to go to Broken Hill in Northern Rhodesia and died in Canada in 1971. A native of Essex, he was a staunch upholder of Richmond customs and traditions, and with his dynamic personality did much to arouse interest in its heritage. In 1946 he wrote and published his *Story of Richmond*, a copy of which was given to every school-child in Richmond to mark the end of World War II.

    David Brooks was also largely responsible for a high compliment paid to Richmond in 1945. At the end of the war the British Council was anxious to re-kindle interest in tourism, and commissioned an exhibition of photographs to tour Europe. Three places were chosen as representative of the British way of life - Salisbury as a cathedral city, Leicester as a manufacturing town and Richmond as a market town. Photographs were taken of contemporary activities to illustrate all aspects of life in those places: over one hundred pictures were taken in Richmond. They give a vivid and unique picture of a place basically the same but so different in detail from the Richmond of today.

    The end of World War II in 1945 was marked by the lighting of the town beacon, and 54 more names were added to the Friary Gardens War Memorial. There were still many shortages of food and fuel when there was another very severe winter in early 1947, with snow and frost persisting for several

Changes in elementary school education are illustrated by these photographs from the National School at Lombards Wynd taken in 1945 and the Richmond Church of England Primary School, taken in 1981.

Looking down Frenchgate 1945 and 1995

weeks. When the snow eventually melted, it over-loaded the street drains and could not escape into the exceptionally high river Swale, causing severe flooding in Bridge Street which resulted in a new storm water pipe being installed just below the Green Bridge. The old tanneries, brewery and other run-down buildings on the river side of the Green were replaced by new council houses, called Bridge Terrace, using the old stone which has meant they have not looked out of place in the famous views of the town from Billy Banks Wood. This started a tradition for particularly well-designed social housing, which continued throughout the 1950s. Near to Bridge Terrace, on the north side of St. James Chapel Wynd, other old buildings were demolished and flats were built around the time of the Festival of Britain in 1951. Earl Edwin Drive off Gilling Road was also planned in a Modern Movement layout. Back in Bargate, more flats were built, Temple Court, using stone from the demolished Whitcliffe Paper Mill, which closed in 1947 after the snow-melt that Spring swept away its weir across the river Swale, the three chimneys being demolished in 1949. The Market Place was opened up by the demolition of the Toll Booth in 1948, on the grounds that it was infested with rats, and it was also obstructing the flow of traffic, particularly buses, of which there were many during and just after World War II.

      One of the most heavily used bus services was that between Richmond and Catterick Camp, a service begun in 1919 by Albert Brand, a businessman who at that time owned The Grove in Frenchgate, and in 1925 he built a garage on part of his land abutting Queens Road, the building now being Calvert's Carpets. Catterick Camp continued to be intensively used during the years of National Service 1948-60. Many men who are middle-aged or elderly at the end of the century still have vivid memories of part of their youth spent in or near Richmond. For thousands of them, arriving by train at Richmond Station was their last taste of normality before they embarked on the rigours of the eight weeks basic training required of National Service conscripts. Trying to climb into a three-ton truck whilst carrying a large suitcase was perhaps the first indignity of many to come.

The sense of discipline created by the uncompromising training staff at the Camp was for many an asset, which stood them in good stead for the rest of their lives. Catterick Camp was then infamous for its cold and wet conditions, and nature continued to play its part in the history of 20th century Richmond. Exceptional weather conditions included, in addition to the winter of 1947, major thunderstorms which deposited huge hailstones in August 1930, and a major flood after heavy snow in 1963, which breached the weir of Easby Mill. This destroyed the appearance of the river as far up as Clink Pool, for shallow and rough water replaced the smooth sheet, which had allowed the boats to operate. On August Bank Holiday 1986 the tail-end of Hurricane Charlie produced a great deluge, particularly in Arkengarthdale, which created tremendous floods and caused great danger and misery to many holiday-makers in the area, especially caravanners and campers.

Richmond has always cherished its links with the military, particularly the Green Howards Regiment, whose Regimental Headquarters and Museum has since 1973 been housed in Holy Trinity Chapel, although the chancel is retained as a chapel of ease. Regimental Secretaries have included Lt. Col. Geoffrey Thomas More Scrope, a very unassuming man despite having a most distinguished Yorkshire ancestry, who died in 1981, and Lt. Col. Neil McIntosh, a charismatic swash-buckling soldier, who took the Museum into the 21st century. Since the Second World War the regiment has had particularly close ties with Norway. In 1940 the Green Howards gallantly went to the aid of that country, which was suffering great hardship at the hands of Germany, and ensured the safe evacuation of many from the port of Aandalsnes. Norwegians still feel great affection for this assistance. In 1942 King Haakon VII of Norway became Colonel-in-Chief of the Regiment, and he was granted the Freedom of Richmond in 1945. The regiment also has the Freedom to march through Richmond with bayonets fixed. King Haakon was succeeded as both king and as Colonel-in-Chief by his son, Olaf V, who was presented with the Freedom in 1983, and was a regular and popular visitor to Richmond until his death in 1991. Now his son King Harald V is Colonel-in-Chief. Because of these ties with Norway, Richmond became 'twinned' with the Norwegian town of Nord-Fron in 1984.

In 1964 the 8th Royal Corps of Signals, based at Catterick, was also presented with the Freedom of Richmond, in honour of which the Station Bridge was renamed Mercury Bridge in 1975, Mercury being their badge. The RAF Regiment, based at RAF Catterick, was also granted the Freedom. Both these military units moved their bases from the area in 1993. However all three put on Freedom marches in the town in that year, during the second mayoralty of Angela Harris, who was also Chief Steward of the Liberal-Democrat Party Conference that summer. In 1999 she was to be given a life-peerage, taking the title of Baroness Harris of Richmond. RAF Catterick closed after the departure of the Regiment, but this soon afterwards was taken over by Catterick Garrison and re-named Marne Barracks. In 1996 the Freedom of Richmond was presented to the company of the new frigate HMS Richmond, launched in 1993.

The Green Howards Barracks in Gallowgate was closed by the Ministry of Defence in 1961. The building was transferred to the Home Office for use as an Approved School, which then became a Community School under the Social Services Department of North Yorkshire County Council. The Barracks was sold in 1983 for private housing, and was somewhat incongruously re-named The Garden Village, and the Gymnasium was eventually taken over as a Sports Hall by Richmondshire District Council which had declined to acquire the Barracks as its headquarters. Other areas developed for private housing in the second half of the century have included Bolton Crofts in the 1960s, Whitefields in the 1970s, and Pilmoor Hill in the 1980s and 1990s. Such expansion put further strain on the town's water supply, and eventually this was switched to a bore-hole at Catterick. Several of the larger old houses were transferred to institutional use in the post-war years. Swale House became local authority offices, Prior House and Earls Orchard became residential field centres run by outside education authorities, and a large house in Quaker Lane became a rest home for the wives of

Durham Miners, named after Sam Watson, the national chairman of the Labour Party who had once spoken in Richmond in 1950. Several developments of sheltered housing for the elderly appeared from the late 1960s starting with Lile Close, then Queens Court, in Queens Road, followed by St. Agatha's in the former premises of the High School for Girls in Frenchgate in 1981, where a new extension was added on the back in a manner sympathetic to its sensitive location next to St. Mary's Parish Church. Anchor Court in Ryder's Wynd was a further sheltered housing development opened in 1985.

Following the success of the purpose-built new High School for Girls, the boys' Grammar School, which had been added to in 1937, was given further extensions including a new hall incorporating an old doorway from St. James' Chapel which had been discovered in 1949-50. A new Secondary Modern School was built on Darlington Road in 1959, the headmaster appointed being Harry Fowler, who in retirement would become the first Town Clerk after local authority reorganisation in 1974. St. Francis Xavier School, a new secondary school for Roman Catholics, was also built on Darlington Road, and would eventually forge links as a joint church school with the Church of England. The old denominational elementary schools became Junior Schools - Church of England in Lombards Wynd, Roman Catholic in Reeth Road, Methodist in Quaker Lane. All three would move into new buildings on or near Darlington Road before the century was out. Further reorganisation of secondary education took place in 1971, when the comprehensive Richmond School absorbed the former Grammar, Girls' High and Secondary Modern schools. The former Grammar School in Station Road became the Low School for the first years only, the Secondary Modern became the Middle School, and the High School the Upper School. The headmaster of the Grammar School, Derek Dutton, became head of the new school, and remained so until his retirement in 1991.

Richmond's parliamentary representation has continued to be of some historic interest, though despite the town's Liberal traditions more recent Members have been Tories. From the

1920s the Member was Sir Thomas Lionel Dugdale, later Lord Crathorne. Chairman of the Conservative Party in the late 1940s, he resigned his seat in 1954 over the Crichel Down controversy. Sir Timothy Kitson was Parliamentary Private Secretary to Prime Minister Sir Edward Heath. Sir Leon Brittan held many government posts, including that of Home Secretary, resigning from the front bench over the Westland affair in 1986. His becoming a European Commissioner in 1988 caused a by-election early in 1989 which could have changed the face of British Parliamentary politics in a different way. The strong local candidate, Mike Potter, standing as a Social Democrat, might well have won the seat and thus kept that short-lived party alive, but instead he was challenged by the Liberal-Democrats, so splitting the 'middle ground' vote. As it was the young Conservative candidate, unknown except for a famous TV clip as a sixteen-year old comprehensive schoolboy receiving a standing ovation led by Margaret Thatcher at the 1977 Conservative Party Conference, won the Richmond seat. His 1989 victory made William Hague the last Conservative to win a by-election in the 20th century. After the Labour Party won the last general election of the century on 1 May 1997 he became Leader of the Conservative Party and thus Leader of the Opposition. A bachelor when he first sat as Member for Richmond, William Hague then married Ffion Jenkins who has ably supported him in his constituency.

The name of Nancy, Lady Crathorne, will always be associated with the restoration of the Georgian Theatre. It was an immense achievement when it eventually re-opened in May 1963. The fact that the old theatre survived almost intact had been discovered during the Second World War by Edwin Bush, History Master at Richmond Grammar School, and David Brooks, the Town Clerk, had the building tidied up sufficiently for local amateur players to present plays on the stage during the Holidays at Home weeks in 1943 and 1944. In the latter year plays were presented by Daniel Thorndike, nephew of Dame Sybil Thorndike, then a lieutenant in the Royal Artillery based at Catterick Camp. However, it was only in 1960 that the Georgian Theatre Trust was established by Lady Crathorne, and then it still had much fund-raising to do before the building could be fully investigated and restored. Since 1963 it has become a much-loved amenity, a venue for an amazing variety of entertainment and cultural activities, and an asset, which a town the size of Richmond would otherwise not have.

It became the Georgian Theatre Royal through the courtesy of Queen Elizabeth II in 1984, it having seen many royal visitors through its doors both in Georgian times and since its revival. It is run by a very small number of paid staff and a huge number of volunteers. In the early days it was devotedly run by Edith Fairbrother, and after her husband Bill retired as Borough Treasurer he became Theatre Manager. During the time of his successor, Gregor McGregor, an adjacent warehouse was converted into a Theatre Museum, officially opened by the TV personality Richard Baker in 1979. Local retired art teacher Bryan Rochford took over for some years, to be followed by Les Jobson, formerly of the Billingham Forum theatre. The Manager up to the end of the century and beyond was Bill Sellars, who had been the producer of the immensely popular BBC TV series *All Creatures Great and Small*. Monica Hill has been the long-serving assistant to several managers. Lady Penelope Zetland, the 3rd Marchioness, was a tireless worker for the theatre. Long-serving stalwart volunteers have included Fay Campion, Frank Dickinson and Lilian Willis. For many years Peggy Holmes ran the box office, followed by Gladys Bramham. Familiar faces regularly serving in the bar have included Betty Freeman, Dick and Olive Severs, and more recently Jim and Sheila Russell. When a coffee bar was added to the facilities, it was run for many years by Pam Grundy. Nancy Crathorne's son, Lord Crathorne, is now Lord Lieutenant of North Yorkshire, and his wife Sylvia is the Chairman of the Trust.

During the 1960s the former Richmond army camp was converted into the Gallowfields Trading Estate. Non-retail businesses were encouraged to re-locate away from the town centre and residential areas, and the availability of grants and suitable premises, including many purpose-built small factory units, has enabled many more businesses to start up. One of the largest businesses established there was the Fairfield Shoe Factory, the town's largest employer in the 1970s. After its closure the shoe-making skills of some of its staff resulted in the opening of Alt-berg, a small factory, which is the country's only specialist maker of boots. The amount of traffic generated by the trading estate, plus the location in Gallowgate of the Fire, Ambulance and Police stations, led to the town's first and only set of traffic lights being installed at the junction of Gallowgate and Pottergate in 1981. The trend towards almost universal car ownership during the century caused great problems in a hill town with narrow streets and many houses some distance away from suitable parking places. The rail link with Richmond was threatened by Lord Beeching's proposals to eliminate most rural lines in 1963, but it was reprieved for some years, finally closing in 1968. However, the passenger station had earlier been included in the Statutory List of Buildings of Special Architectural or Historic Interest, and this was crucial to what happened later. The station complex site was acquired by the Richmond Rural District Council, for recreational use, and the line became part of a popular circular footpath to Easby using the old Iron Bridge.

Discussions about the future of the passenger station included a suggestion that it might become a Museum of Horse-Drawn Carriages, based on the collection of Richmond builder George Shaw, but in the end it became a Farm and Garden Supply Centre. The goods station was demolished and an award-winning swimming pool was built on the site. Designed by the Napper, Errington, Collerton Partnership of Newcastle-upon-Tyne, it was opened in 1975, European Architectural Heritage Year, by the Countess of Dartmouth, daughter of the authoress Barbara Cartland, and later to become better known as Raine, Countess Spencer, step-mother of Diana, Princess of Wales. The engine shed was converted to workshop units in 1988, but these eventually became a gym and health club, a use compatible with the swimming pool. The same firm of Newcastle architects who had produced the pool also designed a new pavilion for the football field on Earls Orchard in 1974, and were commissioned to make proposals for a Country Park from Easby Bridge to Lownethwaite Bridge along the south bank of the Swale, but this was not proceeded with. A new footbridge had been built in 1971, crossing the river from near the site of Whitcliffe Mill to Round Howe. The nearby Hudswell Woods had become National Trust land in 1938.

The First Fruits Ceremony in 1954 with Mayor Miss Ruth Roper and Town Clerk David Brooks

The 1974 reorganisation of local government resulted in Richmond losing its status as an independent borough. The successor authority, Richmondshire District Council, which took over responsibility for Richmond and also four rural districts, is however still based in Richmond, using several buildings in the town centre as offices. The first Chief Executive of Richmondshire District Council was Bert Hodge, from Richmond

Rural District Council, the second was Malcolm Tooze, the last Town Clerk of the old Borough of Richmond. After losing the status of borough, the new Richmond Town Council only has the status of a parish council, but the position of mayor, re-titled the Town Mayor, was retained along with those of Town Clerk, Serjeants-at-mace and halberdiers. The Town Council continues to use the borough council chamber, extended and refurnished in 1956. Many ancient but small charities were amalgamated in 1987 to mint a special coin, the Richmond Shilling, given to pensioners each Christmas. That the pageantry was preserved in 1974 was due to some resurgence of appreciation of the town's heritage, generally out of fashion since the end of World War II. The demolition of the Toll Booth had been followed in the early 1950s by the clearance of cottages at the west end of the Green, once the handsome stable block designed by John Carr for Yorke House, and now the Yorke Square car park. In 1958 a service in the Friary grounds commemorated the 700th anniversary of the founding of the Richmond Grey Friars. In 1969 Church Mill was demolished, despite a vociferous campaign to save it and make it into a museum, and The Batts was made into a recreational area, and the old gas works was cleared shortly afterwards. Grants were available for the removal of 'eyesores', as such historic buildings were then regarded.

    This was the climate in which Richmond and District Civic Society was founded when 35 members of the public attended a meeting in the Town Hall on 24 January 1967, a few months before the Civic Amenities Act of August of that year advocated the setting up of civic societies. The first chairman was the history master at Richmond Grammar School, Tom Carr, and the secretary Audrey Carr (no relation). Audrey and her mother Julia Ghent were to produce several interesting books on the 20th century history of Richmond. The School provided the Civic Society with its next two chairmen, French master Eric Tyson, and physics master Frank Dickinson, who was chairman in European Architectural Heritage Year, 1975. In 1976 Rev. A.A. 'Dick' Harrison took over the reins, followed in 1978 by Peter Wenham, back in his birthplace in retirement having been

Head of the History Department at St. John's College of Education in York. He remained Chairman until his death in 1990. Despite losing its early fight to save Church Mill, the civic society has continued to work long and hard on conservation matters, and has had many successes in encouraging a more sympathetic attitude towards the town's rich heritage, publishing from 1978 an annual journal, *The Richmond Review*, and since 1984 putting up over twenty information plaques around the town. In 1971 Richmond was designated an Outstanding Conservation Area, a status enabling a Town Scheme to be set up in 1976 which, for the next 18 years, stimulated restoration work to the value of over £1 million on Richmond's historic buildings by generating grants from central and local government.

Also in 1971 a summer festival was held to celebrate the 900th anniversary of the town's foundation by Alan Rufus. Concerts, banquets and pageants were put on, notably inside the Castle. This may be seen as the start of the late-20th century tourist boom, which was greatly to benefit the local economy. It was followed by a number of biannual Richmond Festivals, largely organised by musician Dr. A.J. Bull and his son-in-law Tom Carr, and later these became the annual Swaledale Festivals, covering a larger geographical area and offering a wider programme of cultural events. Other popular events are staged regularly by Richmond Operatic Society, founded in 1922, and Richmond Amateur Dramatic Society. Summer floral displays, Christmas lights and the floodlighting of the Castle keep have been introduced as amenity expectations rose. Towards the end of the century as the idea of 'living history' presentations spread from the United States, historical re-enactments have been regularly staged in the Castle.

Richmondshire District Council appointed its first Tourism Officer in 1987, and put up 'Welcome to Richmondshire' road signs the following year. Three elements of the growth of tourism deserve individual mention. The first was the 'Coast to Coast Walk' devised by Alfred Wainwright in 1973, a 190-mile walk from St. Bees Head on the Cumbrian coast to Robin Hood's Bay on the Yorkshire coast, which passes through

Richmond and brings many long-distance walkers for an overnight stay in the town. The second was the screening on BBC Television in 1978 of the programme on Richmond in the first series of Alec Clifton-Taylor's *Six English Towns*. The third was the James Herriot phenomenon. The popular books written by Thirsk vet Alf Wight under the famous pseudonym actually had little or nothing to do with Richmond or the Yorkshire Dales, but the films and TV programmes, shown around the world, used locations in Richmond itself and other local spots, and brought many thousands of devoted fans to the area, from abroad as well as from Great Britain, the number of such visitors reaching a peak in the mid-1980s.

Town meets country. Sheep being
Driven through the town to their
Autumn grazing.

The 'set' of James Herriot's surgery from the first *All Creatures Great and Small* TV series was purchased by the Richmondshire Museum and opened by Alf Wight himself in 1984. Many thousands of Herriot fans have since made their pilgrimage to see it there. The Richmondshire Museum opened in Ryders Wynd in 1978, after a four-year long effort by a group of volunteers to find a suitable building for a museum devoted to the town's heritage. They were persuaded to call it the Richmondshire Museum by the then Chief Executive of Richmondshire District Council, Bert Hodge. As the leading lights of the group which worked so hard to create the Museum included Eric Tyson as Chairman and Peter Wenham as Honorary Curator, it may be seen as one of the several parallel bodies spawned by Richmond and District Civic Society. Others include two now defunct, the Richmond Family Surname Society, and the Richmondshire Preservation Trust, a rolling fund set up in 1978 to restore heritage buildings, which repaired an attractive dovecote at Forcett.

Many good conservation projects were undertaken in the town in the last few decades of the 20th century. Some were small, such as the re-cutting of the inscriptions on the Green Bridge in 1975, others were more costly, such as the rescue of Culloden Tower in 1982 by the Landmark Trust, a national charity which takes on buildings of outstanding importance for which no everyday use is possible and turns them into superior holiday cottages. The restoration was overseen by the leading conservation architect Martin Stancliffe of York, later to become Surveyor to the Fabric of St. Paul's Cathedral. Only a few developments have been proposed which would have threatened the unspoilt character of Richmond, and these have been resisted, such as the hotel, golf-course and time-share complex at Red House Farm, Easby turned down after a public inquiry in 1991. The applicant turned instead to rearing wild boar, and to contain the animals erected a hideous metal fence alongside Love Lane, creating an effect, which outraged those who used the attractive footpath there. The fence was removed and Red House Farm returned to traditional agricultural use. A successful outcome to a happier saga can be recorded for Temple Lodge and the grounds, which once formed the famous landscaped garden to Yorke House. For much of the 20th century this little estate belonged to the family of Richmond clockmaker Robert Murray. His widow and unmarried daughters Jessie, Lettie and Mary continued to live at Temple Lodge until Mary died at the age of 99 in 1991. She bequeathed the estate to descendants of the Rev. Lawson from whom her father had bought it, and Dr. Richard Lawson, his wife Morven and their two children moved up from Devon and energetically began work on the house and estate. The importance of Temple Grounds was recognized in 1995 when it was included in English Heritage's Register of Historic Parks and Gardens.

Some conservation projects have failed, the most significant being that to restore the once-fine grandstand on the former racecourse. This was kept in reasonable repair until the end of the Second World War. Richmond Corporation then removed the lead from the roof and the building quickly deteriorated, so they partly demolished it in 1969 despite its being a listed building. Efforts to interest the Landmark Trust in the building have been unsuccessful, and although the Vivat Trust undertook to take on the project in 1990 they have since withdrawn. The town's noble racing tradition had almost been lost by the Millennium. The trainer J.W. Watts, whose famous horse Teleprompter was formally welcomed back to Richmond by the then mayor, Ron May, after winning the fifth Budweiser-Arlington Million race at Arlington Park, Chicago in 1985, left Richmond in 1997, and his successor, Ann Swinbank, moved to Constable Burton in 1999. Hurgill Lodge, a new stables built by Lord Zetland in 1938, and the base of famous trainer Harry Peacock in the 1940s and 1950s, now stands empty.

A somewhat different 'horse' from Richmond's past was successfully revived in the 1980s. 'Poor Old Horse' or, in dialect, T'Owd Hoss, was an ancient Christmas custom perambulated from one public house to another. Doggerel verse recounts the horse's fate. In its youth it was the pride of its master and was cosseted and well fed, but as it grew old it was neglected and rejected and eventually fit only for the knacker's yard. At the end of the recital the horse rolls on its back with its legs feebly waving in the air.

The chief actor, representing the horse, is clothed in a horse's skin, worn and ragged to indicate its age, with a short stump for a tail. The head and neck can be turned, the jaws open and close and the loud snapping of the teeth during the chorus at the end of each verse is an essential part of the act. Accompanying the horse is a small band, together with two 'huntsmen' with long whips, which are cracked during the performance. In 1999 a painting of a performance of this Christmas tradition, by local artist Bill Ward, who was the chief instigator of the Hoss's revival, was purchased by Richmond Town Council and hangs in the Town Hall.

Another revived institution is the Company of Fellmongers, which was refounded in 1981 by Richmond solicitor Ralph Waggett and Peter Wenham after the record book of that ancient Richmond guild, covering the period 1666-1820, came up for auction in London and was brought back to the town. There was considerable discussion about what form the revived company should take, and who should be eligible for membership, and to the disappointment of this author it was decided that women should be excluded, although invited as guests to some dinners. It still seems a surprising decision to have taken, not only because of the social and economic climate in 1981 but also because women were not debarred by gender in the past. The reason was due in part to the present men-only format of the Company of Mercers, Grocers and Haberdashers, which has survived continuously since medieval times. However, the Fellmongers have revived the educational role of ancient craft guilds by inaugurating awards for apprentices, and they hosted an historic gathering in 1989 when they welcomed to lunch the Lord Mayor of London, Sir Christopher Collett and his Lady, during the 8th centenary of that office.

Most of the Georgian and Victorian shop fronts were removed from the town centre in the 1950s and 1960s. As in most towns, small privately-owned shops have dwindled in number and chain stores increased, though the change has been less marked here than in most places. A chain store was responsible for a major conservation success when Woolworths relocated into Bailey House in 1980. The building work involved shoring up the huge three-storey and eight-bay front wall, which had little foundation as three shop fronts had been inserted into its ground floor, and tying this to a new internal structure which extended out to the rear in a form carefully modelled so as to blend into distant views. This scheme saved a prominent building at the bottom of the Market Place, and also gave the town an enlarged store selling a wide range of merchandise.

Boots also invested in larger premises, in 1991 doubling the size of their shop by extending into the adjacent building previously occupied by the old-established drapers Hodgson's, which closed in 1990. The even older Robson Wood & Co. had closed in 1983. The ironmonger's shop of Robert Spence & Co. had closed in 1970, as had the chemist Newton Clarkson, whose fittings were removed to Preston Park Museum at Stockton-on-Tees. A small shop remembered with particular affection by many was that of Stuart Hayward, the last in a long line of shoemakers, who until his death in 1984 displayed in his window a remarkable collection of photographs of old Richmond and racing memorabilia. There was such consternation when estate agents and building societies started taking over retail units that planning policies were introduced to deter them from the Market Place. The first building society to appear was the Cheltenham and Gloucester, which took over the stationery and toy shop of Austin's in 1977, and then closed its branch in 1998. The rise of charity shops also provoked comment towards the end of the century. Oxfam was the first, in 1969, and remained the only one for over twenty years, but as several others opened in the 1990s at a time when trade in the town was declining, there was hostility from some shopkeepers. Another change in shopping habits was the demise of Wednesday half-day closing. Most shops in Richmond closed on the first Saturday in September 1997 while the nation watched on television the funeral of Diana, Princess of Wales, who had died on 31 August.

Supermarkets were a preoccupation late in the century - were they to be or not to be, that was the burning question. By the 1970s there were three modest-sized supermarkets in the Market Place, Hinton's/Presto/Spar near the top of New Road, the Co-op which had moved from its original 1907 building in Rosemary Lane in the 1950s, and Fine Fare/Gateway/Kwik-Save at the lower end of the Market Place, where the town's most handsome shop frontage, complete with Ionic columns, was demolished in the 1960s for a particularly poor box-like replacement. A hypermarket at Catterick was suggested in 1974, and turned down after strong objections from Richmond traders. Several schemes for a new supermarket were submitted by a Leeds-based developer, David Black, all of which were unsympathetic to the town's architectural and historic character, whatever the merits of having a larger store. His first application was in 1984, to demolish the Fleece Hotel and build on its extensive site, followed the next year by a scheme for that section of Queens Road between Dundas Street and Ryders Wynd. In 1988 he tried to demolish several buildings on the corner of the Market Place and Finkle Street, the site being bought the following year by a different developer who restored all the buildings and created small new shop units in Chantry Wynd.

The next chapter in the supermarket saga began in 1991, with the announced retirement of Derek Dutton as headmaster of Richmond School. The Education Committee of North Yorkshire County Council decided to dispose of The Friary, which the headmaster had occupied as a tied house connected with the boarders' accommodation which dated back to the Grammar School days but which was something of an anachronism with a comprehensive school. With the site went Friary Lodge, large gardens and the field, which generations of schoolboys had worked to turn into a cricket ground. David Black's company quickly submitted a planning application for a supermarket and its attendant car park on the site in 1991. A further application in 1992 included a new doctors' surgery on part of the site, because the building they occupied in Queens Road needed to be demolished to form a new access. Feelings ran high, there were well-attended public meetings, letters in the press, various local authority committees decided both for and against it. A public inquiry was called, and sat for several weeks in May and June 1994 in the inhospitable surroundings of the Richmondshire Sports Hall in Gallowgate. Inspector Harold Stephens was faced with three submissions presented by three barristers and attendant teams, for three different supermarket proposals on three different sites, the other two being on both sides of Darlington Road beyond the town boundary. On the morning the inquiry opened, the barrister representing Deerpark, the company applying for the Friary site, announced that its supermarket would be a flagship Co-op store. The large, bare and cold hall was strangely empty. Where, the inspector asked, were the objectors? Of the relatively few members of the public and councillors who put in an appearance, slightly more were in favour than against.

Early in 1995 the government's decision was announced granting permission for the Friary site. This now had a high market value, and the press reported an offer of £475,000 being accepted in the September. The protesters, spurred into belated action, marched, blew whistles, picketed County Hall, sought grants to keep the field in sports use, and resurrected proposals for the development of the so-called 'brown field' site across Queens Road. The matter was again referred to the government, to decide whether the County Council could sell the land for development, and the announcement was given late in 1996 by Conservative Environment Minister John Gummer that it could. It was reputedly sold for £2.5 million. Construction work began in November 1997, with a new roundabout in Queens Road, and the Co-op Friary Superstore opened in September 1998. Edinburgh Woollen Mills opened in the old Co-op shop in the Market Place in 1998. The Friary boarding house was converted into a new community hospital, opened in March 1999 and opened in July of that year by the Labour Health Minister Frank Dobson, replacing both the Victoria Hospital and the Health Clinic in Quaker Lane. Richmond has since at least the 18th century been served by many skilled and dedicated medical practitioners, and the inauguration of the National Health Service in 1948 probably brought less of an improvement in health provision here where it was already much better than in many places.

The heated debate generated by the prolonged supermarket controversy was largely responsible for the formation in 1995 of the Economic Development Strategy Project, renamed the Richmond Partnership in 1996. Ably led by Jonathan Fry, a young Richmond man and an independent financial adviser, it is a largely voluntary organisation aimed at improving the economic status of Richmond and its environs, and has already had significant success in both Richmond and Catterick Garrison. A Georgian Festival was inaugurated for a weekend early in December, held in each of the four last years of the decade. A Town Centre Forum was established in 1998, with Ken Wilson appointed as Town Centre Manager the following year. A closed-circuit television system to reduce anti-social behaviour as well as crime was switched on on Christmas Eve 1998, and Finkle Street was pedestrianized in 1999. Memories of the 1927 eclipse were revived when there was a partial eclipse of the sun on 11 August 1999. As the Millennium approached, a bronze sculpture of a shepherd and his sheep, based on local artist Mackenzie Thorpe's picture 'Bringing them home' was planned for the Friary Gardens. The Richmond Beacon was lit, and Richmond woke up on 1 January 2000 to another day.

Richmond still has its 'sense of place' and cherishes the pride in simply being Richmond, which it has had for nearly 1,000 years. Despite having a 1999 population of 8,480, slightly more than double what it had been at the start of the 20th century, compared with many places Richmond has retained its character and identity. It has been particularly fortunate in having the economic benefits of Catterick Garrison physically detached from the historic town. Richmond apparently prefers to be a working market town, albeit a quaint one, rather than just a tourist attraction. Yet it is aware of the need to look to its future, that its traditional role as a market town is threatened by large stores and supermarkets, which draw its trade away. Perhaps they are indeed like leeches, sucking its life-blood but, as used in medicine for hundreds of years, also having a beneficial purpose. It seems appropriate to give the final word to the visionary David Brooks, writing in the Souvenir Programme for Holidays at Home week 1-7 August 1943, and quoting from *The Present Crisis* by the American writer and poet James Russell Lowell (1819-91):

> If we were asked to choose a one-word motto for Richmond, it would surely be, "Survival".......The 20th century salutes ......ancient Richmond......Its little flame has glowed steadily through all England's vicissitudes of fortune. Its pages are a Chapter in the Book of England, and it will live on......so long as its people remember that---
>
>   "New occasions teach new duties:
>   Time makes ancient good uncouth;
>   They must upward still, and onward,
>   Who would keep abreast of Truth."

Bibliography

General
Brooks, David *The Story of Richmond in Yorkshire*, Richmond, 1946
Bulmer, Thomas *History, Topography and Directory of North Yorkshire,* Preston, 1890
Clarkson, Christopher *The History and Antiquities of Richmond in the County of York,* Thomas Bowman, Richmond, 1821
Clifton-Taylor, Alec *Six English Towns*, BBC Publications, 1978
Fieldhouse, Roger & Jennings, Bernard *A History of Richmond and Swaledale*, Phillimore, 1978
Hatcher, Jane *Richmondshire Architecture*, Richmond, 1990
(ed.) Page, William *Yorkshire North Riding*, 2 vols., Victoria County History, 1914
Pevsner, Nikolaus *The Buildings of England, Yorkshire: The North Riding*, Penguin, 1966
Plantagenet-Harrison, G. H. de S. N. *The History of Yorkshire, vol. 1 Wapentake of Gilling West*, 1879
Richmond and District Civic Society *Annual Reports 1978-82; The Richmond Review* 1983 onwards; the series here called *Richmond Review.* All volumes contain many articles of local history interest, some are mentioned individually in this Bibliography
Ryder, John (pseudonym) *A Look at Richmond*, Richmond, n.d. c.1978
Speight, Harry *Romantic Richmondshire*, 1897
Whitaker, Thomas D. *History of Richmondshire,* 2 vols., 1823

Chapter 1

Bede *A History of the English Church and People*, Penguin, 1955

Fleming, Andrew *Swaledale, Valley of the Wild River*, Edinburgh University Press, 1998

Hartley, B. R. & Fitts, R. Leon *The Brigantes*, Alan Sutton, 1988

Lang, J.T. & Morris, C.D. "Archaeological Discoveries at Gilling West 1976", *Richmond Review 1978*, pp. 6-9

Lang, James, "The Easby Cross", *Richmond Review, 1994*, pp. 15-17

Longhurst, M. "The Easby Cross", *Archaeologia*, vol. 81, 1931, pp. 43-7

Morris, David *The Swale, A History of the Holy River of St. Paulinus*, Sessions of York, 1994

Stenton, F. M. A*nglo Saxon England*, Oxford University Press, 1971

Victoria & Albert Museum *Annual Review 1931*

Wacher, J.S. *The Towns of Roman Britain*, London, 1974

Webster, Graham "A Hoard of Roman Military Equipment from Fremington Hagg", *Soldier and Civilian in Roman Yorkshire,* ed. Butler, R. M.

Wheeler, Mortimer *The Stanwick Fortifications, North Riding of Yorkshire,* Society of Antiquaries, 1954

[Wilson, Peter *Catterick* - a volume bringing together the findings of archaeological excavations, mainly of Roman Catterick, over 40 years is due out 2000/2001]

Chapter 2

(ed.) Clay, Charles Travis *Early Yorkshire Charters, vols. IV & V, The Honour of Richmond*,YorkshireArchaeological Society Extra Record Series, 1935, 1936

Faull, Margaret L. & Stinson, Marie *Domesday Book, Yorkshire*, 2 vols., Phillimore, 1986

Gale, Roger *Registrum Honoris de Richmond*, 1722

Holinshed, Raphael *Chronicles,* 1586

Morris, David *The Honour of Richmond*, Sessions of York, 2000

Palliser, D.M. "Domesday Book and the 'Harrying of the North', *Northern History* vol.29, 1993, pp. 1-23

Peers, Sir Charles *Richmond Castle, Yorkshire*, HMSO, (various editions)
Renn, Derek *Norman Castles in Britain*, John Baker Humanities Press, 1973
Richmond, Keith C. *Richmonds, People and Places*, Castle Cary, 1984
Watts, Victor "The Place-name Hindrelac", *Richmond Review 1984*, pp. 22-3.
Weaver, John *Richmond Castle and Easby Abbey*, English Heritage, 1989

Chapter 3
Hatcher, C.J. "Medieval Grave Markers from St. Nicholas", *Richmond Review 1990*, p.35
Jennings, Bernard *The Grey Friars of Richmond*, Richmond Friary Seventh Centenary Celebration Committee, 1958
Jennings, Bernard *Yorkshire Monasteries: Cloister, Land and People*, Smith Settle,1999
Lawrance, Henry *A Short History of the Greyfriars of Richmond, Yorkshire*, Thomas Spencer, Richmond, n.d.
Morris, David *The Honour of Richmond*, Sessions of York, 2000
Peers, Sir Charles *Richmond Castle, Yorkshire*, HMSO, (various editions)
Pollard, D.J. *North-Eastern England during the Wars of the Roses*, Oxford, 1990
Richmond, Keith C. *Richmonds, People and Places*, Castle Cary, 1984
Thompson, A. Hamilton *The Registers of the Archdeaconry of Richmond 1361-1442*, Yorkshire Parish Register Society, 1919
Weaver, John *Richmond Castle and Easby Abbey*, English Heritage, 1989
Wenham, Leslie P. "Two Notes on the History of Richmond School, Yorkshire", *Yorkshire Archaeological Journal*, 1950
Wenham, Leslie P. "The Anchoress of Richmond", *A Richmond Miscellany*, North Yorkshire County Record Office Publications No. 25, 1980

Wenham, Leslie P. "The Hospital of St. Nicholas", *A Richmond Miscellany*, North Yorkshire County Record Office Publications No. 25, 1980

Chapter 4
Barr, Bernard   "Fragments of Tudor printed books from Frenchgate, Richmond", *Richmond Review* 1983, p. 34
(ed.) Berry, Elizabeth K. *Swaledale Wills and Inventories 1522-1600*, Yorkshire Archaeological Society Record Series vol. *clii*, 1998
Bush, M.L. "The Richmondshire Uprising of October 1536 and the Pilgrimage of Grace", *Northern History* vol. 29, 1993, pp. 64-98
Cross, Claire & Vickers, Noreen *Monks, Friars and Nuns in Sixteenth Century Yorkshire*, Yorkshire Archaeological Society Record Series vol. *cl*, 1995
Hatcher, Jane   "The Elizabethan Portrait", *Richmond Review 1986*, pp. 40-4
Jennings, Bernard *The Grey Friars of Richmond*, Richmond Friary Seventh Centenary Celebration Committee, 1958
Jennings, Bernard *Yorkshire Monasteries: Cloister, Land and People*, Smith Settle, 1999
Morris, David *The Honour of Richmond*, Sessions of York, 2000
Newman, Christine M. *Robert Bowes and the Pilgrimage of Grace*, University of Teesside, Paper in North Eastern History No. 7, 1997
(ed.) Page, William *The .... Chantries, Guilds, Hospitals etc. in the County of York*, Surtees Society, 1895
Peers, Sir Charles *Richmond Castle, Yorkshire*, HMSO, (various editions)
Richmond, Keith C. *Richmonds, People and Places*, Castle Cary, 1984
Sheils, W.J. *The English Reformation 1530-1570*, Longman, 1989
(ed.) Smith, Lucy T. *The Itinerary of John Leland in or about the years 1535-1543,* 8 vols., George Bell, 1907
Weaver, John   *Richmond Castle and Easby Abbey*, English Heritage, 1989

Wenham, Leslie P. "The Chantries, Guilds, Obits and Lights of Richmond, Yorkshire", *Yorkshire Archaeological Journal*, in 3 parts 1952, 1953, 1954
Wenham, Leslie P. "James Cotterell and his Salt", *Richmond Review* 1979, pp.12-15
Wenham, Leslie P. "The Anchoress of Richmond", *A Richmond Miscellany*, North Yorkshire County Record Office Publications No. 25, 1980
Wenham, Leslie P. "The Hospital of St. Nicholas", *A Richmond Miscellany*, North Yorkshire County Record Office Publications No. 25, 1980
Wenham, Leslie P. "The Dissolution of St. Agatha's Abbey, Easby, 1536", *Journal 8*, North Yorkshire County Record Office Publications No. 27, 1981
Wenham, Leslie P. "Portrait of Queen Elizabeth I", *Richmond Review 1986*, pp. 37-9

Chapter 5
anon. *Evidence of the Great Age of Henry Jenkins*, John Bell, Richmond, 1859
Boddy, G.W. "Players of Interludes in North Yorkshire in the early 17th century", *Journal 3*, North Yorkshire County Record Office Publications No. 7, 1976
(ed.) Jackson, Charles *The Autobiography of Mrs. Alice Thornton,* Surtees Society, 1875
Merryweather, James "The Town Waits", *Richmond Review 1994*, pp. 19-21
(ed.) Morris, Christopher *The Journeys of Celia Fiennes*, Cresset Press, 1947
(ed.) Raine, James *The Correspondence of Dr. Matthew Hutton, Archbishop of York*, Surtees Society, 1843
Spencer, Thomas *Robert Willance: His Miraculous Escape from Death while Hunting on Whitcliffe Scar*, Thomas Spencer, Richmond, 1906
(ed.) Waine, George *The Register of Civil Marriages, 1653-1660, belonging to Richmondshire*, Yorkshire Parish Register Society, 1936

Wenham, Leslie P. *Richmond Burgage Houses 1679, 1773, 1820*, North Yorkshire County Record Office Publications No. 16, 1978

Woodfall, Walter L. *Musicians in English Society from Elizabeth to Charles I*, Da Capo Press, New York, 1969

Chapter 6
(ed.) Andrews, C. Bruyn *The Torrington Diaries*, Eyre & Spottiswoode, vol. 3, 1936

(ed.) Butler, L.A.S. *The Archdeaconry of Richmond in the Eighteenth Century*, Yorkshire Archaeological Society Record Series vol. *cxlvi*, 1990

Elwin, Malcolm *The Noels and the Milbankes: their letters for twenty five years 1767-1792*, Macdonald, 1967

(ed.) Furbank, Owens & Coulson *Daniel Defoe, A Tour Through the Whole Island of Great Britain*, Yale, 1991

Hartley, Ingilby, Hall & Wenham *Alexander Fothergill and the Richmond to Lancaster Turnpike Road*, North Yorkshire County Record Office Publications No. 37, 1985

Hatcher, Jane *George Cuit the elder 1743-1818*, Tennants Auctioneers, Leyburn, 1992

Hill, David *In Turner's Footsteps, Through the Hills and Dales of Northern England*, John Murray, 1984

Historic Manuscripts Commission *Journal in England by Lord Harley, afterward 2nd Earl of Oxford; Journal ..... by Lady Oxford* Report on the MSS of the Duke of Portland at Welbeck Abbey, vol. *vi*, 1901, pp. 134-5; 184

House of Commons *Returns relating to Parliamentary Representation, Borough of Richmond, 1831*

House of Commons *Returns relative to the 120 smallest boroughs at present returning M.P.s, Borough of Richmond*, 1831-2

House of Commons *Returns of Boundary Commissioners, Borough of Richmond*, 1832

House of Commons *Report of Commissioners on Municipal Corporations, Northern Circuits*, 1835

Manton, Jo. *Sister Dora, The Life of Dora Pattison*, Methuen, 1971

Morton, Albert *A Brief History of Freemasonry in Richmond, Yorkshire*, Thomas Spencer, Richmond, 1911

Robinson, W.R. *Guide to Richmond*, Richmond, 1833

Waggett, Ralph W. "The Murder of John Moore", *Richmond Review 1988*, pp. 34-7

Wakefield Historical Society *Samuel Buck's Yorkshire Sketchbook*, Wakefield Historical Publications, 1979

Wenham, Leslie P. *The Letters of James Tate*, Yorkshire Archaeological Society Record Series vol. cxxviii, 1966

Wenham, Leslie P. "The Green Bridge, Richmond, North Yorkshire", *Journal 4*, North Yorkshire County Record Office Publications No. 2, 1976

Wenham, Leslie P. *Richmond Burgage Houses 1679, 1773, 1820*, North Yorkshire County Record Office Publications No. 16, 1978

Wenham, Leslie P. "What was Plasingdale?", *Richmond Review 1980*, pp. 19-20

Wenham, Leslie P. *Roger Strickland of Richmond, A Jacobite Gentleman 1680-1749*, North Yorkshire County Record Office Publications No. 30, 1982

Wenham, Leslie P. "Richmond Market Cross", *Richmond Review 1983*, p. 27

Wenham, Leslie P. "More on Richmond Market Cross", *Richmond Review 1984*, pp. 16-17

Wenham, Leslie P. "Some Scots Jacobite Prisoners in York and Richmond", *Journal 10*, North Yorkshire County Record Office Publications No. 35, 1984

Wenham, Leslie P. *Frances I'Anson, The Lass of Richmond Hill*, Richmond, 1986

Wenham, Leslie P. *James Tate, Master of Richmond School, Yorkshire and Canon of St. Paul's Cathedral, London, Schoolmaster and Scholar*, North Yorkshire County Record Office Publications No. 46, 1991

Wenham, Peter "John Foss of Richmond", *Annual Report 1976*, York Georgian Society, pp. 27-35

Wenham, Peter & Hatcher, Jane   "The Buildings of John Foss", *Annual Report 1977*,   York Georgian Society, pp. 32-43

York Georgian Society *The Works in Architecture of John Carr*, 1973

Chapter 7

anon. *Henry Cooke, papermaker 1773-1973*, Lund Humphries, 1973

Bulmer, Thomas   *History, Topography and Directory of North Yorkshire*, 1890

Hatcher, Jane   *The Industrial Architecture of Yorkshire*, Phillimore, 1985

Pound, Reginald *The Fenwick Story*, Fenwick Ltd., 1972

Wenham, Leslie P. *Richmond, North Yorkshire, The Churchyard*, Richmond, 1976

(ed.) Wenham, Leslie P. *Richmond, Yorkshire, in the 1830s*, Richmond, 1977

Wenham, Leslie P. *Richmond Municipal Reform Association Minute Books 1841-1859*, North Yorkshire County Record Office Publications No. 19, 1978

Wenham, Leslie P. *Richmond in Old Picture Postcards*, European Library, 1983

Wenham, Leslie P. *Around Richmond in Old Photographs*, Alan Sutton, 1989

Chapter 8

Carr, Audrey *You Must Remember This*, Aztec, Richmond, 1987

Carr, Audrey *Well Played (The Story of Richmond High School)*, Aztec, Richmond, 1988

Carr, Audrey *Time Goes By*, Aztec, Richmond, 1989

Carr, Audrey   *Richmond in Old Picture Postcards*, European Library, 1992

Cole, Howard N. *The Story of Catterick Camp 1915-1972*, HQ Catterick Garrison,1972

Eaton, A.E. *From the Dales to Jericho, The Story of J. Alan Broadley, DSO, DFC,   DFM*

Recall Publications, Northallerton, 1999

Ghent, Julia & Blades, Hubert *Remembering Richmond*, Aztec, Richmond, 1985

Hatcher, Jane *Richmond: Then and Now, The Town in 1945 and Fifty Years On,* Darlington and Stockton Times, 1995

Thorpe, Lesle "Richmond in the Twenties and Thirties", *Richmond Review 1983*, pp.   8-10

Wenham, Leslie P. *Richmond, Yorkshire 1945, A Photographic Study*, 2 vols., Castle Print, Richmond, 1984 and 1985

Wilcox, Alan *The Richmond Meet 1892-1992*, Richmond Meet, 1992

Wright, Malcolm *The Richmond Sixteen*, Tyne Tees Television, 1995

Corn Watermills
Hatcher, Jane "The Corn Watermills of Richmond", *A Richmond Miscellany*, North Yorkshire County Record Office Publications No. 25, 1980

Dundas Family
Ashcroft, M. Y. "The Zetland (Dundas) Archive, *Annual Report 1971*, North Riding Record Office, 1971

Education
Fieldhouse, Roger "The History of Adult Education in Richmond and Swaledale", *Journal 5*, North Yorkshire County Record Office Publications No. 13

Wenham, Leslie P. "Two Notes on the History of Richmond School, Yorkshire", *Yorkshire Archaeological Journal*, 1950

Wenham, Leslie P. *The History of Richmond School, Yorkshire*, Arbroath, 1958

(ed.) Wenham, Leslie P. *Richmond, Yorkshire, in the 1830s*, Richmond, 1977

Guilds
Waggett, Ralph Whitell *A Transcript of the Archives of the Company of Mercers,   Grocers and Haberdashers of Richmond,*

Yorkshire 1580-1980, Company of Mercers, Grocers and Haberdashers, Richmond, 1987

Wenham, Leslie P. *The Company of Fellmongers of Richmond, Yorkshire: A History* Company of Fellmongers of Richmond, 1982

Horse Racing
Fairfax-Blakeborough, J. *Northern Turf History*, vol. 1, Allen & Co., 1948

Huggins, M.J. *'Kings of the Moor', North Yorkshire Racehorse Trainers, 1760-1900*, Teesside Polytechnic, Papers in North Eastern History No. 1, 1991

Wenham, Leslie P. "The Horse 'Hopeless'", *Richmond Review 1978*, pp. 22-3

Hutton Family
(ed.) Raine, James *The Correspondence of Dr. Matthew Hutton, Archbishop of York*, Surtees Society, 1843

Meet (Cyclists')
Wilcox, A.M. *The Richmond Meet 1892-1992*, Richmond, 1992

Military History
Cole, Howard N. *The Story of Catterick Camp 1915-72*, HQ Catterick Garrison, 1972

Green Howards Regimental Museum *The Green Howards Museum, Richmond*, various editions

Turton, Robert Bell *The History of the North York Militia*, Patrick & Shotton, 1907

Mining of Lead and Copper
Hatcher, Jane "A True Story" (The Yorke Copper Mine), *Richmond Review 1984*, pp. 20-2

Hornshaw, T.R. "The Richmond Copper Mine", *Journal 3*, North Yorkshire County Record Office Publications No. 7, 1976

Morris, David *The Dalesmen of the Mississippi River*, Sessions of York, 1989

Raistrick, Arthur & Jennings, Bernard *A History of Leadmining in the Pennines*, Davis   Books Newcastle-upon-Tyne, 1983

Wenham, Leslie P.   "Billy Banks Wood Copper Mine", *A Richmond Miscellany*, North Yorkshire County Record Office Publications No. 25, 1980

Parliamentary Representation

Carroll, Roy   "Yorkshire Parliamentary Boroughs in the 17th century", *Northern History* vol. 3, 1968

Fieldhouse, R.T. "Parliamentary Representation in the Borough of Richmond", *Yorkshire Archaeological Journal* vol. 44, 1972, pp. 207-16

Wenham, Leslie P.   *Richmond Burgage Houses 1679, 1773, 1820*, North Yorkshire County Record Office Publications No. 16, 1978

Religious Denominations (Churches and Chapels)

Beadle, Harold L.   *Methodism in Richmond 1750-1950*, Richmond Methodist Church, 1984

Curnock, Nathaniel *The Journal of the Rev. John Wesley*, 8 vols., Epworth Press, 1938

Hall, David S.   "The Quakers in Richmond and Swaledale", *Cleveland and Teesside Local History Society Bulletin No. 20*, 1973

Howell, Mark A.   "The Richmond Theatre and the Quaker Meeting House", *Richmond Review 1986*, pp. 15-17

Sullivan, Arnold M.   *The Story of Richmond Parish Church, Yorkshire*, Richmond, 1950

Wenham, Leslie P. "A Richmond Quaker", *Richmond Review 1978*, pp. 21-2

Wenham, Leslie P. "Quaker Burial Ground", *Richmond Review 1980*, pp. 14-15

Wyman, Sr. Clare Veronica & Minskip, Dominic   *A History of the Catholic Mission in Richmond*, Richmond, 1992

Religious Houses (Monasteries)
Colvin, H.M. *The White Fathers in England*, Oxford, 1951
Hill, Rosalind M. T. *The Labourer in the Vineyard: The Visitations of Archbishop Melton in the Archdeaconry of Richmond*, Borthwick Papers No. 35, University of York, 1968
Jennings, Bernard *The Grey Friars of Richmond*, Richmond Friary Seventh Centenary Celebration Committee, 1958
Jennings, Bernard *Yorkshire Monasteries: Cloister, Land and People*, Smith Settle, 1999
Lawrance, Henry *A Short History of the Greyfriars of Richmond, Yorkshire*, Thomas Spencer, Richmond, n.d.
Wenham, Leslie P. "The Anchoress of Richmond", *A Richmond Miscellany*, North Yorkshire County Record Office Publications No. 25, 1980
Wenham, Leslie P. "The Hospital of St. Nicholas", *A Richmond Miscellany*, North Yorkshire County Record Office Publications No. 25, 1980
Wenham, Leslie P. "The Dissolution of St. Agatha's Abbey, Easby, 1536", *Journal 8*, North Yorkshire County Record Office Publications No. 27, 1981

(Georgian) Theatre Royal
Boddy, G.W. "Players of Interludes in North Yorkshire in the early 17th century", *Journal 3*, North Yorkshire County Record Office Publications No. 7, 1976
Georgian Theatre (Richmond) Trust Ltd. *The Georgian Theatre, Richmond, Yorkshire*, 1972
Howell, Mark A. "The Richmond Theatre and the Quaker Meeting House", *Richmond Review 1986*, pp. 15-17
Rosenfeld, Sybil *The XVIII Century Theatre at Richmond, Yorkshire*, York Georgian Society, Occasional Papers No. 3, 1947
Rosenfeld, Sybil *The Georgian Theatre of Richmond, Yorkshire*, The Society for Theatre Research, London, 1984
Wenham, Leslie P. "Richmond Parish Registers 1771-1842: References to the Players of Richmond", *Richmond Review 1978*, pp. 23-5

Wenham, Leslie P. "Theatre Royal, Richmond 1818", *Richmond Review 1980*, pp. 21-4

Willmott, Carl "Thomas Snagg(e), minor player at Richmond Theatre 1788-92", *Richmond Review 1993,* pp. 25-7

Yorke Family
Ashley Cooper, Anne *Yorke Country*, published by author, 1988

Bagley, F.H. "Culloden Tower Gates, Richmond", *Richmond Review 1982,* pp. 13-17

Hatcher, Jane "Culloden Tower", *Richmond Review 1982*, pp. 10-12

Hatcher, Jane "A True Story" (The Yorke Copper Mine), *Richmond Review 1984*, pp. 20-2

Hepworth, Val *The Temple Grounds, Richmond, North Yorkshire*, Yorkshire Gardens Trust, 1999

INDEX

Acrige, John 88-89
Adam, Robert 126, 145
agriculture 5, 14, 27, 41, 43, 47, 166, 230
Aidan 2
Aislabeck 91, 151-152, 174
Alan Niger I 18, 23, 29-30
Alan Niger II 24, 26, 33
Alan Rufus 18-19, 21-23, 26-30, 91, 128, 140, 227
Albert 173, 175, 192
Albert Place 175
Alcuin 2
Aldbiggin 14, 30, 98
aldermen 82-83, 96, 102, 108-111, 114-116, 121, 134, 140, 193
Alexandra 199
Alexandra Way 174
Alfred 2
Allen, George 127
Alt-berg 225
Amateur Dramatic Society 228
America 57, 93, 99, 126, 128, 188, 202, 212, 228, 231, 237
Anchor Court 222
Anchorage Hill 30, 98
anchoress 30, 51, 75
Ancram, earl of 141
Andrews, George Townsend 179, 181
Aneirin 9
Anglian period 1-2, 8-13
angling 90-91, 120, 161, 212
Anglo-Saxon period 15-17, 22, 29
Anne, queen 95, 125, 130, 142
Anne Boleyn 58, 63

Anne of Bohemia 34
apprentice bell 3, 105
archaeology 5, 8-9, 37, 40, 45, 50, 55, 132-133, 164, 209
archdeaconry of Richmond (see also Consistory Court) 29, 47-48, 52, 64, 73, 78, 81, 83, 105, 119, 121, 140, 142, 148, 170
Archer, William 111
archery 164
architects -
   Adam, Robert 126, 145
   Andrews, George Townsend 179, 181
   Campbell, Colen 128
   Carr, John 138, 144, 150, 227
   Clark & Moscrop 186-187
   Clarke Hall, Denis 215
   Garrett, Daniel 138
   Goldie, George 186-187
   Harrison, Thomas 156-157
   Hoskins, George 193
   Moscrop, W.J. 186-187
   Napper, Errington, Collerton Partnership 225
   Rutherford, 213
   Scott, Sir George Gilbert 185
   Smythson, Robert 101-102
   Stancliffe, Martin 230
Arkengarthdale 66, 134, 220
armorial bearings of Richmond 112, 114, 127, 193
Arrowsmith, James, upholsterer 163
Arthur 1, 8-9, 34, 62
Arthur of Brittany 33-34

Arthur Tudor 62
Arthur's Oven 9
arthurian legend 8-9
artificers, statute of 79
artists - Cuit, George 156-157, 159, 162
    Harman, Robert 104, 124, 128-129, 132-133, 138
    Hedley, Ralph 193
    Hulsbergh, Henry 128
    Ibbetson, Julius Caesar 193
    Joy, Jessey Margretta 193
    Kip, Johannes 128
    Robinson, William Ripley 69, 193
    Sanderson, William 194-195, 197
    Speed, Harold 205
    Speede, John 98, 100
    Thorpe, Mackenzie 236
    Turner, Joseph Mallord William 163, 196
Aske 85-87, 121, 131, 138, 145-146, 163, 186
Aske, Robert 65-66
assemblies 143-144, 153-154, 172
Athelstan 15-16
athletics 212
audit money 44
augmentations, court of 65, 75
Augustine 2
Austin's shop 233

Back Flags 191
Back of the Friars 191
Backhouse ings 212
Baden-Powell, Lord Robert 205-206

Bailey (outer, also ward) 26, 29, 37, 40, 61, 108, 122
Bailey House 40, 233
Baker, John, painter 143
Baker, Richard 224
Bampton, abbot Robert 65-66, 71-72
Bank Yard 157, 165
banks 147, 165, 187
Bannockburn, battle of 31, 37
Bargate (also ward), (see also Green) 38-39, 53, 60-61, 80, 108, 122, 151, 187, 192, 219
Barley Cross 45, 129
Barnard Castle 35, 43, 66, 81, 130-131, 198
Barningham Moor 5
Barracks 184, 209, 215, 221
bars (gates in town wall) 38-40, 60, 91, 98
Bath 78, 155
Bathurst family 106-107, 133-135
Batts 227
Beacon 41, 58, 89, 216, 236
Beast Market 129
Beatrice Plantagenet 34-35
Becket, archbishop Thomas 31
Bedale 22, 36, 43, 76, 103-104, 138
Bede 2, 10
Beeching, Lord 203, 225
Bégard Abbey 24, 33, 46
Bell, John, printer 188
Bell, Matthew, printer 169, 188
Belleisle 144
bells 3, 27, 52, 55, 70, 89-91, 105, 142, 210
Bend Hagg Farm 212
Bennison & Walsh 150

Bernicia 2, 9-10
Beveridge, Sir William 202
Bigod, Sir Francis of Healaugh 65
Billy Banks Wood 9, 133, 138, 147-148, 161, 205, 212, 219
Billyngham, William 50
Binckes, John 111
bishops of Richmond 210
Black, David 234
Black Death 32, 43
Black Prince 32
Blackburne, Rev. Francis 141-142, 159
Blair, Tony 202
Blegborough, Henry 150
Blytheman, Augustus 165
Blytheman, William 64
boating 212
Bogg, Edmund 194
Boggy Lonnen 10, 149
Bolton, duke of 128
Bolton Crofts 40, 221
Bolton-on-Swale 119
Boots chemist 233
Bordelby 30
Bosworth, battle of 32, 56-57
Boudicca 1
boundaries 3, 9-10, 67, 82, 87, 148, 150-151
boundary riding 3, 82-83, 87, 96
Bowes family 65, 85-87, 98, 101, 121
Bowes Hall 121, 165
Bowes Hospital 98
Bowman, Thomas, printer 163, 169
Bradley, Thomas, surveyor 167
Bradrigg, Henry 109-110

Bradwell, Joseph 191
Bramham, Gladys 224
Brand, Albert 219
Branson, George, stonemason 151-152
Branson, William 149
brewery 167, 219
Bridge Street 122, 147, 151, 219
Bridge Terrace 219
bridges - Green 38, 45, 53-54, 61-62, 149-151, 161, 205-206, 219, 230
    Lownethwaite 167, 226
    Station/Mercury 4, 67, 221
Brigantia 1, 6
British Council photographs 216-218
Brittan, Sir Leon 223
Brittany 18, 24, 33-34, 46
Broadley, Alan 215
Brockell, Tryphosa 155
Brompton-on-Swale 30, 38, 191
Bronze Age 1, 5-6
Brooks, David 216, 223, 226, 237
Brough Hall 36, 82, 156, 170, 186
Browne, William 109
Bruno, Helena 187
Buck, Samuel & Nathaniel 139-141,148, back end-paper
Bull, Dr. Arthur James 214, 228
Bulmer, Thomas 194
burgage houses 122, 134, 146
burgage rights 122, 134, 146, 184

burgesses 26, 37, 41, 43-44, 79-80, 82, 89-90, 96, 115, 134-135, 140
Burgh, Thomas de 36
Burghley, Lord 87
Burley's or Hutchinson's Wynd 165
Bury St. Edmund's 19, 23, 30
Bush, Edwin 223
Butler, Samuel 153-156, 183
bye-laws 82, 89-90

Calvert, Sir George 99, 128
Cambridge 106, 130, 157, 159
Camden, William 91
Campbell, Colen 128
Campion, Fay 224
Canute 16-17
Carleton, John 149
Carlisle 10, 137
Carr, Audrey 227
Carr, John of York 138, 144, 150, 227
Carr, Katherine 214
Carr, Tom 214, 227-228
"Carroll, Lewis" 182
Carter, Edward 149
Carter's Lane 151
Carter's Yard 165
Cartimandua 1, 6
Castle 5, 8, 14, 16, 18-30, 33-37, 40-41, 44, 54, 60-61, 98, 107, 120, 124, 128, 131, 133, 140, 160-161, 172, 184, 196, 205, 208-209, 215, 228, plate 2
Castle Bank 8, 132
castle guard 23
Castle Walk 132-133, 161
Castle Wynd 210
Castle Yard 91, 109, 205

Cataractonium 8
Catraeth 9
Catterick 8-10, 36, 38, 135-136, 146, 170, 221, 234
Catterick Bridge 5, 8-9, 132, 198, 215-216
Catterick Camp/Garrison 32, 153, 206-207, 210-211, 214-215, 219-221, 223, 236
CCTV 236
Cemetery 192
census 194
Chaloner, Thomas 110
Chamberlain, Neville 202
chamberlains 105, 117, 142
Chandley, S., jockey 198
Channel (Frenchgate) 38, 183, 194
chantries 54, 64, 74-75, 79-80, 88
Chantry Wynd 234
Chapel Wynd 53, 219
charities 97-98, 106, 168, 227
charity shops 233
Charlemagne 2, 13
Charles I 72, 93-94, 99, 106, 110, 133
Charles II 94-95, 106, 112, 114-115, 124, 126, 133, 148, 169
Charles Stuart 136-137
charters 26, 29, 41, 44, 80, 82, 114-116, 128, 134, 140, 168-169, 213
Chaucer, Geoffrey 32
Chaytor, Jane & John 118
Cheltenham & Gloucester Building Society 233
Chester 73, 76, 78, 157
Church Wynd 179

Churchill, Winston 202
churchyard 80, 91, 96, 106-107, 160-161, 165, 169, 172, 183, 192-193, 210
cinemas 211
civic plate 82-84, 96, 114-118, 127, 148, 193, 203
civic society 227-228, 230
Clarence, George, duke of 34
Clark & Moscrop 186-187
Clarke Green 91, 179
Clarke Hall, Denis 215
Clarkson, Christopher 52, 69, 118, 137, 147, 163, 193
Clarkson, Newton 233
Clarkson, Rev. Thomas 155
Cleveland 37, 41, 144, 212, 224, 233
Clifton-Taylor, Alec 229
Clink Bank and Pool 91, 99, 104, 129, 179, 220
Clints 95, 106
clocks 28, 53, 105
Close, James 115
Close, Robert 131-132
close rolls 35
Coal Hill 177
Coalsgarth 174, 215
coast to coast walk 228
coat of arms of Richmond - see armorial bearings
Coates, William, shoemaker 99, 101
Coatsworth, Robert, painter 156
Cogell, Henry, miller 67
Cohu, Jean Rougier, schoolmaster 186
Collard, Avalon, play director 213

college of chantry priests 54
Conan 24, 26, 33-35, 140
conduit 91, 129, 150
Congregationalists 187-188
conscientious objectors 208
conservation 196, 225, 227-228, 230-231, 233-235
consistory court 47-48, 105, 119, 140, 142-143, 170, 186
constables of Corporation 82, 108-109, 122
constables of Richmond Castle 25, 27, 35-36, 49
Constance 24, 33-35
convent 187
Conyers, John 105
Conyers, Ralph 81
Conyers, William 65
Cooke, Henry, papermaker 167, 187
Cooke, James, papermaker 195-196
Cooke, Leonard, grocer 190
Co-op 234-235
copper mining 148, 205-206
Cornforth Hill 39, 151, 192
Coronation Place 215
Corporation of Richmond 26, 42, 75, 79-80, 82, 88-91, 98, 105, 110, 112, 114-116, 128, 134, 137, 140-144, 151, 154, 163, 166, 168-169, 174, 177, 180-181, 184, 190, 200, 203, 205, 211, 226, 231
cottage hospital 192
Cotterel, James 83-84
council housing 215, 219
Council of the North 72, 83, 85

courts (see also augmentations, court of) 59, 65, 67, 79, 82, 115-116, 143
Coverham Abbey 49
Cradock, Sir Joseph 121
Cradock, Thomas 116
Cradock Hall 121-122
Cranmer, archbishop Thomas 63, 74, 76
Crathorne, Lady 223-224
Crathorne, Lord 223
Cravengate 53, 149, 153, 163, 167
Cresswell, Estcourt Sackville 170
cricket field 198, 211-212
Crimean War 174, 184
Croft 129, 153, 182
Croft family 169, 174, 183, 207
Cromwell, Oliver 94, 106
Cromwell, Thomas, vicar-general 63,72
Cuit, George, artist 156-157, 159, 162
Culloden, battle of 126, 137-138
Culloden Tower 126, 138-139, 213, 230
Cumberland, duke of 126
Cumberland, earl of 112
curfew bell 3, 28, 53, 105
cyclists (see also Meet, cyclists') 191, 198

Dakyn, Dr. John 76-78
Danby, Sir Thomas 110
D'Arcy family (see also Holderness, earl of) 120, 131, 134-135, 138, 145-146
Dark Ages 1-2, 8-12

Darlington 30, 81, 126, 186, 191, 193, 211, 213
Darlington & Stockton Times 188
Darlington Road 29, 222, 235
Daville, William 134
Dawson, Charles 144
defences 37-40, 42
Defoe, Daniel 129-130, 148
Deira 1-2, 9-10
Delaire, Rev. Peter 169-170
Dere Street 1, 8
Devlin, 229
dialect 5, 13, 38-39
Diana, princess of Wales 225, 233
Dickinson, Frank 205, 224, 227
Disraeli, Benjamin 174
dissolution of the monasteries 58, 63-68, 70-72, 74-75, 78-79, 84
divine right of kings 93
Dobson, Frank 235
Dodgson, Charles Lutwidge 181-182
Domesday Book 14-15, 27-28
dovecotes 146, 230
Downholme 128
drummer boy legend 98
Dublin 2, 83, 189
ducking stool 103-104, 129
Dugdale, Thomas Lionel 222-223
dukes of Richmond 63, 95, 124, 132-133, 140
Dundas family (see also Zetland) 145-147, 153, 155-156, 165, 173-175, 195
Dundas Street 165, 187, 234
Dunn, Thomas 150

Durham 52-53, 81, 84-85, 110, 194, 198, 213, 222
Dutton, Derek 222, 234
dye house 45-46, 166

Eadgar Atheling 17
Earl Edwin Drive 219
Earl's Orchard 21, 221, 225
earls of Richmond 19, 24, 33-37, 41, 45-46, 54-55, 57, 60, 140
Easby 5, 12-13, 29, 35, 47, 64, 87, 98-99, 111, 132, 156-157, 179, 195, 210, 225, 230
Easby Abbey 49-51, 64-67, 71-72, 75, 106, 132, 141, 147, 156, 161-163, 185, 194
East Anglia 18, 23, 30
East Field 14, 47, 166
Ebenezer Chapel 187
eclipse 213, 236
Edinburgh 9
Edmund, king of East Anglia 30
Edward I 31, 35, 37, 41
Edward II 31, 37
Edward III 31-32, 34, 41, 213
Edward IV 32, 34, 56
Edward VI 58, 74-75, 79, 82
Edward VII 199, 201
Edward VIII 202
Edward the Confessor 16-17
Edwin 2, 10, 17-18, 23, 27-28
Egglestone Abbey 35, 49
Eleanor of Aquitaine 31
Eleanor of Brittany 33
elections 122, 134-135, 167, 195, 201-202

Elizabeth I 58, 63, 75, 79-82, 84, 86-87, 91, 93, 98, 101, 114, 134, plate 4
Elizabeth II 202, 224
Elizabeth, queen mother 202
Elizabeth of York 57, 60, 62
Ellerton, William 50
Ellerton-on-Swale 119
Ellerton Priory 68
Elsworth, John 147
Empire Day 201
enclosure 166
English Heritage 6, 26, 209, 231
Enisant Musard 27
Eudo 18
European Architectural Heritage Year 225, 227
European Union 202
Eyles, James 213

Fairbrother, Bill & Edith 224
Fairfax, Sir Thomas 94
Fairfield Shoe Factory 224-225
fairground 198
fairs, annual 32, 41, 82, 89-90, 115, 141
Falls - see Foss Head
Farm & Garden Supply Centre 225
Farmer, Stephen 149
Faucenberg, Lord 153
fee farm rent 26, 41, 43-44
Fellmongers 118, 147, 232
Fenwick, John James 191
festivals 214, 219, 228
feudalism 23, 32, 43
Fiennes, Celia 119-120, 138
Finkle Street 38-39, 54, 60, 62, 122, 162, 188, 191, 234, 236

Firby, George Henry 214
First Fruits 3, 226
Fitzalan, Brian 36
Fitzrandal, Ralph 50
Flint, James 191
Flints Terrace & Yard 191
Flodden Field, battle of 61, 119
floods 4, 149, 195, 219
Fontenais, land of 26
football & football field 21, 212
Forcett dovecote 230
Foss, John stonemason 162-3
Foss Head 4-5, 46, 120, 133, 161, 167, 195-196
Foster, W.W. 213
Fothergill, Alexander, surveyor 149
Fowler, Harry 222
Fox, George 117
Foxe, John 32, 76-77
France (see also Brittany) 31-32, 35, 46, 63, 94-95, 135, 150, 165, 170, 208
Francis, St. 50
Freedom of Richmond 128, 163-164, 220-221
Freeman, Betty 224
freemasonry 155, 190, 192
Fremington Hagg 6
French, Joe 211
French Revolution 126, 150, 170
Frenchgate (also ward) 27, 30, 38, 49, 60-62, 96, 98, 108, 121-122, 147, 151, 163, 165, 175, 183, 187, 191, 197, 209, 215, 218-219, 221
Frenchgate Head 151, 175, 209
Frenchgate House 209

Friars Wynd 39, 54, 118, 154, 167, 170, 190, 193
Friary 69-70, 85, 102-103, 121, 161, 186, 227, 234-235
Friary Community Hospital 235
Friary Gardens 209, 216, 236
Fry, Jonathan 236

Gale, Roger 127-128, 193
Galliers, -, policeman 180-181
Gallow Field 14, 47, 166
Gallowfields Trading Estate 224-225
Gallowgate 104, 121, 135, 174, 184, 192, 209, 215, 221, 225, 235
gallows 104-105
gaols 76, 89, 116
Garden Village 221
Garrett, Daniel 138
Garvin, James Louis 190
gasworks 167, 175
Gatherley Moor 131, 150
Geoffrey Plantagenet 33-34
geology (see also copper mining, lead mining) 4, 52, 188, 191, 206-207
George I 125, 127
George II 125-126
George III 126, 173
George IV 126, 173
George V 201-202, 215
George VI 202, 215
Ghent, Julia 227
Gilling Road 219
Gilling sword 12
Gilling West 10-14, 16, 18, 29, 38, 91, 111, 131 148, 191, 193, 210

Gladstone, William 174
Gododdin 9
Godwin 16
Goldie, George 186-187
golf 212, 230
Gosling, Robert 118, 127
Gower family 81, 84
grandstand 144-145, 213, 231
Great North Road 1, 8, 38, 129
Great War - see World War I
Greathead, Matthew 192
Green (Bargate Green) 45-47, 120-121, 138, 149, 167, 187, 212, 219, 227
Green Howards Regiment 184-185, 207, 209, 220-221
Green Howards Regimental Museum 96, 220
Green Howards Road 215
Gregory 2
Grey, Earl 159
Grey Friars 39-40, 50-51, 61, 68-70, 85, 102, 132, 161, 172, 209, 227
Grove, The 147, 157, 187, 219
Grundy, Pam 224
guilds 32, 44-45, 112, 115, 118, 143, 193
Gummer, John 235
Gunpowder Plot 93, 95

Hadrian's Wall 1, 8
Hague, William 223
halberdiers 40-41, 227
halberds 3, 41
Halley's Comet 16
Hanoverians 125-127, 133, 136, 138, 145
Harald Hardrada, king of Norway 17

Harley, Robert 130-133, 139
Harman, Robert 104, 124, 128-129, 132-133, 138, front end paper
Harold Godwinson 16-17
Harris, Baroness Angela 221
Harris, Col. George 171
Harrison, Rev. A.A. 'Dick' 227
Harrison, Thomas 156-157
harrying of the north 15, 28-29
Harthacanute 16
Haslam, -, innkeeper 131
Hastings, battle of 18
Hastwell, Robert 211
Hauxwell 183
Hayward, Stuart 233
hearth tax of 1673 122, 124
Hedley, Ralph 193
Heighington, Robert 81
Henrietta Maria, queen 93-94
Henry I 15
Henry II 24, 31, 33, 35, 54
Henry III 31, 34-35, 41
Henry IV 32, 34, 140
Henry V 32
Henry VI 32, 43-44
Henry VII (Tudor) 32, 34, 57, 59-62, 82, 140
Henry VIII 57-58, 60, 62-63, 66, 68, 72, 74, 82, 88
Henry Fitzroy, duke of Richmond 63
heraldry - see armorial bearings
Hermitage 187
'Herriott, James' 224, 229-230
Hey, Robert, inventor 212
Hickson, John 137
Hidcote, Gloucestershire 204
High Row 175
Hill, Monica 224

Hill House 85, 120-122, 147, 153, 189
Hillings, Commissary 77
Hindrelac 1, 16, 27, 47
Hinton's 234
Hipswell 32, 108, 206-207
Hitler, Adolf 202
HMS Richmond 221
Hodge, Bert 226, 230
Hodgson, Minnie 214
Hodgson, Robert 105
Hodgson, William 149
Hodgson's shop 233
Hogg, Tristram 150
Holderness, earl of (see also D'Arcy family) 141, 145-146
Holinshed, Raphael 37
Holly Hill 10, 149
Holmes, Peggy 224
Holy Trinity Chapel 29, 53-54, 60-62, 88, 91, 105, 120, 137, 142, 164, 170, 177-178, 186, 190, 213, 220
Honour of Richmond 18, 22-23, 33-34, 52, 55, 59, 63, 127-128
Hook, James 189
Hope, Sir William St. John 194
Hornby 29, 119, 132, 141, 146, 187
Hoskins, George 193
hospitals - see charities, cottage hospital, Friary Community Hospital, Victoria Hospital
'Hoss', Poor Old 231-232
House of Correction 103
houses - Bailey House 40, 233
 Belleisle 144
 Bowes Hall 121, 165
 Cradock Hall 121-122

Frenchgate House 209
Friary 69-70, 85, 102-103, 121, 161, 186, 227, 234-235
Grove, The 147, 157, 187, 219
Hermitage 187
Hill House 85, 120-122, 147, 153, 189
Hurgill Lodge 231
Kimber House 165
Lennox House 190
Minden House 163
Oglethorpe House 121-122, 135-136, 147
Prior House 147-148, 183, 189, 221
Ronaldshay House 214
Sandford House 151
Silvio House 144
Terrace House 190
Wellington House 148
Yorke House 120-122, 138-139, 148, 161, 166, 227, 231
Zetland House 175
Howard, Sir George, armoury master 79
Hudswell 10, 207
Hudswell, William de 46, 50
Hudswell Pele Tower 46, 121, 138
Hulbergh, Henry 128
Humber 1, 17, 28
Hunt, Mrs. Alfred 196
Hunton, Wensley 194
Hunton & Garget 194
Hurgill Lodge 231
Hurgill Road 38, 53, 144, 148, 151, 191
Hurst 8

Hutchinson, Martha & Ralph 189
Hutton family 52, 69, 88, 101-103, 105, 116, 144, 156, 167, plate 4

I'Anson, Frances 189-190, 213
I'Anson, Thomas 148, 189
I'Anson, William 189
I'Anson, William Arthur 190
Ibbetson, Julius Caesar 193
Iceni 1
Incledon, Charles Benjamin 189
Independents' Chapel 188
India 171, 174, 185
industry 45-47, 55, 59, 67-68, 70, 103, 118, 129, 140-141, 147-148, 166-167, 196, 224-225
Innes, Captain 108
inns and hotels -
    Bishop Blaize 148, 154, 192
    Black Bull 192
    Black Lion 39
    Blue Bell 192
    Dainty Davy 144
    Fleece 193, 234
    Freemasons' Arms 192
    Holly Hill 10
    King's Arms 133-134, 164
    King's Head 94, 106, 131, 133-134, 139, 160, 164, 179, 183, 197, 205, 211
    Nag's Head 148
    Town Hall Hotel 143
    Unicorn (old) 107
Ireland 167, 173-174, 187, 195
Iron Age 1, 6

Jackson, George 146
Jackson, Henry 111
Jackson, Rev. John 102
Jacobite rebellions 125, 127, 136-137, 145
James I 59, 86, 93, 95, 99, 110, 125
James II 95, 125, 135
James, Lady Serena 204
James, Hon. Robert 204
Jarrow hunger marches 201, 214
Jehovah's Witnesses 210
Jenkins, Henry 119
Jervaulx Abbey 66
Jobson, Les 224
John (king) 31, 34
John, duke of Bedford 34
John of Gaunt 32, 34, 36, 57
John I earl of Richmond 34-35, 41
John II earl of Richmond 36-37
Johnson, Robert, R.C. priest 186
jousting 21
Joy, Jessey Margretta 193

Katharine of Aragon 58, 62-63, 75
Kay, George 8
Kay, John 111
Keirincx, Alexander 99, plate 5
Kent 2, 31, 63, 171, 212
Kent, duke of 173, 175
Kilner, Francis Charles 210
Kimber House 165
King, Richard 112
King Street 134, 164, 191, 203
Kip, Johannes 128
Kiplin Hall 99, 128

Kirby, Stephen 111
Kirkby, Sarah 117
Kirkby Ravensworth 78, 210
Kitchener, Lord 208
Kitson, Sir Timothy 223
Knight, bishop William 78
knights 8-9, 21, 23, 36, 37, 62, 79, 82, plate 3
knitting 118-119, 129-130, 147
Knox, John 85-86

Lambert, William 106
Lancaster (see also Roses, wars of) 47, 105, 149-150, 157
Landmark Trust 78, 139, 230-231
Lass of Richmond Hill 189-190, 213
Lawrence, Alexander 185
Lawrence, John Laird Mair 185
Lawson family of Brough Hall 82, 156, 186
Lawson family of Temple Lodge 231
lay subsidy 42
Layton, Dr. 63-64
lead mining 8, 84, 134, 144, 147-148, 167, 206
leather market 129
Leeds 8, 73, 103, 234
Leeds, duchess of 187
Leigh, Dr. 63-64
Leland, John 60-61
Lennox, Charles duke of Richmond 124
Lennox House 190
Lennox Lodge 190, 192
Leslie, David 107-108, 121
Lestor, James Brown 192
"Lewis Carroll" 182

library 164
Lile Close 191, 222
Lile Cottage 191
Lindisfarne 2
Lizst, Franz 183
Lloyd-George, David 201
Lombards Wynd 165, 217, 222
London 6, 13, 17-18, 36, 58-60, 76, 79, 93-94, 130, 135, 145, 151, 157, 159-160, 179-180, 185, 189-190, 230, 232
Love Lane 230
Low Church Wynd 179
Low Scales Farm 10
Lowell, James Russell 237

McGregor, Gregor 224
McIntosh, Neil 220
Macmillan, Harold 202
MacNally, Elizabeth 189
MacNally, Frances 189
MacNally, Leonard 189
Maison Dieu 54, 151, 190
Major, John 202
Manchester, earl of 94
Manley, Charles 180-181
market 3, 26-27, 32, 38, 41, 43, 45, 82, 89-90, 116, 119-120, 132, 141-142, 148, 168, 175-178, 206
market cross (see also Obelisk) 45, 103, 111, 113, 120, 129, 151, 176
Market Hall 142, 184, 211, 214
Market Place 26-27, 30, 37, 39-40, 45, 54, 61-62, 89-90, 98, 107, 142-143, 151, 154, 157, 159-161, 163, 165, 167, 170, 175-180, 187-188, 190-192,

197-198, 200, 209-211, 213, 219, 233, 234, plates 7 & 8.
Marlborough, duke of 95
Marrick 68, 101
Marske-by-the-Sea 145
Marske-in-Swaledale 65, 88, 101-103, 106, 144
Marston Moor, battle of 94, 107
Mary I (Tudor) 58, 62, 75-79, 81-82, 88
Mary II (Stuart) 95, 128
Mary, queen of Scots 58, 81, 86
Masonic Hall 192
Matthew, prior John 67
Maxwell, Peter Constable 187
May, Ron 231
mayors 3, 40, 105, 115-116, 127, 134, 140, 147-148, 150, 162, 193, 203, 205, 213-214, 216, 221, 226-227, 229, 231
Mechanics Institute 55, 164, 188
medical practitioners 151, 163, 172, 235-236
Meet, Cyclists' 198, 210
Melbourne, Lord 173
members of Parliament 82-83, 85, 106, 110, 120-121, 127, 133-135, 138, 141, 146, 168, 195, 222-223
Mercers, Grocers & Haberdashers 112, 118, 232
Mercia 15-16
Metcalfe, James 115
Metcalfe, John 116
Metcalfe, Thomas 149
Methodists & their chapels 159-160, 187, 197

Middleham 34, 43, 50, 55-56, 61-62, 104
Milbank(e) family 116, 129, 153-154
militia (see also North York Militia) 184, 205
millennium 25, 231, 236
Millgate 163, 185, 197
mills - Castle 46, 167, 195
    Church 67-68, 166, 227-228
    Easby 212, 220
    Green 46, 166
    St. Martin's 67-68, 166, 179
    Whitcliffe 46, 147, 166-167, 187, 212, 219, 226
Minden House 163
misericords 71
Moore, John 148
Morcar 16-17
Mordaunt, Henry 127
More, John, chantry priest 80
Morton, Albert 203
Moscrop, W.J. 186-187
Municipal Reform Association (see also Reform of municipal government) 191
murage grants 37-38
Murray, Robert & family 231
museum (in Tower Street) 55, 188
music (see also waits) 183, 214

Napoleon 126
Napper, Errington, Collerton Partnership 225
National Service 219-220
National Trust 204, 226
navvies 179-180
Nelson, Lord 166
Neolithic period 5

Nevill, Charles earl of Westmorland 81
Nevill, Ralph earl of Westmorland 34, 50, 52, 54
New Road 151, 234
Newbiggin 27, 30, 38, 62, 76, 136, 147, 160, 165, 178, 181, 186, 192, 197, 229
Newcastle Chronicle 190
News Chronicle 215
Newton 14, 26-27
Nicholson, Francis 128
Norbert, St. 48
Norfolk, duke of 66
Norman conquest 10, 14-15, 17-19, 21, 27-28, 91
North York Militia 152-153, 159, 161-162, 172, 184, 205
North Yorkshire & South Durham Cyclists' Meet 198
Northallerton 47, 81, 119, 154, 175, 195
Northern Echo 195
Northern Rebellion 81-82, 85, 88, 101
Northumberland, duke of 188
Northumberland, earl of 81
Northumbria 2, 9-13, 15-16, 28-29
Norton family 107-108, 121, 159
Norway 17, 220-221
Nottingham 94
Nuns' Close 53

Oat cross 129
Obelisk (market) (see also Market Cross) 151-152, 170
Observer, The 190
Oglethorpe House 121-122, 135-136, 147
Olliver 186
Olliver Ducket 146, 213
Operatic Society 187, 228
Oswine 10
Oswiu 10-11
Out Moor 144, 166
Outhwaite, Mary 103
Oxfam 233
Oxford 58, 76, 157, 159-160, 182
Oxford, earls & countess of 130-133, 139

pageant 213
Palgrave, Francis Turner 183
pancake bell 3
paper making 166-167, 187, 195, 212
parish church 27, 29-30, 51-52, 54-55, 61, 71, 75, 80, 87-88, 102, 105-106, 114, 117, 121, 127-128, 141-142, 164, 185, 209-210
parish registers 72, 76, 91, 105, 107-108, 111, 153
Parkin, John 150
parliament (see also member of) 30, 63-64, 82, 93-94, 103, 110, 122, 125-126, 135, 146, 166, 184
Partnership (Richmond) 236
Parvinge, John 106-107
Pattison, Dorothy Wyndlow 183
Pattison, Rev. Mark James 183
Paulinus 2, 10
Peacock, Anthony 66
Peacock, Harry 231

Peel, Sir Robert 173, 181
Peirse, Billy 144
Pennines 2, 4
Pennyman, Sir William 110
Penrith 91
pensions, old age (see also augmentations, court of) 201, 203
Pentecostal church 210-211
Pepper family 85, 102
Percy, Thomas, earl of Northumberland 81
Peter de Braine 34
Peter of Savoy 34
Petrie, Mr. S. 198
Pilgrimage of Grace 65-66, 72, 78, 85
pillory 45, 129
Pilmoor Hill 221
Pinckney's Hospital 98
pinder 182
Pinder, Thomas 211
pinfold 175
pipe rolls 34-35
place names 2, 4-5, 10, 14, 39, 53
plagues & plague stone (see also Black Death) 91, 108-109
Plantagenet-Harrison, G.H.D.S.N. 193
Plantagenets 31-35
Plasingdale 133
plate - see civic plate
players (drama) 111-112, 153-156, 223
Plummer, Peter, waller 8
Plummer, Robert, stonemason 151
'Pocket' Borough 135, 146, 195

police 180-181, 225
poll tax (14th century) 32, 43
Pontefract 32
poor law 79, 116, 126
population 27, 43, 47, 91, 165, 186, 194, 236
portrait of Queen Elizabeth I 58, 87-88, 98, plate
postal services 173, 203
Potter, Mike 223
Pottergate 121, 135, 151, 191, 225
'prentice bell 3, 105
printing 32, 163, 169, 188
Prior House 147-148, 183, 189, 221
Pulleine, John James 210

Quaker Lane 8, 53, 84, 117, 151, 203, 213, 221-222, 235
quakers 117-118, 149, 154
quarrying 8, 70, 132
Queens Court 222
Queens Road 187, 191, 209, 211, 219, 222, 234-235

races, racecourses & racehorses 116-117, 144-145, 153, 166, 172, 184, 198, 231
RAF Regiment 221
railway station 4, 179, 181, 184, 198-199, 206-207, 219, 225
railways - Reeth line 206
    Richmond line 179, 188, 190, 225
    Stockton-Darlington 126, 158
Raine, Jonathan, stonemason 8
Raw, Leonard 147

Readshaw family 147, 157
recorders of Richmond 82, 85, 115-116, 140
rectors of Richmond 83, 87, 128, 141, 172
rectory 141, 172
Red Cross 207
Reeth Road 5, 163, 167, 187, 191-192, 215, 222
Reform of municipal government 126, 169, 174, 181, 191-192
Reform of parliament 126, 135, 159, 167
Reformation 32, 58, 62-64, 72
Restoration of Charles II 112-114, 116-118, 121, 148
Rheged 10
Rhodes, Cecil 193
Richard I, the Lionheart 31
Richard II 32, 34, 54
Richard III 32, 24, 55-56
Richmond, Surrey 57, 59-60, 93, 171, 189
Richmond Family Surname Society 230
Richmond place-name 2, 24, 44, 91
Richmondshire 14, 37, 65, 91, 107, 111, 129, 140-141, 152, 169, 195
Richmondshire District Council 182, 214, 221, 226, 228, 230
Richmondshire Museum 12, 44, 55, 91, 194, 200, 230
Richmondshire Preservation Trust 230
Rimington, Major-General M.F. 207
Rimington Avenue 207

Ripon 71, 81, 132, 154, 170, 188
Ripon & Richmond Chronicle 188
Roald 35-36, 49-50
Robinson, W.S., goldsmith 193
Robinson, William 216
Robinson, William Ripley 69, 193
Robson Wood & Co. 191, 216, 233
Rochford, Bryan 224
Roman Catholic Church 186, 210
Roman Catholic Emancipation 126
Romans 1, 6, 8-9, 132
Ronaldshay House 214
Ronaldshay Recreation Ground 203-204
Roper, Ruth 214, 226
Rosemary Lane 144, 234
Roses, wars of 32, 34, 55, 57, 59
Round Howe 147, 226
Royal Oak Day 114
Ruport, prince 94, 107
rural district councils 225, 227
Ruskin, John 196
Russell, Jim & Sheila 224
Rutherford, Mr. 213
Ryder, the misses 209
Ryder's Wynd 40, 179, 187, 211, 222, 234

Sager, Joseph 160
St. Agatha's (Frenchgate) 215, 222
St. Agatha's Abbey - see Easby Abbey

St. Anthony's Chapel 53, 61
St. Blazius 148
St. Edmund's Chapel 30, 52, 54, 75, 98
St. James' Chapel 53-54, 61, 75, 80, 90, 105, 222
St. James' Chapel Wynd - see Chapel Wynd
St. Martin's (civil parish) (see also mills) 179, 195
St. Martin's Priory 29-30, 49, 66-68, 78, 161, 207
St. Mary' Abbey, York 29, 66-68, 72, 77-78
St. Mary's Parish Church 27, 29-30, 51-52, 54-55, 61, 71, 75, 80, 87-88, 102, 105-106, 114, 117, 121, 127-128, 141-142, 164, 185, 209-210
St. Nicholas (Hospital & house) 51, 54-55, 75-76, 84, 107-108, 121-122, 141, 151, 204
St. Thomas' Chapel 30
St. Trinian's 165
Sandbeck 10
Sanderson, Dr. Robert 68
Sanderson, William 194-195, 197
Sandford House 151
scandinavian influences 2, 10-13, 16, 39
Scarbrough, earl of 204
schools - Convent 187
    Corporation 164
    Grammar 52-53, 69, 79-80, 84, 86, 88-89, 102, 106-107, 114, 128, 131-132, 137, 141, 168, 170, 172, 156-159, 181-183, 186, 215, 222-223, 227, 234
    High School for Girls 215, 222
    Kirkby Ravensworth 78
    Methodist 222
    National 165, 217, 222
    Richmond Comprehensive 222
    Richmond Hill 221
    St. Francis Xavier 222
    Roman Catholic 222
    Secondary Modern 222
Scientific Society 164, 188
Scolland 20-22, 36
Scorton 5, 99
Scotch Corner 38, 46, 153
Scotland (see also Mary, queen of Scots) 16, 27, 30, 33, 38, 59, 61, 81, 85-87, 93, 95, 98-99, 127, 130, 136-137, 145, 157
Scots Dike 9-10
Scott, Sir George Gilbert 185
Scottish army 107-109, 121
Scottish raids 29, 37-38, 41
Scottish wars 31, 37-38, 42, 61, 94
scouts 205
Scrope family 36, 50, 65, 72, 136, 220
seals 42, 80, 115, 128
Sedbury 131, 153
Sellars, Bill 224
serjeants-at-mace 82-83, 114-115, 127, 227
Severs, Dick & Olive 224
Shambles 45, 89-90, 129, 142, 177-178, 184
Shaw, George, builder 225

Shaw, George, clothier 103
sheltered housing 215, 222
Shepherd, Miss D.O. 215
shillling, Richmond 227
Shrove Tuesday 3
shops - Austin's 233
  Boot's 233
  charity 233
  Clarkson's 233
  Hayward's 233
  Hinton's 234
  Hodgson's 233
  Oxfam 233
  Robson Wood 191, 216, 233
  Spence, Robert 39, 190, 233
  Spencer, Thomas 188-190
  supermarkets 235
  Woolworths 40, 192, 233

Sidgwick, Richard 65
Signals Regiment 221
Silvio House 144
Simpson, Anne Elizabeth 183
Simpson, James Brown 192
Simpson, Thomas 183
"Sister Dora" 183
Siward 16
Skaife, Thomas 109
skating 212
Skeeby 5, 38
slavery, abolition of 126, 155
Sleegill 10, 30, 78, 149, 195
Smith, Douglas Rucker 186
Smith, Rev. Sidney 159
Smithson, Francis 117
Simpson, James 188
Smithsonian Institution 188
Smurthwaite, John 197
Smythson, Robert 101-102

Snell, Richard & John 76, 229
Snowden, James 186
South Africa 174, 193, 203
South Sea 'Bubble' 125
Spanish armada 58, 88-89
Speed, Harold 205
Speede, John 98, 100
Speight, Harry 193
Spence, Robert, ironmonger 39, 190, 233
Spencer, Charles, gunsmith 212
Spencer, Thomas 188-190
Staindrop 52
Stamford Bridge, battle of 17-18
Stancliffe, Martin 230
Stanfield, Clarkson 155
Stanfield, James Field 155-156
Stanwick 6-7, 9-10, 188
Stapleton, Miles, 35
Stapleton family 187
Station Road 179, 181, 190
Stephen of Brittany 18, 23-24, 29-30, 33, 140
Stephens, Harold 235
stocks 45
Stockton 126
Stokoe, Thomas Henry 186
stonemasons 8, 20-21, 36, 70, 149-151, 162
street lighting 151, 167-168, 175
streets - Albert Place 175
  Aldbiggin 14, 30, 98
  Alexandra Way 174
  Anchor Court 222
  Anchorage Hill 30, 98
  Back Flags 191
  Back of the Friars 191
  Bank Yard 157, 165

Bargate 38-39, 53, 60-61, 80, 108, 122, 151, 187, 192, 219
Boggy Lonnen 10, 149
Bridge Street 122, 147, 151, 219
Bridge Terrace 219
Burley's or Hutchinson's Wynd 165
Carter's Lane 151
Carter's Yard 165
Castle Wynd 210
Castle Yard 91, 109, 205
Channel (Frenchgate) 38, 183, 194
Chantry Wynd 234
Chapel Wynd 53, 219
Church Wynd 179
Coal Hill 177
Cornforth Hill 39, 151, 192
Coronation Place 215
Cravengate 53, 149, 153, 163, 167
Dundas Street 165, 187, 234
Earl Edwin Drive 219
Finkle Street 38-39, 54, 60, 62, 122, 162, 188, 191, 234, 236
Flints Terrace & Yard 191
Frenchgate 27, 30, 38, 49, 60-62, 96, 98, 108, 121-122, 147, 151, 163, 165, 175, 183, 187, 191, 197, 209, 215, 218-219, 221
Friars Wynd 39, 54, 118, 154, 167, 170, 190, 193
Gallowgate 104, 121, 135, 174, 184, 192, 209, 215, 221, 225, 235

Garden Village 221
Gilling Road 219
Green Howards Road 215
Hurgill Road 38, 53, 144, 148, 151, 191
King Street 134, 164, 191, 203
Lile Close 191, 222
Lombards Wynd 165, 217, 222
Love Lane 230
Low Church Wynd 179
Maison Dieu 54, 151, 190
Millgate 163, 185, 197
New Road 151, 234
Newbiggin 27, 30, 38, 62, 76, 136, 147, 160, 165, 178, 181, 186, 192, 197, 229
Pottergate 121, 135, 151, 191, 225
Quaker Lane 8, 53, 84, 117, 151, 203, 213, 221-222, 235
Queens Court 222
Queens Road 187, 191, 209, 211, 219, 222, 234-235
Rimington Avenue 207
Rosemary Lane 144, 234
Ryder's Wynd 40, 179, 187, 211, 222, 234
St. James' Chapel Wynd 53, 219
Station Road 179, 181, 190
Temple Court 219
Terrace, The 190
Thornhill Dykes 165
Victoria Road 154, 175, 181-182, 191, 193, 198, 211-222
Waterloo Street 165
West Terrace 213

Yorke Square 138, 227

Strickland, Roger 135-137
strike, general 201, 212-213
Sunday schools 164, 187
supermarkets (see also shops) 235
Surtees Society 194
Swale 4-5, 8-10, 19, 29, 38, 44-46, 61, 67, 76-77, 90-91, 98, 120, 129, 131-133, 138, 140, 147, 149, 160-162, 166-167, 171-172, 179, 212, 219-220, plate 1
Swale House 182, 209, 221
Swaledale 4-5, 8, 19, 38, 41, 53, 65, 88, 129-130, 147-148, 167, 176, 206
"Sweet Lass of Richmond Hill" 189-190
Sweyn, king of Denmark 17
swimming 212, 225
Swinbank, Ann 231

Taschella, Rita 183
Tate, James I 155-159, 167, 181-182
Tate, James II 155, 159, 181-183
taxation 27, 32, 42, 59, 93-94, 118, 122, 124
Taylor, Christopher 112
Tees 1, 28, 33, 35, 47
Teesdale 'marble' 52
telephones 203
television 209, 229-230
Temple, Anthony, schoolmaster 159
Temple Court 219

Temple Lodge & Temple Grounds (see also Yorke House) 138, 197, 213, 231
Tennyson, Alfred, lord 183
Tenter Bank 47, 213
Terrace, The 190
Terrace House 190
Terry, William 163-164
Thatcher, Margaret 202, 223
Theatre 118, 153-156, 172, 183, 192, 223, plate 6
Thompson, Francis 'Matabele' 193
Thompson, Potter 8-9
Thompson, Thomas 193
Thompson family of Cornforth Hill 192
Thoresby, Ralph, antiquary 8
Thornaby, William 118
Thorndike, dame Sybil 223
Thornhill Dykes 165
Thornton, Alice 107-108
Thorpe, Mackenzie 236
Thorr 27
Tinkler, Isabella, bookseller 162,
Tippoo Sultan 171
Toll Booth 45, 82, 90, 142, 178, 219, 227
Tooze, Malcolm 227
Torrington, Viscount 160-163
Tosti 16-17
tourism 188, 203, 228
Tower Street 55, 98, 164, 188
Town Centre Forum 236
town clerks 115, 124, 192, 207, 212-213, 216, 222, 227
Town Council 227, 231

Town Hall 44, 87-88, 90, 137, 143, 154, 168-169, 177-178, 181, 193, 197, 205, 227, 232
town mayor 40, 87, 227
town walls 37-40, 42, 60-61, 91, 118
traffic 27, 38-39, 200, 203, 225
tram-lines (Friars Wynd) 39, 190
Trinity Chapel - see Holy Trinity Chapel
Trinity Church Square 142, 213
Tudor, Edmund (see also Henry VII) 34, 57
Turner, Joseph Mallord William 163, 196
turnpike roads 149, 151, 167
twinning 221
Tyson, Eric 227, 230

Urswick, Walter de 36

Venutius 6
Victoria 173-175, 179, 188, 191, 194, 199, 201
Victoria Fountain 200
Victoria Hospital 199, 235
Victoria Road 154, 175, 181-182, 191, 193, 198, 211-212
Vikings 2, 10-13, 16, 29
Vivat Trust 231

Wade, George, builder 214
Wade, George, schoolmaster 164
Waggett, Ralph 232
Wainwright, Alfred 228
waits 40, 112
Walburn 65
Wales 31, 35, 62

Walker, Gerald 203
Wallis, Fielding 155, 157
Wallis, Jane 155
Wallis, Margaret 155, 157
walls (defensive) 37-40, 42, 60-61, 91, 118
Walpole, Sir Robert 125
Walsingham, Sir Francis 87
Wandesford, Alice 107-108
wapentake 13-14
war memorials 209-210, 216
Warburton, John 140
Warcoppe, Thomas 79
Ward, Bill 232
wards (zones of town) 108
waste (ground) 27-28
watch (see also police) 40, 168
water supply 40, 45, 50, 61, 90-91, 150-152, 168, 174, 200, 214-215, 221
Waterloo, battle of 165
Waterloo Street 165
Watson, Sam 222
Watson, William 165
Watts, J.W. 231
Wayne, Christopher 151
weather 4, 9-10, 16-18, 42-43, 116, 149, 195-198, 214, 216, 219-220
Wedgwood, Josiah 126
welfare state 202, 235
Wellington, duke of 126, 204
Wellington House 148
Wellington Place 53, 214
Wenham, Leslie Peter 14, 194, 212, 227, 229-230, 232
Wenham, Peter Charles 212
Wensleydale 4, 25, 34, 41, 43, 47, 50, 55, 65, 72, 104, 107,

111, 128, 134, 136, 149-150, 159, 176, 189, 198, 231
Wesley, John 159-160
Wessex 15-17
West Field 14, 47, 91-92, 166
West Terrace 213
West Wood 207, 211
Westmorland, earls of 34, 50, 52, 54, 81
Wetwang, William 115
Wharton, Lord 131, 146
Wharton, Mr. 133
Wharton, William 75, 79
Wheeler, Sir Mortimer 6
Whitaker, Thomas D. 163, 193
Whitby 2, 75, 154
Whitcliffe Pasture 41, 44, 47, 122, 135, 144, 166
Whitcliffe Scar 95, 189
Whitefields 221
Whiting, James, policeman 181
Whyomar 29-30
Wight, Alf 229-230
Wilfrid 2
Willance, Elizabeth 106
Willance, Robert 95-98, 189
Willance's Leap 95-98, 189
William I, of Normandy, Conqueror 3, 15, 17-18, 23, 27-28, 31, 128, 140
William II, Rufus 15
William III 95, 128
William IV 126, 173
William the Lion, king of Scotland 33
Williams, Randall 211
Willis, Lilian 224
wills 48, 73-74, 83, 97, 99, 101, 103
Wilson, Harold 202

Wilson, Ken 236
Wilson, Robert 114
Winchester 62
window tax 124
Winn, Francis 147
Wise, William 175
Wolsey, cardinal Thomas 63
Wood, Edward 188, 191
woodworkers 19, 28, 45, 70-71
wool house 89-90, 142
Woolworths 40, 192, 233
workhouse 163
World War I 198, 201, 206-207, 211, 215-216
World War II 184, 198, 202, 209-210, 214-216, 219-220, 223, 227, 231, 237
Worsley, Thomas Taylor 165
Wray family 84, 107
Wycliffe, John 32-33, 72
Wyvill, Sir Marmaduke 134-135

York (see Roses, wars of) 1-2, 6, 12, 16-17, 28-29, 35, 51, 56-57, 64-67, 72, 79, 83, 88, 93-94, 103-104, 116, 119, 130, 133, 137-138, 142, 163, 179, 181, 188, 213, 228, 230
Yorke family 120-121, 127, 134-135, 138-139, 141, 146, 148, 156, 161, 166
Yorke House (on the Green) and its grounds (see also Temple Lodge & Temple Grounds) 120-122, 138-139, 148, 161, 166, 227, 231
Yorke Square 138, 227
Yorkshire Archaeological Society 194

Young Men's Christian Association 210

Zetland, earls, marquesses and marchioness of (see also Dundas family) 175, 192, 195, 200, 203-204, 224
Zetland Christian Community Centre 212
Zetland House 175

THE NORTH EAST PROSPECT OF RICHMOND IN THE COUNTY OF YORK